M000218539

Daily Manna

Daily Manna

by

William L. Banks

*My voice You shall hear in the morning, O L*ORD*;*
in the morning will I direct it to You, and I will
look up.

Psalm 5:3

CLC ❖ PUBLICATIONS
Fort Washington, Pennsylvania 19034

Published by CLC Publications

U.S.A.
P.O. Box 1449, Fort Washington, PA 19034

GREAT BRITAIN
51 The Dean, Alresford, Hants. SO24 9BJ

AUSTRALIA
P.O. Box 213, Bungalow, Cairns, QLD 4870

NEW ZEALAND
10 MacArthur Street, Feilding

ISBN 0-87508-756-6

Copyright © 2005
William L. Banks

Quotations from:
The *New King James Version* of the Bible,
Copyright © 1982 by Thomas Nelson, Inc.
unless otherwise indicated.

Scripture verses marked "NASB" are from the
New American Standard Bible,® Copyright ©
1960, 1962, 1963, 1968, 1971, 1972, 1973, 1975,
1977, 1995 by The Lockman Foundation.

Scripture verses marked "TLB" are taken from
The Living Bible, Copyright © 1971. Used by
permission of Tyndale House Publishers Inc.,
Wheaton IL 60189. Used by permission.

This printing 2005

All Rights Reserved

Printed in the United States of America

~

FOREWORD

As the Israelites of old gathered manna, daily food for their physical bodies, you may gather *manna*, God's written Word, as daily food for your soul.

Pastor Banks, a scholar of words, will give you an inspirational message for each day. In addition, you will receive information that will help you to defend the faith. Pastor Bank's insights into God's Word will make you hunger for more even after being satisfied for the day.

May you find your daily portion. In *Daily Manna* you will find rest from your labors, strength for every task, hope for the future, and spiritual satisfaction in a barren, materialistic society. I am glad that my former pastor has written this excellent devotional book. My heart was warmed and challenged as I read the manuscript.

Rev. King A. Butler

ACKNOWLEDGMENTS

The author and publisher wish to express gratitude to the following who have granted permission for the privilege of including selections in this volume:

Hope Publishing Company for the hymn *"Master, the Tempest Is Raging"* by Mary A. Baker. Copyright 1941. Renewal 1969 by Hope Publishing Co., Carol Stream, IL 60187. All rights reserved. Used by permission.

MCA Music for *"It Is No Secret (What God Can Do)."* Words and music by Stuart Hamblen. Copyright 1950 by Duchess Music Corporation, New York, NY. Copyright renewed. Used by permission. All rights reserved.

The Rodeheaver Company for the hymns *"He Lives"* by A. H. Ackley. Copyright 1933 by Homer A. Rodeheaver. Renewed 1961, The Rodeheaver Co. All rights reserved. Used by permission. *"Wonderful"* by A. H. Ackley. Copyright 1938 by Homer A. Rodeheaver. Renewed 1966, The Rodeheaver Co. All rights reserved. Used by permission.

January 1

In the beginning God created the heavens and the earth.
(Genesis 1:1)

I am amazed how seldom I hear the doctrine of God the Creator mentioned in our churches. Perhaps that is part of the damage done by the evolutionists. I certainly resent those who teach evolution as if it were fact when it is only hypothesis.

From Genesis to Revelation the Bible speaks of God the Creator. "He has made the earth by His power; He has established the world by His wisdom, and has stretched out the heavens at His discretion" (Jeremiah 10:12). ". . . and worship Him who made heaven and earth, the sea and springs of waters" (Revelation 14:7).

Perhaps the lack of emphasis on God as Creator is a natural outcome of humanism, where man is made central and not God. The truth of God's creatorship is neglected in an age of materialism. We are in love with things, while ignoring the One who made all things, and that is idolatry.

All existing things were made from nothing. The universe was created *ex nihilo*. In other words, the world was not made out of matter that previously existed. God did not have to have something in order to make something.

"By faith we understand that the worlds were framed by the word of God, so that the things which are seen were not made of things which are visible" (Hebrews 11:3). That is accepted by faith. Because men are spiritually blind, it is impossible for them to give intelligent consent to that dogmatic pronouncement.

By faith we see that God made the worlds out of nothing, and He did so by the word of His power. What a humbling matter that is. Surely our voices cry out: "You are worthy, O Lord, to receive glory and honor and power; for You created all things, and by Your will they exist and were created" (Revelation 4:11).

January 2

. . . and I was afraid. (Genesis 3:10)

We are all sinful creatures. One inevitable fruit of sin is fear. When God called unto Adam, "Where are you?" Adam replied, "I heard Your voice in the garden, and I was afraid" (Genesis 3:9–10). Sin had broken the fellowship and substituted fear for joy.

How often men must be told by God not to fear! "Do not be afraid, Abram; I am your shield, your exceedingly great reward" (Genesis 15:1). "Do not fear him [Moses]; for I have delivered him [Og, the king of Bashan] into your hand" (Numbers 21:34). "Fear not [Hagar]; for God has heard the voice of the lad [Ishmael] where he is" (Genesis 21:17). "Do not be afraid [Joshua], nor be dismayed" (Joshua 8:1).

"Peace be with you [Gideon]; do not fear; you shall not die" (Judges 6:23). "Do not be afraid, Zacharias; for your prayer is heard" (Luke 1:13). "Joseph, son of David, do not be afraid to take to you Mary your wife" (Matthew 1:20). "Do not be afraid [Simon Peter]; from now on you will catch men" (Luke 5:10). "Do not be afraid, Paul; you must be brought before Caesar" (Acts 27:24).

Surely the command needs to be obeyed, for fear is a characteristic of this present age. Evidence of that truth is seen in both what we do and what we do not do—our commissions and omissions. We fear crime—purse-snatchers, robbers, burglars, murderers. So we stay home, double-lock our doors, bar our windows, and turn on the television to look at the robbers, burglars, and murderers!

These are times to test our faith. May we so live this day that others will know that "God has not given us a spirit of fear; but of power and of love and of a sound mind" (2 Timothy 1:7). Like Adam, we have been clothed with the protection of God's righteousness in Jesus Christ.

January 3

And Enoch walked with God; and he was not; for God took him. (Genesis 5:24; see also Hebrews 11:5)

We are not told much more about Enoch than that. He is one of the many wonderful characters of the Bible we would like to have known. Nothing is said of artistic achievements, military exploits, intellectual attainments, whether he had political clout, or was wealthy. We do not know.

The one thing that distinguished him was faith. If he was mediocre or average, faith lifted him out of that mediocrity and put his name in Sacred Writ so that millions might know there was a man by the name of Enoch who walked with God and never saw death.

Marriage did not stop Enoch from living in such a way that God was pleased. He fathered sons and daughters. Evil times did not stop Enoch from living in such a way that God was pleased.

Enoch's day was a time of moral looseness and deterioration. Enoch lived on the very margin of the Flood, when, according to Genesis 6:5, "The wickedness of man was great in the earth, and . . . every intent of the thoughts of his heart was only evil continually."

Enoch is to be commended. His righteous living came in an unrighteous age. He lived clean in dirty times. That speaks to our hearts today!

Finally, see Enoch as a picture of the possibility that not all Christians will pass through physical death (1 Corinthians 15:51–52). Enoch would say, "Look up; and keep looking up!" Soon you will see Christ standing on a cloud, with outstretched arms and nail-pierced hands, commanding you to come on up a little higher.

January 4

And they said, "Come, let us build ourselves a city and a tower whose top is in the heavens; let us make a name for ourselves." (Genesis 11:4)

Note man's *arrogance* in the words: "Let us build . . . let us make." That incident at Babel shows men's complete disregard for God's will, almost daring the Lord to interfere with their plans.

Second, see their *ambition* in their desire for "a name." Without God, ambition becomes self-reliance, self-sufficiency, and self-glorification. Men, however, were not created to make a name for themselves but to praise God's name.

Ambition not guided by the Holy Spirit has an improper motive, is likely to use improper methods to achieve its aim, and is never satisfied once its goal is reached.

Third, is the matter of *astrology*; the tower was to be open unto the heavens. That is, upon the ziggurats, or terraced towers, were zodiac signs that they might worship the hosts of heaven—the sun, moon, and stars. God hates astrology (Deuteronomy 18:10–12), for the study of horoscopes is an attempt to be independent of God, a failure to rely upon Him.

Keep in mind that the Lord's antidote for arrogance is humility. The sinner saved by grace does not leave God out of his plans. The alternative to unholy ambition is the leading of the Holy Spirit. The answer to astrology is the Word of God.

God's Word assures us that Jesus Christ is able to make all things work together for our good. There is nothing—no height, no depth, nor any other creation—that can separate us from the love of God shown in Christ Jesus our Lord (Romans 8:38–39).

January 5

And Lot lifted his eyes. . . . Then Lot chose . . . .
(Genesis 13:10–11)

Lot had accompanied Abram, his uncle, from Egypt. God blessed Abram materially, and he became the owner of many cattle and much silver and gold. Lot too, being in Abram's company, was blessed. When the large flocks of sheep and herds of cattle put a serious strain upon the natural resources and bitter strife developed among the herdsmen, Abram came to Lot with a plan.

Lot's eye: Abram left it up to his nephew to pick whatever land he wanted. Lot immediately accepted the offer, without praying, without offering his uncle first choice. Lot's greed and selfishness led him to depend solely upon what he could see. So he chose the well-watered valley of Jordan.

Lot's environment: In the territory Lot chose were the corrupt cities of Sodom and Gomorrah, wherein dwelt wicked men. Lot looked toward Sodom, pitched his tent toward Sodom, and ended up living in Sodom. Second Peter 2:7–8 speaks well of Lot to that point, but Lot's greed made him insensitive to the claims of God. A deliberate choice of an evil environment, not to witness against it but to enjoy it or use it for worldly advantage, is spiritually devastating.

Lot's end: The first warning came when he was captured by King Chedorlaomer and had to be rescued by Abram. The second event was his escape from the burning city. His sons-in-law mocked and died. His wife lingered and looked back; she was turned into a pillar of salt. Lot ended up with nothing but his two daughters who later got him drunk and committed incest.

Lot chose for himself. Christ wants to choose for you. Let Him. He who shed His blood so that you might have life eternal will enable you to enjoy life abundant today.

January 6

But his wife looked back behind him, and she became a pillar of salt. (Genesis 19:26)

After teaching a Sunday school class the teacher asked for comments. One little boy said, "My mother looked back once while she was driving."

The teacher asked, "What happened to her?"

The boy replied, "She turned into a telephone pole."

Looking back can be dangerous. You recall that after the angels of the Lord blinded the homosexuals of Sodom, the next morning the angels led Lot, his wife, and their two daughters out of the city.

They were all warned: "Escape for your life; do not look behind you" (Genesis 19:17). As God rained down fire and brimstone out of heaven upon the cities of Sodom and Gomorrah, Lot's wife looked back—she lingered—and was turned into a pillar of salt.

Such judgment may seem harsh to the sophisticated modern, but God had a reason for His condemnation. Lot's wife evidently showed an infatuation with the carelessness and sensuality of the city. She suffered spiritual schizophrenia; her loyalty was divided. In other words, her treasures were in Sodom; where your treasures are, your heart is also.

Looking back may indicate the heart's desire to be back. Sometimes the old nature craves the leeks, onions, and garlic of Egypt, the company of Gomorrah. Sad to say, our hearts may feel no pangs, no guilt, no grief, no shame because of such longings. Here indeed is a first step in backsliding.

"Remember Lot's wife" (Luke 17:32), and strive by the power of the Holy Spirit to keep your eyes upon Jesus Christ as you reach forward to what lies ahead (Philippians 3:13).

~

January 7

Then they called Rebekah and said to her, "Will you go with this man?" And she said, "I will go." (Genesis 24:58)

When Abraham was well up in age, about 140 years old, he sent out his servant to find a wife for Isaac. The servant's name is not mentioned, although he probably was Eliezer (Genesis 15:2). Having sworn to do as Abraham commanded, he went to the city of Nahor in Mesopotamia. There he prayed that the Lord would help him in the selection of a wife for his master's son, thus showing a deep sense of spiritual responsibility.

Before he had finished praying, the beautiful virgin Rebekah came to the well where the servant was; when she had filled her pitcher, the servant asked her for a drink of water. She complied, furnishing water for his camels as well. Later the servant announced his mission. When Rebekah was asked to go back with him, she consented.

They traveled the long journey back. As was the custom, when Isaac approached the returning caravan Rebekah lighted off the camel and covered her face with a veil; the unveiled bride was not to be seen by the groom until the marriage rites were completed.

We see here a picture of Christ and the Church. The servant is a type of the Holy Spirit, who does not speak of Himself, but of Jesus Christ (John 16:13). Rebekah is a type of the Church, the called-out virgin bride. Having never seen the groom, she takes the word of the servant and starts off to meet her husband.

You and I are on that journey now. It is long and hazardous. We travel through an unfriendly world. One day we shall see Him whom we have never seen before. Because we love Him and believe in Him we are able to rejoice with great joy along the way.

January 8

And he was afraid and said, "How awesome is this place! This is none other than the house of God, and this is the gate of heaven!" (Genesis 28:17)

Those are the words of Jacob after he experienced the dream of the ladder that reached from earth to heaven. Perhaps here for the first time in his life he was personally conscious of God's presence. He was afraid: "How awesome is this place!"

The word rendered *awesome*, *dreadful*, or *terrible*, means "to be feared and reverenced." Other scriptures speak of a great and awesome God (Daniel 9:4) whose name is terrible among the nations (Malachi 1:14); yea, the LORD Most High is awe-inspiring (Psalm 47:2) in His works (Psalm 66:3) and in His deeds toward the children of men. He is fearsome to the kings of the earth (Psalm 76:12); His name is holy (Psalm 99:3), and He in His own good time will send that great and terrible day of judgment.

To Jacob that was a very sacred spot. He was greatly impressed by the experience. Here was the place where God dwelt. Jehovah had made His presence known. Yea, He was a God very near.

I think we must agree with Jacob that the house of the Lord is the gate of heaven. Where God showed Himself to Jacob there was shown also to him a way that opened into heaven.

One cannot get to God's heaven without God, and no man comes to the Father but through Jesus Christ. He that tries to get in some other way is a thief and a robber.

Today the church is where God's people meet to worship Him in spirit and in truth. It is a place of reverence. When we come into the church our hearts ought to say, "How awesome is this place! This is none other than God's house, the gate of heaven!"

January 9

Then Jacob was left alone; and a Man wrestled with him until the breaking of day. (Genesis 32:24)

Returning home after a twenty-year absence, Jacob was afraid of Esau. He split his caravan, prayed for deliverance, and was left alone. A man came and wrestled with Jacob. Note that God initiated the struggle, for the Lord had been working with and on Jacob for a long time. The lesson Jacob must learn is this: Stop relying upon self.

Self-dependence and reliability are basic ingredients for spiritual failure. Self-sufficiency is characteristic of lostness. Jacob, as a believer, must learn to put off the old man and put on the new man.

God made us for Himself, to use for His own glory, to live for Him. That was something Jacob had to learn. To bring Jacob to his knees, God had to cripple him. It was the only way for Jacob to find himself—it took that to turn all of the craftiness and cunning of the years into subjection to the will of God. The Man with whom Jacob wrestled touched his thigh and dislocated the bone from its socket. God was intent upon taking away that which hindered Jacob from growing in the Lord.

So it was that in time Jacob, the swindler, cheat, slickster, full of scheming self-sufficiency, became one who had power with God. His name was changed, indicating a new relationship with the Lord. Changing character is a struggle. Jacob found it to be a humbling process and a very personal one. God was the God of Abraham and Isaac, but Jacob needed a personal encounter to discover that the Lord would help him find himself.

When Jacob realized his own helplessness and God's omnipotence, his own weakness and God's strength, his own inferiority and God's superiority, his heart yielded, and he received a blessing from the Lord.

January 10

Your name shall no longer be called Jacob, but Israel.
(Genesis 32:28)

Only God can give men names that are really good, names that befit good character. Christian character comes only from the Lord. A good name from God's point of view is based upon one's relationship with the Lord. Only a good God can give good names.

Now the Lord desires that men become like Him in order that their names too might be good. The names He gives are not "nicknames"—additional names like those of our boyhood days: Butch, Cue Stick, Flash, Fiddle, Peanut, and so on. To this day, if someone hollers, "Hey, Ducky!" I will turn, expecting to see someone from yesteryear who knew me as a boy.

When God changes your name it indicates a genuine change in character, an alteration in values and attitudes. It means a change in position or relationship with the Lord. There is something new on the inside. A new name means a new era, a new period in a man's life, the occurrence of some great event. The Lord uses a change of name to direct attention to the change of character of the person with whom He deals.

God is still in the name-changing business! To make sure you have a good name, you must be born again. If any man is in Christ Jesus he is a new creation; and every new creature must have a new name.

It does not matter what men call us on this earth. We are but pilgrims, sojourners, strangers just passing through. Rejected by the world, despised by demons, hounded by the devil, ill-treated by wicked men, we have new names the world knows nothing about. When we stand before the Lord may we hear Him say, "Well done!" and then receive a white stone on which is written a new name that no man knows except our Savior and us.

January 11

And the Angel of the LORD appeared to him in a flame of fire from the midst of a bush. So he looked, and behold, the bush was burning with fire, but the bush was not consumed. (Exodus 3:2)

God is *powerful*. The burning bush was not consumed and was another example of the power of God. It was a miracle needed to attract Moses' attention. It was a sign required to show him that God within was greater than affliction on the outside.

God is *personal*. Moses learned that Jehovah was a personal God. When the Lord saw that Moses turned aside to see, God called unto him out of the midst of the bush and said, "Moses, Moses!" (Exodus 3:4). I am reminded of the little girl who had just learned what is sometimes called the "Lord's Prayer." One night her mother overheard her saying, "Our Father, who art in heaven, how did you know my name?"

He knew Moses by name. He is a personal God who takes time out to deal with us personally, individually. The God and Father who made a different pattern for every snowflake, for every leaf on every tree, for every fingerprint, for every human voice, and who knows every star by name—surely knows us, each one by name. He has numbered the very hairs of our heads.

God is *pure*. The third thing Moses learned in that encounter with the Lord was that God is pure. After Moses answered, "Here I am" (Exodus 3:4), God had to restrain him from coming any closer. "Moses, do not draw near this place. Take your sandals off your feet, for the place where you stand is holy ground" (Exodus 3:5).

Today we see Jesus Christ, our powerful Savior who rose from the dead, a Savior who knows each one of us personally, a Savior who is pure and holy. Unlike the situation in Moses' day, Calvary has opened the door, and we can enter into the very presence of a holy God.

January 12

Moreover He said, "I am the God of your father—the God of Abraham, the God of Isaac, and the God of Jacob." (Exodus 3:6).

This full title, the God of Abraham, the God of Isaac, the God of Jacob, first appears in Exodus 3 and is found there three times (vv. 6, 15, 16). A peculiarly Jewish title, it reminds us of the agreement, or covenant, God set up.

It is a title that links Jehovah in a very personal, intimate way with Israel. It connects the Jews with God as His very own people. It is a title that brings to mind God's personal dealings and experiences with men of clay.

Above all, I see the grace of God in this title. It indicates that the Lord deals with men where He finds them. God is fully aware of what we are—frail, fragile pieces of clay. Consider the various situations of Abraham, Isaac, and Jacob: idol worship, polygamy, and concubinage; lust, fear, deceit, lies, scheming, plotting, failure to wait on the Lord.

Yet a holy God considered their weaknesses and by His grace used their faults and failures to further His program for Israel and for the rest of the world. He talked to them in dreams, visions, and face to face; answered their prayers, wrestled with their pride; touched their hearts, calmed their fears; protected their families; made their enemies to be at peace with them; prospered their livestock; increased their holdings of land; enlarged their vision, developed their character; changed their names, sanctified them; blessed their posterity; broadened their faith; and wrote their names down in the Lamb's book of life.

January 13

And God said to Moses, "I AM WHO I AM." And He said, "Thus you shall say to the children of Israel, 'I AM has sent me to you.'" (Exodus 3:14)

God knew about the terrible time the Jews were having there in Egypt. He heard their groans, felt the sting of the lash across their backs. He remembered the covenant He had made with Abraham, Isaac, and Jacob.

Moved by compassion and concern for His people, Jehovah caught the attention of Moses shepherding his father-in-law's sheep by appearing in a flame of fire from a bush that was not consumed. "Moses, I want you to go to Pharaoh and bring the children of Israel out of the land of Egypt!"

Then said Moses, "When I tell them the God of their fathers sent me, and they ask, 'What is His name?', what shall I tell them?" And God replied, "I AM THAT I AM. Tell them, 'I AM sent me to you.'" (Exodus 3:12–14).

What a name! One so simple, yet so profound, so inexhaustibly deep. Apparently it comes from the verb *to be*, although some scholars suggest it is derived from the verb *to become*. Because the tense is imperfect or indefinite, the name may also be rendered: I WAS WHAT I WAS, or I WILL BE WHAT I WILL BE.

As the God who *was*, His eternality is expressed. He always was, always has been; He is the Eternal One. As the God who *is*, He is a very present help. He knows our condition, our troubles, problems, heartaches; as I AM, He is available at all times. He not only knows what we need and when we need it, but because He *is*, He supplies that need.

Finally, because He is the God who *shall be* we rejoice that the future is in good hands.

January 14

The LORD will fight for you, and you shall hold your peace.
(Exodus 14:14)

When a man relies solely upon himself or upon other human aid, what is he really saying to God? Is it not: "I don't need you!"? One man who became angry with me during a marriage counseling session said, "I don't need your help. I wear pants just like you do! I'm a man!"

How many men dare shake their fists in God's face and declare by their action: "I don't need You! I can take care of myself! I'm a man!"

Such a man is deluded. His discernment is dim. He does not realize that his attitude invites the aid of wicked men who mean him no everlasting good. For often evildoers will help for a while only because it enables them to get what they want.

Israel's desire to fight her own battle was also an expression of ingratitude. In spite of every deliverance wrought by God, every foe vanquished, every victory won, we tend to forget and want to settle scores ourselves.

Another danger of fighting our own battles is that we may become like the allies with whom we associate. That can be a major cause of weakness. Some of us sell our souls for help from sinners. We offer material gifts and ourselves for physical aid to combat that which is basically not flesh and blood, but spiritual wickedness.

Failure to see the true enemy moves us to use sticks and stones and to try to break bones. However belligerent the enemy becomes today, however vicious his attack, remember that God has promised to fight your battles for you. Let Him!

January 15

The LORD is my . . . song. (Exodus 15:2)

The devil hates to hear Christians sing, especially when they live the life they sing about. Paul and Silas, although in jail, at midnight prayed and sang praises unto God. I can see the devil over in some dark corner of the dungeon with his fingers in his ears and crying out, "Shut up! Stop your singing!" However, it was to no avail, for the Lord in heaven heard and moved to set His children free. The prison foundation shook, and the two prisoners were released.

We saints belong to a singing family. "Sing the wondrous love of Jesus, / Sing His mercy and His grace; / In the mansions bright and blessed, / He'll prepare for us a place" (Eliza E. Hewitt).

"Sing them over again to me, / Wonderful words of Life; / Let me more of their beauty see, / Wonderful words of Life" (Philip P. Bliss). "Nearer, my God, to Thee, / Nearer to Thee! / E'en though it be a cross / That raiseth me; / Still all my song shall be, / Nearer, my God, to Thee" (Sarah E. Adams).

"Rejoice, rejoice, O Christian, lift up your voice and sing / Eternal hallelujahs to Jesus Christ the King!" (Alfred H. Ackley).

"Take my feet and let them be / Swift and beautiful for Thee; / Take my voice and let me sing / Always, only, for my King" (Frances R. Havergal). "O for a thousand tongues to sing / My great Redeemer's praise, / The glories of my God and King, / The triumphs of His grace" (Charles Wesley).

Yes, music runs in our Christian family, and we have got something to sing about. Indeed, we have *Someone* to sing about. That is the meaning of this text. He is my song. Is He yours? He is the object of my song, the theme of my singing:

> Jesus, Jesus, Jesus —
> Sweetest name I know,
> Fills my every longing,
> Keeps me singing as I go.
> *Luther B. Bridgers*

January 16

And He has become my salvation. (Exodus 15:2)

Israel was delivered from being trampled under by horses and chariots of Pharaoh and from a watery grave or re-enslavement in Egypt. Today there are Christians who need to be delivered. They have been redeemed by the blood but not by power. That is ridiculous, for there is power in the blood. However, it is not God's fault that some saints cannot say, "The LORD is my salvation."

We are suggesting that the Lord did not die on the cross to save us from the penalty of sin and then leave us to live on our own against the power of sin. No. He saved and still saves—that is the thing we are impressed with here.

He who lifted up Joseph from a pit and placed him in Pharaoh's palace, who saved David from the spear of Saul, who saved king Hezekiah from death and added fifteen more years to his life, who saved Simon Peter from sinking to his death beneath the waves, who saved Paul and Silas out of the dungeon—that same resurrected Savior lives forevermore to deliver us too.

He will solve your problems, dear saint. Just cast your cares upon Him, for He cares for you. As He made a way for Israel out of no way so that they could cross the Red Sea in safety, so will He deliver you and give you the victory.

Then you too will be able to add your voice to the multitudes who can sing: "The LORD is my strength, my song, and my salvation!" Remember today, in whatever Red Sea experiences you may have, that Jesus Christ is Savior, not just from the penalty of sin, but also from the power of sin and the persecution of sinners.

January 17

The LORD is a man of war; the LORD is His name.
(Exodus 15:3)

Those words are found in the beginning of the song of the redeemed Israelites who had escaped the pursuing Egyptians. Now it was time to glorify God. Note that Moses is not mentioned. The Israelites realized that they had absolutely nothing to do with the victory. God did it all. Indeed, Jehovah is the hero of that battle; He is the man of war.

Now Goliath is called a "man of war from his youth" (1 Samuel 17:33). When King Saul sought soothing music and asked for a man that could play the harp well, a servant said, "Look, I have seen a son of Jesse the Bethlehemite, who is skillful in playing [the harp], a mighty man of valor, a man of war" (1 Samuel 16:18). Therefore, a way was made for the young man David.

We are tempted to add names like Alexander the Great, Napoleon Bonaparte, Robert E. Lee, John Pershing, George Patton, and Douglas MacArthur. None of these compare, however, with Jesus Christ, the general who led the children of Israel out of bondage.

He is a buckler, shield, defender, fortress, battle-axe, high tower; a God who shoots arrows, whose Word is a sword, and who makes the clouds His chariots. "He teaches my hands to make war, so that my arms can bend a bow of bronze" (Psalm 18:34). He is "the LORD strong and mighty, the LORD mighty in battle" (Psalm 24:8).

Never forget that all genuine Christians are engaged in a warfare—not physical, not against other men, but against spiritual wickedness in high places. As you go forth this morning, wearing the whole armor of God, willing to endure hardness as a good soldier, remember that the hero of the hour is Jesus Christ. Follow the resurrected Savior today, obey the Captain of your salvation, and discover that He always leads His soldiers in triumph (2 Corinthians 2:14).

January 18

And they went three days in the wilderness and found no water. Now when they came to Marah, they could not drink the waters of Marah, for they were bitter. (Exodus 15:22–23)

After the singing, shouting, and dancing were over, after the celebration of their deliverance from Egypt, the Jews went out into the wilderness of Shur. Within three days the beautiful harmonious symphony of victory and triumph had degenerated into the cacophony of complaint. What happened?

It was testing time. The Lord Jehovah wanted to prove Israel's trust in Him for the supply of her material needs. The Israelites had gone three days in the wilderness and found no water. Three days without sight of a tree, without shade from the glaring, scorching rays of the sun. Doubtless there was present the fear of dying from thirst.

Then water was discovered! Pulses skipped, hearts throbbed, hopes leaped, steps hastened, and parched tongues and dry lips anticipated refreshment. But, alas! The water was brackish, bitter, unfit for human consumption.

"And the people complained against Moses, saying, 'What shall we drink?'" (v. 24). It was testing time for Israel; though she had sung in triumph three days earlier, she now complained bitterly. The sweet song of victory turned to a bitter tune of murmuring.

God provided the solution by having Moses cast a tree into the bitter waters, and the waters were made sweet. That tree represented the cross of Christ (Galatians 3:13). We learn from that incident that there may be bitter experiences for us even today. Let us pray that we will keep our eyes on Christ and allow Him to keep us consistent in times of testing.

~

January 19

I will utterly blot out the remembrance of Amalek from under heaven. (Exodus 17:14)

What provoked that devastating announcement? What moved Jehovah to declare such relentless war against Amalek from generation to generation? Basically, it was because the Amalekites refused to accept the fact that it was God who worked wonders for the Israelites. They despised Israel and held Israel's God in contempt.

One of the things that made the fighting dreadful was the fact it was intra-family fighting—the Amalekites and Israelites were relatives. Amalek was a grandson of Esau (Genesis 36:12); and, of course, Esau was the brother of Jacob, whose name became Israel (Genesis 32:28).

Second, the attack was unprovoked. Israel had done nothing against the Amalekites. Third, we learn that their attack was sneaky (Deuteronomy 25:17–18). Amalek dared not try a point-blank frontal attack, but sought to pick off the Jews like some satanic sniper. Those who lagged behind—the stragglers, the feeble, the tired, the weary, the worn out, the crippled—were wiped out.

Fourth, note the last clause of Deuteronomy 25:18: "and he did not fear God." They were idol worshipers in common with the Canaanites and had no fear or knowledge of the true God.

We Christians can learn something here. We see that we too are in a warfare against a malicious foe. Like Moses, Aaron and Hur, we must stretch out our hands in prayer and discomfit Amalek with the sword, the Word of God. Fly high the banner of the Lord today, and let men know that in Jesus Christ there is victory over every foe.

January 20

You shall not take the name of the LORD your God in vain, for the LORD will not hold him guiltless who takes His name in vain. (Exodus 20:7)

The God of the Bible has revealed Himself by more than four hundred different names and titles, and each one shows some aspect of His person, character, plans, and relationship with mankind. For example, there are such designations as: almighty, eternal one, holy, I AM THAT I AM, Jehovah, jealous, LORD of hosts, rock, and strong tower. Some names of Christ are: Branch, Bridegroom, Lamb of God, Bright Morning Star, Cornerstone, and Redeemer.

Failing to understand the significance of a name, some men make a big to-do over what name should be pronounced over a candidate for water baptism. It is almost as if they believe in baptismal regeneration.

Of course, water baptism does not save anyone. It is simply a symbol of what the Holy Spirit has done already. If a man's heart has not been changed by God, baptizing that man "in Jesus' name" certainly will not save him. The saying is, he goes down a dry sinner and comes up a wet sinner.

Whatever name He uses, it stands for God; He *is* His name. He makes known to us His attributes—His deity, humanity, glory, grace, honor, love, mercy, perfection, power, providence, purpose, wisdom and will—by His name.

In short, the name of God stands for the cumulative revelation of all that is made known through His different personal names. No one name fully describes Him. If we take all of the names and titles in the Bible and lump them together into one big name, we would still fall short of describing God adequately.

Yet each name is *God*; He *is* His name. You see why it is so wrong to take God's name in vain, to use it thoughtlessly, or use it to substantiate a falsehood.

January 21

Behold, I send an Angel before you to keep you in the way and to bring you into the place which I have prepared. (Exodus 23:20)

The Place was promised. Sometime earlier Jehovah had revealed Himself in the burning bush to Moses and then commissioned Moses to return to Egypt and seek the freedom of the Israelites. In reminding Moses of the covenant established with Abraham, Isaac and Jacob, it is again evident that the land the Jews were to inherit had been promised to them by the Lord. "For all the land which you see I give to you and your descendants forever," said God to Abraham (Genesis 13:14–15, 17).

The Place was prepared. Because the Canaanites and other pagans lived there, it became necessary for God to remove them. A sovereign God has the right to move whom He pleases, having determined the times before appointed and the bounds of the habitations of the nations (Acts 17:26). Ripe for judgment because of their idolatry, those nations were dispossessed by God.

The People were protected. An angel (I believe it was Jesus Christ appearing as the Angel of the LORD) was needed to guard the Jews, for the pagans were not willing to give up any territory. As an obedient people, they would discover that the Lord would indeed watch over them and give them victory.

What was true of Israel in the Old Testament is true of Christians in the New Testament church age. Although the promised land is not to be equated with heaven, where there will be no warfare waged, it is true that the Lord Jesus promised He would prepare a place for His own (John 14:2–3). Daily we walk with the assurance that what the Lord started, He will finish. He will not desert us. Nothing can separate us from Him.

All the way my Savior leads me; What have I to ask beside?
Can I doubt His tender mercy, Who through life has been my guide?
Heav'nly peace, divinest comfort, Here by faith in Him to dwell!
For I know whate'er befall me, Jesus doeth all things well.

Fanny J. Crosby

January 22

You shall not offer strange incense on it.
(Exodus 30:9; Leviticus 10:1)

Men must be taught how to worship God, and God Himself must be the instructor. In the matter of incense burning and its smoke ascending up to God in heaven, we have a symbol of prayer and praise. The altar upon which the incense burned was a type or representation of Jesus Christ.

Incense is called strange, unholy, alien when it is not prepared in the prescribed manner (Exodus 30:34–38) or when it is offered in the wrong way, a way not according to the will or instruction of God (Leviticus 10:2–3).

Cain was the first to fall into that trap. The only worship acceptable to the Lord involved the shedding of blood through animal sacrifice that looked forward to the death of Christ at Calvary. However, Cain wanted to worship God the way Cain wanted to worship God. He brought vegetables, the products of his own toil, and showed he was a religious man satisfied with his own sufficiency and ability.

Strange incense then indicates an inadequate concept of sin. The warning to worship God in spirit and in truth goes unheeded. Wherever there is incorrect and unacceptable worship, there is the beginning of idolatry; and presumptuousness moves men to worship the creature instead of the Creator.

Nadab and Abihu, two older sons of Aaron, took it upon themselves to kindle a fire upon the altar. Whatever their motives, they acted contrary to the will of God, and they were destroyed. The true Christian is made aware of the fact that God desires to be worshiped in spirit and in truth.

Sincerity is not enough. Knowledge is needed—obedience to the Word of God. Where there is reverence, respect for holiness, and a desire to worship the Lord the way He wants to be worshiped, there are blessings unspeakable.

January 23

You cannot see My face; for no man shall see Me, and live.
(Exodus 33.20)

While Moses was up on Mount Sinai talking with the LORD, the people grew restless, rebellious. A golden calf was made and worshiped. When Jehovah saw it He became angry and threatened to destroy the people and raise up a new group through Moses. However, He exercised restraint. About three thousand men were killed in disciplinary judgment, after which Moses again made intercession.

Ordered to resume the journey, Moses was encouraged to the point where he boldly yearned for a fuller revelation of God: "Please show me Your glory" (v. 18). Moses wanted to see the face of God.

Now according to the Bible, God has a nose (Exodus 15:8; Amos 5:21), a mouth (Deuteronomy 8:3; Matthew 4:4), ears (Numbers 11:18; James 5:4), eyes (2 Chronicles 16:9; Hebrews 4:13). He also has a face. Not to see God's face is a sign of disfavor, disapproval, showing His anger or judgment. On the other hand, to see His face means approval, favor, benediction, familiarity, intimacy, and personal acceptance.

What Moses desired long ago and it was impossible to obtain, we have today in Christ. Standing on the solid rock, we can see God's face. John said: "We beheld his glory, the glory as of the only begotten of the Father, full of grace and truth." In Christ God is elucidated, analyzed, exegeted, and unfolded (John 1:18)—so much so that on one occasion Christ could say to Philip: "He who has seen Me has seen the Father" (John 14:9). And again: "He who sees Me sees Him who sent Me" (John 12:45). Today thank God that through the eyes of faith you can see the Lord Jesus Christ and bask in the sunshine of His favor.

January 24

Moses did not know that the skin of his face shone while he talked with Him. (Exodus 34:29)

It is impossible to encounter God and remain unaffected. Enoch met God; he walked with Him and was snatched up into heaven. Jacob met God and his leg was crippled. Balaam's donkey met the Lord and talked about it. Zacharias, father of John the Baptist, met Him and was struck dumb for nine months. The disciples on the Emmaus road met Him, and their hearts burned within them. Paul met Him on the road to Damascus and was blinded for three days.

Moses too was affected. Having spoken with God, he came away with his face reflecting the glory of God. Of course, God is light and dwells in the light that no man can approach. It is not strange that Moses' face reflected some of this glory. It is impossible to be with the Lord and not become like Him.

Note that Moses did not know his face was shining. "He was glorious in all eyes but his own" (F. B. Meyer). The Israelites recognized the shining was a sign from God and were afraid to come near. Moses put a veil on his face. A veil symbolizes secrecy, concealment; it represents that which is transitory.

Moses wore no veil when in God's presence, nor when teaching the people, but put it on whenever he stopped speaking to God or for God. That was in order that the Israelites might not view the "end," the fading, transitory glory of the law given by Moses. The law was only temporary; eventually it would end. We know now that all things find their fulfillment in Christ. All the fullness of the Godhead dwells in Him bodily, and in Him we are complete. Through Christ the veil is taken away. God grant that our unveiled faces will be radiant this day for Jesus Christ as we are changed from glory to glory (2 Corinthians 3:18).

January 25

I am the LORD your God, who brought you out of the land of Egypt, that you should not be their slaves; I have broken the bands of your yoke and made you walk upright. (Leviticus 26:13)

In slightly more than half of the books of the Old Testament mention is made of the redemption of Israel from the land of Egypt: "I saved you . . . I redeemed you . . . I brought you up . . . I brought you out." That is the constant refrain of grace.

Why that recurrent reminder to Israel? Was it that a disobedient people needed to be reminded of their redemption? Indeed, the fact of their deliverance from slavery in Egypt became the basis of all of Jehovah's appeals to the Jews.

God had broken the yoke of severe oppression, for He did not want His people to be slaves. Likewise our bands were broken at Calvary. We are exhorted to remain free in the freedom with which Christ has freed us (Galatians 5:1). Sin shall not have dominion over us to re-enslave us (Romans 6:14).

When the yoke of bondage was removed, the Israelites were able to stand upright. When Christ broke our yoke, He enabled us to walk with dignity. That is what true freedom does for the believer.

The God we serve wants us to be truly free. Redemption opens the eyes of the blind; it frees us from sin's dominion; it delivers us from feelings of guilt, from deception and slavery to circumstances. Our Lord desires that we enjoy the heritage of an enlarged soul.

Make up your mind today to walk with your head held high. You are a citizen of heaven, not a slave in Egypt.

January 26

We remember the fish which we ate freely in Egypt; the cucumbers, the melons, the leeks, the onions, and the garlic. (Numbers 11:5).

How soon we are removed from the remembrance of God's grace to us. Hear the Israelites on the way from Sinai to Kadesh Barnea complaining: "We remember what we had in Egypt!" Longings returned for those sensuous pleasures once enjoyed. Out of fellowship with God, the things of the world and the old life again become attractive.

We lust, we remember, we seek. Moved by the immoral mixed multitude in their midst, the memories of the Israelites were stirred. They remembered the bread they ate to the full, but not the backbreaking bondage; they remembered the cucumbers, but not the cruelty; the delicacies, but not the despair; the fish, but not the loss of freedom; the fleshpots, but not the frustration.

They remembered the choice garlic, but forgot the chain gangs. They recalled the leeks but not the lashes, the meat but not the meanness and murder, the melons but not the moans, onions but not oppression, tasty radishes but not the taskmasters' roughness, the water but not the whips and rigors of the work.

You may meet someone today, or some event may occur, that will take your mind back to yesteryear when you lived without Jesus Christ. You will indeed remember some good things and some bad things. Surely the old life had death as its goal (Romans 6:21).

In Christ there is life eternal and life abundant. The remembrance of what used to be serves only to heighten your concept of God's grace. Be moved to rejoice and thank the Lord for bringing you out of Egypt's land and Pharaoh's hand.

January 27

Let us go up at once and take possession, for we are well able to overcome it. (Numbers 13:30)

After forty days the twelve spies Moses sent out returned to Kadesh Barnea, bringing with them grapes, pomegranates, and figs. They showed them to all the congregation, remarking, "It [the land] truly flows with milk and honey, and this is its fruit."

At that point ten of the spies began to give undue prominence to the strength of the Canaanites and started an evil report. "It's a good land all right, but giants live there!" Their exaggeration of what they deemed insurmountable difficulty had its effect upon the people and caused their hearts to melt.

Then Caleb spoke up. Perhaps Joshua was too closely associated with Moses to be very effective at that point, but Caleb could serve as a more independent and objective witness. He sought to quiet the people. "Let us go up at once and take it; we can do it!"

However, the ten spies prevailed and persuaded the people that the Canaanites were too strong—that compared to the Anakim the Jews were but grasshoppers. "No," they warned, "the land devours its inhabitants." That expression suggests that something about the land led to the early death of its inhabitants—war!

Because of their rebellion and unbelief they were made to wander in the wilderness a total of forty years (Numbers 14:33–34). All those twenty years old and upward died, their carcasses wasted in the wilderness. Of that generation, only Caleb and Joshua entered into the promised land. The ten spies who brought the majority report died by the plague before the Lord. Let us be determined today not to let the lack of faith rob us of God's blessing or delay its bestowment.

January 28

And all the children of Israel complained against Moses and Aaron. (Numbers 14:2)

It was at Kadesh Barnea that the Israelites rebelled against Moses and Aaron. Therefore, they rebelled against God. If your leader is God's man and is Spirit-led in what he asks you to do, refusal to obey is disobedience to God, not just disobedience to a mere mortal man.

So it was at Kadesh Barnea. You recall that only Caleb and Joshua in their minority report urged the people, "Let us go up at once and possess the land; for we are well able to overcome it." The rest of the spies had no such faith, and the report they brought concerning the land of Canaan struck fear into the hearts of the Jews.

"If only we had died in the land of Egypt! If only we had died in this wilderness! Would it not have been better for us to return there?" They cried the blues, murmured, and complained until the Lord became sick to His stomach and wanted to wipe them all out.

Moses pleaded for mercy upon them, and God did not strike them dead. Whereas travel through the wilderness was a necessary part of God's plan to discipline the Israelites, the thirty-eight years of wandering were unnecessary. Their misery was the product of their own unbelief.

How true that is today—we go through rough places in life of necessity. Man that is born of woman is of few days and full of trouble. But the road is often made rougher because of our faithlessness, lust, and disobedience. Our prayer today is: "Lord, help us to be satisfied and thankful for all You have done for us."

January 29

Gather the people together, and I will give them water.
(Numbers 21:16)

Finally Aaron was dead; Miriam had died earlier. The wanderings ended; the marches began. As the long trek approached its end, they entered a region where, because of its aridity, water was welcomed. At Beer, which means well, the LORD spoke to Moses the words: "Gather the people together, and I will give them water."

"Gather together" is a call to worship. It is ever God's desire that His people gather to and about Himself. The center of worship is not the preacher; it is not the choir or chorus; it is not the collection of money. The center of worship is Jesus Christ Himself.

We gather together to praise God in song, in testimony, in offerings, in the reading of His Word, in preaching, and in prayer. God desires that. The Lord loves it, wants it, demands it; all glory, honor, praise, power, and majesty belong to Him.

Note that the text speaks not only of a gathering, but of a giving. There is something we get in coming together that we cannot obtain in the same measure otherwise. We must recognize that we serve the God who said, "I will give them water."

He is the God who said in Isaiah 41:17–18: "The poor and needy seek water, but there is none; their tongues fail for thirst. I, the LORD, will hear them; I, the God of Israel, will not forsake them. I will open rivers in desolate heights, and fountains in the midst of the valleys; I will make the wilderness a pool of water, and the dry land springs of water."

Let the Lord quench your thirst today. Hear the Lord say: "If anyone thirsts, let him come to Me and drink" (John 7:37).

January 30

And be sure your sin will find you out. (Numbers 32:23).

Reuben and Gad made known their desire to possess the land already conquered but still outside of the area promised to Israel by God. Intrinsic to their request was self-interest. They had a lot of cattle, and the land was excellent for grazing. That was foremost in their minds.

Moses was displeased. He saw through their request and feared that if those two tribes were allowed to remain on that side of the Jordan, morale would break down.

At that point Reuben and Gad countered with an offer to stay where they so desired but to fight along with the rest of the Israelites until the entire land was secured. "We will not return to our houses until everyone of the children of Israel has received his inheritance" (v. 18).

Moses reminded them of the seriousness of their promise and that God would take them at their word. "Okay, do it!" said Moses. "But if you don't do it, behold, you have sinned against the LORD. Be sure your sin will find you out."

The principle remains true today. Some people do not believe that their sins will be uncovered, but God's Word is true. Sometimes in life our sins find us out. Yet sometimes it seems men get away with murder in this life. What then?

"And as it is appointed for men to die once, but after this the judgment . . ." (Hebrews 9:27). "And books were opened . . . and the dead were judged according to their works, by the things which were written in the books" (Revelation 20:12).

Thanks be to God that the Christian need not worry about the final judgment. Only rewards face us. Jesus Christ became sin for us and paid the full penalty when He died in our place. That sin whose wages is eternal death will never find us out.

January 31

You shall remember that you were a slave in the land of Egypt, and the LORD your God redeemed you; therefore, I command you this thing today. (Deuteronomy 15:15)

Here the LORD instituted the sabbatic year, the year of release. Creditors were to release their debtors from obligation. The poor were to be helped, and Israelite slaves were emancipated every seventh year. A Hebrew who remembered what it was like for his people to be in slavery in Egypt became more willing to obey God's command concerning the sabbatic year.

It is not always wrong or detrimental spiritually to look back. It is not always perilous to walk down memory lane and recall the experiences of the past. In fact, you should remember from time to time from where you have come; recall the clay from which you were dug. You will find it a humbling experience.

The apostle Paul informed the saints at Corinth that certain kinds of men would not inherit the kingdom of God, then added: "And such were some of you" (1 Corinthians 6:9–11). Again he said in Ephesians 2:11–12: "Therefore remember that you, once Gentiles in the flesh . . . that at that time you were without Christ . . . having no hope . . . without God in the world."

Knowledge of the past may be helpful. Knowledge that you have come through many dangers, toils, and snares heightens in your heart the concept of God's amazing grace. It is good once in a while to look back. He who brought you out of Egypt is able to guide your feet on the way to the promised land. Surely the Lord Jesus who provided for you in the past will guide your every step today and in countless days ahead.

February 1

When a prophet speaks in the name of the LORD, if the thing does not happen or come to pass, that is the thing which the LORD has not spoken; the prophet has spoken it presumptuously; you shall not be afraid of him. (Deuteronomy 18:22)

According to the Word of God, to prophesy and have that prophecy fail to come to pass is an indication God is not in it. God's test is simple: If the prediction does not come to pass, then its source is not God. The LORD is not the author of lies, falsehood, or error. To flunk this test is to be branded a liar: "The prophets prophesy lies in My name. I have not sent them, commanded them, nor spoken to them; they prophesy to you a false vision, divination, a worthless thing, and the deceit of their heart" (Jeremiah 14:14).

All of us are curious about the future. We want to know what is going to happen to us. Many books of the Bible provide us with much information about the future, and we thank God for His Word.

Christians are warned that false prophets within Christendom will continue to rear their sheep-disguised wolves' heads. "Then many false prophets will rise up and deceive many" (Matthew 24:11). We are exhorted to test the spirits by the Holy Spirit (1 John 4:1).

You might outrightly reject a false prophet who makes no pretense to believe in God. But the religious psychics are more dangerous; they are a more subtle menace. No matter who is involved, the failure of a verifiable prediction exposes the predictor to the wrath of God.

God says to each of us: Instead of worrying about today or tomorrow, lean on Him who holds today and tomorrow in His hands. On Jesus Christ alone build all your hopes, for all other ground is sinking sand.

February 2

Be strong and of good courage, do not fear nor be afraid of them; for the LORD your God, He is the One who goes with you. He will not leave you nor forsake you. (Deuteronomy 31:6)

The command to "be strong" first appears in the Bible in this text. The Hebrew verb used means "to grow firm or strong," signifying "to be courageous or confident." In his final words to Israel Moses counseled: "Be strong and of good courage, do not fear." To Joshua he said: "Be strong and of good courage." Jehovah spoke likewise to Joshua (Joshua 1:6–7, 9).

When the sun stood still and the Israelites defeated the kings of the Amorites, Joshua had the five kings brought out of a cave. He ordered the captains to put their feet upon the necks of the kings and then said to the people: "Do not be afraid, nor be dismayed; be strong and of good courage, for thus the LORD will do to all your enemies against whom you fight" (Joshua 10:25).

David's last charge to his son Solomon was: "I go the way of all the earth; be strong, therefore, and prove yourself a man" (1 Kings 2:2). Azariah the prophet warned King Asa: "But you, be strong and do not let your hands be weak, for your work shall be rewarded!" (2 Chronicles 15:7). When the king heard those words, he took courage and started a reformation; the idols were put away, and the altar of the LORD was renewed.

Haggai, sent to encourage the returned Jews to build the LORD's Temple, said: "'Yet now be strong, Zerubbabel . . . and be strong, Joshua . . . and be strong, all you people of the land . . . for I am with you,' says the LORD of hosts" (Haggai 2:4).

We are to be strong for many reasons, but the most frequently given reason in God's Word is this: Be strong because God is with you, and He will not forsake you.

February 3

For then you will make your way prosperous, and then you will have good success. (Joshua 1:8)

Ask a dozen different people the meaning of success, and you will get perhaps a dozen widely differing answers. If answers are similar and you then ask, "How is that success achieved?" you are liable to get even more differences of opinion.

The dictionary defines *success* as "the achievement of something desired, planned, or attempted"; it is the gaining of fame or prosperity. It is easy to see that some people define success in terms of money, position, power, prestige, or possessions.

Even in those terms *success* is relative. Definitions of success are not only too materialistic, but they are highly subjective without any absolute yardstick whereby success may be truly measured.

The Christian has an absolute standard: the Bible. In it we find that the word *success* occurs only once (in the King James Version). Joshua was chosen to succeed Moses, and the Lord Jehovah promised to bless Joshua if he would stick with God's Word. "This Book of the Law shall not depart from your mouth, but you shall meditate in it day and night."

The word rendered *success* comes from a verb meaning to be prudent, clever, to have insight, act circumspectly, have understanding. How do you like that for a definition of success? True success is tied up with the Word of God.

If you will study, meditate, believe and obey the Bible, God will prosper you. You will see that the central character in the Book is none other than Jesus Christ. Believe in the Word made flesh and discover that you are a successful person.

February 4

Now therefore, I beg you, swear to me by the LORD, *since I have shown you kindness, that you also will show kindness to my father's house, and give me a true token.* (Joshua 2:12)

Soon after assuming command, Joshua sent out two spies to the city of Jericho. As it turned out, the two men found their way to the house of Rahab, the prostitute. When the King of Jericho heard about the spies, he sent soldiers to Rahab's house. She admitted that some men had been there but said they had left.

Rahab lied, for she had hidden the two spies upon the roof of her house with the stalks of flax. After the soldiers had gone, Rahab requested a pledge of faithfulness from the two spies. "Show me you mean business—that you will keep your end of the deal—since I have shown kindness to you."

Before they left, the men told her to bind a scarlet rope in the window from which they were let down. That would identify her house when the city was attacked. Then she was to bring all of her relatives into the house. Rahab did as she was told. The men escaped and returned to Joshua.

When the walls of the city crumbled, Rahab and her family were saved. God's wrath fell upon the inhabitants of Jericho for their gross immorality and wickedness, their child sacrifice and idolatry. But Rahab escaped.

That scarlet cord was a true token, a sure sign. Symbolic of the shed blood of Jesus Christ, it provided an escape from the wrath of God. Faith in the shed blood of the Lamb of God remains the way of deliverance. Rahab believed in the LORD, the God of the Israelites, and the scarlet rope symbolized deliverance. Let us thank God for the sure sign He has given us that when He sees the blood He will pass over us.

February 5

Now therefore, give me this mountain . . . (Joshua 14:12)

Caleb was forty years old when he was sent out as a spy. Forty years in the wilderness, plus five years in the Promised Land, made him eighty-five years old. When the land was to be parceled out to the tribes of Israel, Caleb did not hesitate to make his request—a request based upon the fact that he wholly followed the LORD God of Israel.

The root meaning of "to follow wholly" is "to fill in or fill up," and thus to overflow or do something in abundance. Caleb was a man who did not hold back on God. He was not of double mind or heart or tongue. For him, fellowship with God was put above all other things. Caleb had his priorities straight.

Because Caleb abandoned himself to God, the LORD "abundanced" him. He blessed him with long life. Even at eighty-five years of age Caleb would say, "I am as strong this day as I was forty-five years ago when Moses sent me to spy out the land; as my strength was then, so now is my strength for war, both for going out and for coming in."

Having followed wholly after God, Caleb could make the request: "Give me this mountain." He could claim a glorious inheritance. *Hebron*, which became Caleb's, means "fellowship" or "communion."

Put God first in your life and you will find yourself enjoying life right here on earth, right now rejoicing in all that the Lord has for you. When your loyalties are divided, you live beneath your privileges. Your prayer requests become a waste of time. The God who gave His only Son desires to freely give us all things richly to enjoy. Follow Him with your whole heart, and like Caleb you too can request: "Give me this mountain!" and it will be yours.

February 6

Choose for yourselves this day whom you will serve. . . . But as for me and my house, we will serve the LORD. (Joshua 24:15)

Every day is election day. Life is full of confrontations and decisions that will not admit of compromise, neutrality, procrastination, or fence-straddling. Adam and Eve were faced with doing God's will, his or her own will, or Satan's prodding will.

Cain and Abel had to decide whether to worship God in God's way or their own. Abel decided for God and paid for it with his life. Abram was confronted with the command to pack up his bags and leave home to go where he knew not. Lot's wife had a decision to make. Her feet moved, but her heart stayed in Sodom; she was turned into a pillar of salt.

Moses too had a choice to make, and he gave up the fleeting pleasures of Pharaoh's palace. Ruth and Orpah, daughters-in-law of Naomi, had a decision to make. Ruth said, "Your people shall be my people, and your God, my God."

On Mount Carmel the prophet Elijah challenged the Israelites with "How long will you falter between two opinions? If the LORD is God, follow Him; but if Baal, follow him." The three Hebrews had to decide whether to bow or burn. Daniel chose to pray to the LORD and become prey for the lions.

Naaman the leper had to make up his mind to either wash or waste. The rich young ruler was confronted with possession of goods or peace with God, but his choice left him sorrowful. Demas had to elect to walk with Paul or run with the world.

Life is not lived in a vacuum. To choose Christ is to choose life—abundant and eternal. To elect Him as King of one's life is to fulfill one's purpose in life—it is to please God and to respond properly to the love of God.

February 7

And they gave Hebron to Caleb, as Moses had said. Then he expelled from there the three sons of Anak. (Judges 1:20)

Some men, after getting what they want, neglect the Lord. But Caleb did not change after his request was granted. Some men put on a front until they achieve their goals. It is disappointing that once these men have achieved their goals they return to their evil ways. But not Caleb, for even after obtaining his mountain (Joshua 14:12), he wholly followed after the Lord.

Note that with every blessing there is responsibility. If you request, "God, give me this mountain," and He gives it to you, be aware of the fact that some evil giants may live on your land and in your territory. It is a fact that in order to possess your inheritance and really enjoy your privileges in Christ here on earth requires kicking the giants off your property.

If you wholly follow the Lord Jesus Christ, you will be able to fulfill your obligation to expel the giants. Giants there are in the land—big and bad enough to give anyone a grasshopper complex.

There are giants of anxiety, of fear, of insecurity, of loneliness; there are giants of immorality, shackling habits, sickness and disease, discouragement, and backbiting. Sometimes you feel like giving up.

The wholehearted Christian is able to expel giants who, like Goliath, seek to kill the abundant life, hide the light, water down the testimony, stifle the witness, discourage the heart, strike fear into the soul, rob you of your joy, and cause you to doubt the love of God.

When you wholly follow the Lord, no man or devil can prevent you from receiving and enjoying your earthly inheritance.

February 8

Now Jephthah the Gileadite was a mighty man of valor, but he was the son of a harlot . . . . (Judges 11:1)

Humble Beginning. Jephthah was born of a prostitute. His father, Gilead, had other sons by his wife after the birth of Jephthah. In time the legitimate sons got together and put Jephthah out. "You shall have no inheritance in our father's house!" they cried and expelled him.

The man destined to be the ninth judge of Israel, chased from his home, went to the land of Tob. By the grace of God he was to become a man of influence, power, and authority. Forced from his home, going from disgrace to grace, he ended up in the Hall of Faith (Hebrews 11:32).

History Buff. When war broke out between the children of Ammon and the children of Israel, the elders of Gilead went to the land of Tob to fetch Jephthah. Agreeing to be their captain, Jephthah gave the king of Ammon the historical background concerning the ownership of the land then in dispute. His message shows he believed the Scriptures; he took God at His word. Israel had conquered the territory and held it undisputed for 300 years.

Hero of Battle. The king of Ammon disregarded Jephthah's message. At that point God the Holy Spirit came upon Jephthah, and the valiant warrior invaded the territory of the enemy. He struck them with a very great slaughter, for the LORD gave them into his hand.

In that way Jehovah God rewarded Jephthah's faith. Jephthah was a witness to God in a time characterized as one in which everybody did what was right in his own eyes. Let us follow today in the footsteps of Christ, our hero of battle, and we too shall be led in triumph.

February 9

And the Angel of the LORD said to him, "Why do you ask My name, seeing it is wonderful?" (Judges 13:18)

When Manoah's wife told him a man had spoken to her and predicted she would have a son, Manoah went to the LORD in prayer. He asked the LORD to send back the man so he could be given more information. God answered his request, and so Manoah was informed exactly what would happen and what was to be done.

Not knowing who the man was, Manoah offered him food and expressed a desire to prepare a burnt offering. That was declined, with the added injunction, "If you prepare a burnt offering, you must offer it to the LORD."

Then Manoah said, still not knowing it was the Angel of the LORD, "What is your name, that when your words come to pass we may honor you?" And the Angel of the LORD said unto him, "Why do you ask My name, seeing it is wonderful [secret; incomprehensible]?"

So Manoah fixed the offering and presented it on the rock to the LORD, and as the flame went up from the altar, the Angel of the LORD ascended in the flame. When Manoah and his wife saw this, they fell on their faces to the ground.

Manoah said to his wife: "We shall surely die, because we have seen God." At that point Manoah's wife showed the calmer judgment and pointed out to her husband that if the LORD had wanted to kill them He would not have accepted the offering, nor showed them what they saw, nor spoken to them that which they heard.

Later she gave birth to a son and named him Samson. Here in a theophany, Christ appeared to Manoah and his wife as the Angel of the LORD. The title *Wonderful* clearly indicates that He is God. Rejoice today in our wonderful Savior and be strong in Him.

> A wonderful Savior is Jesus my Lord,
>> He taketh my burden away;
> He holdeth me up, and I shall not be moved,
>> He giveth me strength as my day.
>>>> *Fanny J. Crosby*

February 10

Then she lulled him to sleep on her knees. (Judges 16:19)

See Samson lying with his head in Delilah's lap. She is infuriated because he has deceived her, toyed with her, and lied about the source of his strength. But eventually he gives in to her continuous nagging: "I'm a Nazirite; no razor's ever touched my head. If I'm shaved I shall become weak and be like any other man."

Then Samson fell asleep, and Delilah called in a barber who shaved off the seven locks of Samson's head. When he awoke he did not know that the LORD was departed from him. Trying to subdue the Philistines, he was captured, his eyes were put out, he was bound with bronze fetters, and was made to grind meal between millstones. Samson had thought he was strong, but he became a slave; spiritually blind, he was made physically blind. Because of his lust, he lost.

See the lesson God would teach us. When you break fellowship with the Lord, when you fail to pray and to read the Bible, you get out of touch with the will of God. You become ignorant of His character, His ways, methods, outlook, and the resources He makes available to you. The whole armor is forgotten; you miss the manna from heaven He supplies to feed your hungry soul.

Out of touch, you forget that He is a shelter from the stormy blast, an oasis in the desert, a bridge over troubled water, an ark of safety in floodtime.

Pray today for that spiritual strength that gives discernment, for the Christian does not have to fall for sin's deception. Through prayer and Bible study we can keep our heads out of the devil's lap.

February 11

Therefore I also have lent him to the LORD; as long as he lives he shall be lent to the LORD. (1 Samuel 1:28)

We see here a remarkable thing. A mother, Hannah, was saying goodbye to her first-born, her only son, a boy for whom she had fervently prayed. Here was a woman who had been taunted because of her barrenness, ridiculed by a rival for the affections of their common husband, accused of being intoxicated by the priest when she was actually praying to God.

Now with joy in her heart she turned over that which was dearest to her: "Here, Lord, You take him!" After enduring years of persecution, perhaps even questioning God about the fruitlessness of her womb, looked at with quiet scorn by the other women there in the town of Ramah, she gave up the son for whom she had prayed.

The baby she had carried within her for three-quarters of a year; whom she had nursed, hugged, bathed, fed, clothed, cuddled, caressed, and loved—the most precious thing in her life was now dedicated to Jehovah.

I could not help but think of the love of God at this point. He too gave up that which was most precious to Him, His only begotten Son, Jesus Christ—the Son who had glory with the Father before the world was, the Son for whom a body was prepared, the Son who said, "Father, send Me."

Surely it pierced the Father's heart to hear the cry from Calvary, "My God, My God; why have You forsaken Me?" Can you see the Father turning away His face from Him who became sin? Now it is all over; Hannah is in glory. Samuel, her son, who was mightily used of God, is in glory. Jesus Christ is there too, seated at the right hand of God the Father.

February 12

Speak, LORD, for Your servant hears. . . . (1 Samuel 3:9–10)

When Samuel first heard the voice early that morning, he thought it was Eli calling him. "Here I am," said Samuel.

But Eli said, "I did not call you. Lie down again."

Then a second time, and a third time, God came and called, "Samuel! Samuel!"

Rest assured that the LORD knows your name. Christ said that the good shepherd calls his own sheep by name (John 10:3). God knows who you are. Some weeks ago children across from my house were out in the street shouting and playing close to midnight. It was difficult for me to study with such noise, so I went over to them and after inquiring as to the whereabouts of their parents, told them they should play in the day and sleep at night. One little boy looked up at me and said, "Who you?"

God knows "who you." He reads every thought and imagination of the heart. He knows your downsitting and uprising: yes, He has numbered the very hairs of your head. In short, your relationship with God is personal and individualized.

It dawned upon Eli, after Samuel came to him the third time, that the voice had been the voice of the LORD. After such a long period of spiritual drought, a new prophetic era was to be inaugurated.

"Samuel, go back and lie down. If He calls you again, you say, 'Speak, LORD, for Your servant hears.'" Samuel obeyed.

The Lord came and stood—God presented Himself—and called as He had done at other times, "Samuel! Samuel!"

Then Samuel answered, "Speak, for Your servant hears." Surely no man can be a spiritual success unless he wants to hear God speak. The desire must be there, even as the poet wrote:

> Speak, Lord, in the stillness
> While I wait on Thee;
> Hushed my heart to listen
> In expectancy.

> *E. May Grimes*

February 13

And the LORD *. . . delivered you out of the hand of your enemies on every side; and you dwelt in safety.* (1 Samuel 12:11)

Here Samuel rehearsed Jehovah's past deliverance of Israel and pointed out how often He had given the Jews the victory over their enemies. God works in many different ways on our behalf. Sometimes He forces foes into feigned submission. Sometimes He puts down enemies by causing them to give up—to consider their cause futile, a waste of time, or not worth the effort. God changes their plans and changes their minds.

Some are afflicted and physically removed or toppled from office and positions of power and authority; some are put to death. God can cause your persecutor to become your protector, your foe to become your friend.

Laban was restrained from harming Jacob. "Be careful that you speak to Jacob neither good nor bad," God commanded Laban in a dream by night (Genesis 31:24). Esau had intended to kill Jacob, but when they met "Esau ran to meet him, and embraced him, and fell on his neck and kissed him, and they wept" (Genesis 33:4).

Korah, Dathan, and Abiram rebelled against Moses, but God opened the earth and they were swallowed up (Numbers 16). Jehoshaphat became king of Judah, "and the fear of the LORD fell upon all the kingdoms of the lands . . . so that they did not make war against Jehoshaphat" (2 Chronicles 17:10). Haman was an enemy; he ended up dangling from a rope. Saul of Tarsus was a persecutor of the Church, and he became a preacher of Christ.

Sometimes the road of life is not smooth; there are detours along the way. Sometimes we must go through the Red Sea, enemy territory, the wilderness, up rough mountains, and down into the valley of the shadow of death. Still God delivers.

February 14

The LORD has sought for Himself a man after His own heart.
(1 Samuel 13:14)

To be a man or woman after the heart of God is to yearn to know the mind of God; it is to want to think God's thoughts; it is to want to please Him; it is to know His will and to do His will. Imagine that text describing David—the adulterer, the murderer, the one so constantly engaged in warfare and bloodshed! (Acts 13:22).

Do not let David's faults blind you to the grace of God that worked in this man's life. Three things come to mind to aid us in the description of a man after God's own heart.

First, note David's confidence, a confidence that moved him to cry out (Psalm 70:1, 5), to call on God when in trouble (Psalm 27:1–3), but also to give God credit for every success (1 Samuel 17:36–37).

Second, note David's contrition. He was of a contrite heart—one humbled by guilt and repentant for his sins, broken in spirit. Some people are very hard to crack. Nobody can convince them they are wrong. So hardheaded are they that they resist the convicting power of the Holy Spirit. There is for them no forgiveness, no godly sorrow, no confession. After David committed adultery with Bathsheba, the LORD sent the prophet Nathan to announce, "You are the man!" Convicted by the Spirit, David confessed his sin. Read Psalm 51:1–7, 10. His contrition led to cleansing.

Third, note that David was Jehovah's choice to rule Israel, whereas Saul was the people's choice, motivated by their fleshly pride. God picked the one man in all Israel who came closest to fulfilling what Israel needed.

We see that there was a spiritual sensitivity that caused David to be mindful of his relationship to the LORD and made him desirous of fulfilling all of God's will.

February 15

Would you build a house for Me to dwell in?
(2 Samuel 7:5)

See, first of all, David's noble ambition. It was for once a time of peace. One day while sitting at home David said to Nathan the prophet, "See now, I dwell in a house of cedar, but the ark of God dwells inside tent curtains. I want to build a house for the Lord."

Nathan encouraged the king and said, "Go, do all that is in your heart, for the Lord is with you."

Second, see David's submissiveness. It came to pass that God turned down David's request. Nathan had to go back and tell David that God had said, "You shall not build Me a house." That did not mean the Lord was angry.

Indeed, God had been good to David. From a lowly, unknown shepherd boy, David was exalted by God above his brothers; given the victory over Goliath, the giant Philistine; made king in the place of Saul; and led in triumph in many battles.

So Nathan reminded David of God's goodness and grace. It was at that point the Lord promised to bless David's seed, and the Davidic covenant was established. Partly fulfilled in Solomon, it remains to be completed in Jesus Christ, David's greater descendant.

Third, see David as a man of prayer. How many of us have something in our hearts, and, when turned down by the Lord, go directly to God in prayer, thanking Him and acknowledging His sovereignty?

David humbled himself, then praised God in prayer for all His goodness and grace. "Lord, do what You said You would do. Let Your name be magnified. Your words are true. Bless!"

May all our ambitions be submitted to God in prayer that His will might be done.

February 16

O my son Absalom—my son, my son Absalom—if only I had died in your place! O Absalom, my son, my son! (2 Samuel 18:33)

So strong was Absalom's rebellion that David was forced to flee for his life. Absalom certainly had no honor for his father. In time David decided to leave Jerusalem, convinced that that was the safest step. It was not cowardice on his part, nor suspicion of disloyalty. Possibly there was a desire to spare the city the ravages of war. However, he mainly wanted to escape Absalom's approaching armies; it was a decision made by a calculating, experienced army general and agreed upon by his followers.

Later, as the battle scene shifted to the forest of Ephraim, David's soldiers destroyed Absalom's army. Some twenty thousand men were killed. Absalom, no longer on a horse or in a horse-drawn chariot, fled on a mule. As he rode through the forest his head was caught firmly in the thick boughs of a great oak tree, and he was left dangling in the air.

When informed of Absalom's predicament, Joab found him and thrust three spears into the heart of Absalom. His body was dumped into a pit in the forest and covered with a huge pile of stones. Thus ended the tragic life of Absalom, buried ignominiously in the woods of Ephraim.

How heart-rending is the cry from David's lips upon hearing of the death of his rebellious son! David would have died in Absalom's place had it been possible. In David's willingness to die for Absalom there is a picture of Christ's willingness to die for us—sons of disobedience, children of wrath.

David could not do as he desired; it was too late. But where David failed, thank God, "greater than David" succeeded.

February 17

And he said: "The LORD is my rock and my fortress and my deliverer; the God of my strength, in whom I will trust; my shield and the horn of my salvation, my stronghold and my refuge; my Savior; You save me from violence." (2 Samuel 22:2–3; see also Psalm 18:2)

Those words were spoken by David at the peak of his prosperity. He was happy; the people were united. David's enemies were defeated; the surrounding countries acknowledged David's royal power. In the past there were the persecutions of a maddened King Saul; David's life had been in constant jeopardy.

There were narrow escapes, civil strife, international intrigue. Neighboring nations, jealous of David's and Israel's increasing power, joined together to destroy the Jews. But now all that had changed.

Yet David did not forget from whence he had come. Neither should we Christians forget. Washed in the blood of Jesus Christ, we follow Him in victory. We should walk confidently, strengthened by the knowledge that our God is a deliverer, rock, fortress, strength, shield, refuge, high tower, and Savior.

His power cannot be proscribed or circumscribed. With God for us, who dares go against us? Remembering that, we saints should not groundlessly conjure up in our own imaginations fears, calamities, and all kinds of worries as if the LORD is asleep.

No. We are to hold our tongues, keep our integrity, avoid traps, play it cool when others are hot, rise above the crowd, and avoid the gang mentality of going along with the crowd. We will discover, as did the psalmist, that the LORD is all we need.

March on to victory, for as that song of deliverance says, our God is able to save.

February 18

The speech pleased the LORD, that Solomon had asked this thing. (1 Kings 3:10)

One night while Solomon was in Gibeon, the LORD appeared to him in a dream. "Ask! What shall I give you?" said the God of all grace.

Solomon replied, "I don't know how to go out or come in. I don't know how to properly govern these Your great people; I don't know how to rule them with the dignity that befits a king, or how to behave in a royal manner. So if you please, Sir, give Your servant an understanding heart. Give me knowledge and wisdom to judge Your people, that I may discern between good and bad. Otherwise, how would I ever be able to rule this great people of Yours?"

Within the bounds of reason, Solomon could have gotten whatever he wanted. But he wanted what God wanted him to want. That is the secret of how to please the LORD: "The speech pleased the LORD, that Solomon had asked this thing."

What does that incident in Solomon's life say to us? One greater than Solomon has come. His name is Jesus Christ. He is the one who gave Solomon all that he received, but who has given us much more. For He shed His own blood, more precious than silver or gold, and washed away our sins, cleansed us from guilt, removed all condemnation, opened our blind eyes, and loved us into His kingdom.

With nail-pierced hands Jesus Christ stands and asks, "What would you like Me to give you?"

I pray to God that you will give the right answer every time the Lord stops by and asks, "What would you like Me to give you?" I pray that you have learned to want what He wants you to want.

May your heart respond, "Father, make me more like Jesus!"

February 19

"How long will you falter between two opinions? If the LORD *is God, follow Him; but if Baal, follow him." But the people answered him not a word.* (1 Kings 18:21)

For those Israelites, Mount Carmel was a place of decision. They were at the crossroads of life, at the fork in the road, and a choice had to be made. How sad that they remained silent. Even today the sin of indecisiveness is widespread.

I am reminded of a politician who was asked about a certain issue, "Are you for it or against it?"

He replied, "Well, some of my friends are for it. Some of my friends are against it. And I'm for my friends." Unfortunately, in spiritual things there is no neutrality. Life is such that you must make a choice. There is no alternative.

If you do not choose the God of the Bible, Jesus Christ, then whatever choice you make, you are against Him. To remain silent is not to choose Him. So there is no détente, no fence-straddling, no peaceful coexistence; no eat-your-cake-and-have-it-too.

Noah had either to build an ark of safety or attempt to swim; Abraham's choices were to pack up or stay put. For Job, it was curse God and die or praise Him and live. For Joseph, it was fornicate or flee. For Lot's wife: choose Sodom and salt, or safety; the Hebrew boys: bow or burn; Judas: betray or be loyal; and for Paul: persecute or preach.

So it is in life. You are either a sheep or a goat; real or phony; serving God or mammon. You reap either of the flesh or of the spirit; and when you die, you will end up like either Lazarus or the rich man in Luke 16.

You are going to either heaven or hell; you are either saved or lost. If you are a Christian, rejoice; you have made the right choice.

February 20

*Then the fire of the LORD fell and consumed the burnt sacri-
fice, and the wood and the stones and the dust, and it licked
up the water that was in the trench.* (1 Kings 18:38)

Mount Carmel was a place for the demonstration of
God's power. How often the Lord has to demonstrate His
power in order to make us come to a proper decision about
Him. So it was here with Elijah and the people of Israel.

Satan is powerful, but God is all-powerful. Only with
God's permission could the devil have responded with fire
in that contest. However, the true God let it be known that
Baal, the god of fire, had fizzled out.

Idol worshipers are deluded. As Elijah poured on the
sarcasm, Baal's devotees tried all the harder to work up
some response from their god. As they pranced and danced
and cut themselves, Elijah mocked them. In today's language he may have said, "Cry a little louder. Perhaps he's
listening to loud rock music or the battery in his hearing
aid went dead! Maybe he fell asleep watching TV!" Nothing happened. No fire fell from heaven to burn up the sacrifice.

On the other hand, Jehovah demonstrated His power
there at Mount Carmel. The most adverse circumstances
mean nothing to Him. Three times, four barrels of water
were poured on the burnt sacrifice. Elijah prayed and fire
fell, consuming the burnt sacrifice—wood, stones, and
dust—and even licked up the water.

At Mount Calvary was another sacrifice. There the
power of God's love was shown. Darkness fell, the earth
quaked, mountains shook, and cemeteries opened. Three
days later Christ stepped forth from the tomb to announce
that He had all power in His hands. That event too has
caused millions of men to make a proper decision.

February 21

And he prayed that he might die, and said, "It is enough!"
(1 Kings 19:4)

Now Elijah was "a man with a nature like ours" (James 5:17). He was not some iron man with unfeeling nerves of steel. He knew that the wicked queen was not bluffing; frightened, he made a hasty retreat.

We do not all react the same way when frightened or scared; perhaps you would have stayed right where you were. When the empress threatened Chrysostom, he said: "Go tell her I fear nothing but sin."

When Basil was sent word that the emperor would be the death of him, Basil said: "I would he would. I shall but go to heaven the sooner."

On one occasion Luther said, "I care neither for the Pope's favor nor fury."

Elijah made a brief stop in Beersheba, a southern city of Judah. He had fled from the North to the South. Fearing detection by Jezebel's spies, he retreated into the wilderness and sat down under a juniper tree. He was discouraged, disappointed.

Elijah had hoped that the failure and destruction of the false prophets, the success of Jehovah, and the ending of the drought would turn the people's minds to God. We do not always know God's intentions or purpose for our lives. Elijah wanted to die, and he never did die. Over 2,800 years have passed, and Elijah has not yet tasted death. As long as God has work for you to do, stay where you are.

Whatever your troubles are, commit yourself to Jesus Christ. Elijah was refreshed by God, fed a meal, and given water. Today you may fall at the foot of the cross and find refreshment there. Thus nourished we can continue to serve until the Lord Jesus says, "It is enough!"

February 22

What are you doing here, Elijah? (1 Kings 19:9, 13)

The prophet had made haste to retreat from the vengeful Jezebel. He had requested to die, and the LORD, in refusing the request, refreshed him instead. In the strength of that refreshment Elijah went to Mount Horeb, entered a cave, and lodged there. It was there that God came to him and said, "What are you doing here, Elijah?"

Such a question causes reflection. It makes one think, pricks the conscience, stirs up feelings of guilt and shame.

"What are you doing here, Elijah?"

"I have been very jealous for the LORD God of hosts."

Elijah's answer showed his disappointment over the way things had turned out. He had hoped after the victory over the phony preachers and their idol god, Baal, on Mount Carmel, and after the return of the rain, ending the drought, that everybody would turn to Jehovah and worship Him only.

Elijah had made up his mind how God was going to work. He attempted to second-guess God; when things did not turn out as he had hoped, the prophet experienced disappointment and shame. From Elijah's experience we should learn not to despair if things seem dark and the Lord does not speak to our hearts by wind, earthquake, or fire. He also speaks in a still, small voice and whispers sweet peace to His own.

February 23

So she said, "Did I ask a son of my lord? Did I not say, 'Do not deceive me'?" (2 Kings 4:28)

The rich woman in Shunem had shown great hospitality to the prophet Elisha. In return for her kindness the prophet predicted that the childless woman would have a son, and it came to pass. Some years later, the boy died in his mother's lap. Immediately she determined to go to the prophet Elisha, and, finding him, she said: "Sir, did I ask you for a son? Didn't I tell you not to get my hopes up?"

She felt it was better not to have had the boy at all than to have had him and lost him. What has been your attitude when gifts have been bestowed and circumstances prevented you from exercising those gifts? When blessings seemed to turn into cursings? Sorrow into sadness? Laughter into crying? When health is turned into sickness and feast becomes famine?

What then? How do you react? Do you pout like King Ahab when he could not get Naboth's vineyard? Do you curse God as Job's wife suggested? Do you get drunk as did Belshazzar? Do you plot and scheme like Haman? Do you cry your heart out as did David over the death of his son Absalom?

Do you backslide like Demas and return into the world? Do you deny your relationship with the Lord as did Simon Peter? Do you, like Judas, betray those who have been loyal to you? How do you react? That woman had the answer. The boy had died in her lap, but she put the problem in God's lap.

We learn not to despair when we have done what God told us to do and things do not seem to turn out right. Hold to God's unchanging hand! He will finish what He started. Work in the confidence that He who began a good work in you will complete it.

February 24

Man of God, there is death in the pot! (2 Kings 4:40)

The famine embracing the city of Gilgal was an opportunity for God to use His prophet Elisha. And so He did use him. While teaching the student prophets who sat before him, Elisha said to his servant, "Put on a big pot of stew for them." One of the men went out into the field to get some herbs.

Probably not natives of that district, the pupils of the prophet were not familiar with what grew there. One man gathered a lap-full of wild cucumber, egg-shaped gourds that looked like another variety that is edible. What the man brought back was the kind that had a bitter taste, producing colic, violent diarrhea, and that if eaten in quantity could produce death.

The man was sincere but ignorant. One can be sincere and wrong; in fact, one can be sincerely wrong. Not knowing what he had, he sliced them into the stew. Fortunately, after the stew was poured out and the men tasted it, they exclaimed to Elisha that it was poisonous. The bitter taste was the giveaway.

To some people in our churches today there is no such discernment. They cannot tell the difference between poison and soda pop or lightning and a lightning bug. Elisha knew that there was danger of being too hasty in time of famine. Christians must not be pressured into making hasty decisions. Do not put just anything in the stew because you are hungry.

Calamities occur in life, emergencies come up, but we must be careful how we respond. Elisha told his students to feast in the famine, but they had to learn that God's help was needed. Our own attempts to save ourselves and to solve our problems all too often are not much more than putting poison in the pot.

February 25

And Elisha prayed, and said, "LORD, I pray, open his eyes that he may see." (2 Kings 6:17)

The Syrians were well aware that it was the prophet Elisha who leaked their secrets to the king of Israel. So the king of Syria ordered Elisha captured. It did not dawn upon him that if Elisha knew the secret plans to ambush the Israelite soldiers, surely he would know of any plan to take him.

Informed that Elisha was in the city of Dothan, the king of Syria sent soldiers with horses and chariots to guard the city gates. When Elisha's servant woke up and saw the city surrounded, he pushed the panic button. "Alas, my master! What shall we do?"

Fear is the product of unbelief; unbelief is a form of blindness that produces a multitude of things that further intensify the blindness. The servant did not know it was the intention of Jehovah to teach both Syria and Israel lessons.

Syria needed to be punished for its idolatry and for fighting the people of God. Israel needed to learn how easy it was for the LORD to maneuver and defeat the wicked. The people of Israel needed to know that their God could help them control their evil ways and live pleasing to Him.

The prophet answered the frightened servant in a response so classic that it has etched itself upon the hearts of countless numbers of saints. "Do not fear, for they who are with us are more than those who are with them." More? More what? More in number? More in power? More in strength? More! Whatever God's more is, it is enough.

> Open my eyes, that I may see
> Glimpses of truth Thou hast for me;
> Place in my hands the wonderful key
> That shall unclasp and set me free.
> Silently now I wait for Thee,
> Ready, my God, Thy will to see;
> Open my eyes, illumine me,
> Spirit divine!   *Clara H. Scott*

February 26

And he did what was right in the sight of the LORD, and walked in all the ways of his father David; he did not turn aside to the right hand or to the left. (2 Kings 22:2)

Josiah was one of the good kings of Judah. Three characteristics of his reign were:

(1) *He repaired the Temple*. Carpenters, builders, and masons were given money to buy timber and hewn stone to repair the Temple ruined by neglect. Levites gathered the money the people brought into the house of the LORD (2 Chronicles 34:9–11).

(2) *He respected the Word of God*. Hilkiah, the high priest, found the Book of the Law and told Shaphan, the scribe, who in turn read it to King Josiah. So moved was the ruler that he sent men to inquire from Huldah the prophetess the will of God.

Huldah predicted that Josiah would not see the judgment awaiting Judah because his heart was tender and he humbled himself and showed repentance upon hearing God's Word ("You shall be gathered to your grave in peace"). Consequently Josiah read the Law to the people, then made a covenant before God to do with his entire heart and soul what the Word said to do.

(3) *He ruined the idols*. Josiah was ruthless in his reformation of the spiritual life of his people: he burned the vessels of Baal, the Asherah, and the "host of heaven." He killed the priests who had burned incense to the gods, goddesses, and the zodiac. He crushed the idols that had been placed in the house of the LORD, burned them, beat them into dust, and scattered the dust on the graves of their devotees. The houses of the homosexuals and cult prostitutes were broken down along with the images; all the mediums were removed.

What a testimony that man's life was! He repaired the Temple, respected the Word of God, and ruined the idols. "Nor after him did any arise like him" (2 Kings 23:25).

February 27

Who then is willing to consecrate his service this day unto the LORD? (1 Chronicles 29:5, KJV).

During a period of peace in the land, David hit upon the idea of building a great temple for the Lord. Whereas Nathan the prophet approved, God disapproved. We learn that we should seek God's advice first, and not decide what we want to do without acknowledging Him or seeking His will. Even in good things, ask Him first.

However, God predicted, "[David's seed] shall build a house for My name" (2 Samuel 7:13). So it came to pass. David encouraged Solomon, even giving vast sums of his own personal treasury. By leading in the giving, he sought to encourage all the people. Then came the question: "Who is willing to consecrate his service this day unto the Lord?"

The Hebrew phrase rendered "to consecrate his service" is literally "to fill the hand," a technical term used when candidates for the priesthood were ordained. When the elements of the sacrifice were placed in the hands of the participants, the "consecration" (Leviticus 8:27) took place.

What a joy it is to have full hands for God. When we give generously and willingly to the cause of the gospel, there is rejoicing. "It is more blessed to give than to receive," said our Lord (Acts 20:35).

God loves a cheerful giver—not giving until it hurts, but giving because it feels good. How can we really repay Him who shed His blood for us, blood more precious than silver or gold? How shall we fill our hands for Him whose hands received those cruel nails?

February 28

He had no war in those years, because the LORD had given him rest. (2 Chronicles 14:6)

Asa was not too far removed time-wise from King Rehoboam under whose reign the nation divided. Recall the lineage: David, Solomon, Rehoboam, Abijah, Asa. The man Asa ruled for forty-one years in the city of Jerusalem, about 911–870 B.C. By the grace of God, in spite of the evil reigns of his grandfather and his father, Asa's heart was perfect with the Lord all his days.

What a wonderful testimony! How refreshing to read of that man's efforts to clean up Judah: he took away the altars of the foreign gods; he removed the high places; he broke down the stone images of Baal; he cut down the Asherim, wooden symbols of a Babylonian goddess, and burned them; he took away the images of the sun gods.

As a result of his efforts to eliminate idolatry, God gave him peace in the land. Note that the LORD gave the peace, not men. The peace men create is no more than a temporary truce between thieves. Peace that men make may be no more than dirt swept under a rug, or a skeleton locked up in a dark, dank, dirty closet. There is no peace for the wicked (Isaiah 57:21).

True peace was God's reward for Asa's moral reform efforts. We learn that one way to have peace is to get rid of idols. It is a fact that Jesus Christ who bought you with His own precious blood wants first place in your life.

Let Him rule in your heart today and experience afresh the peace of God and the rest of God that passes all understanding. Satan leaves only for a season, but thank God for that season! When he returns, may he find Christ still ruling in your heart, and peace flowing like a river.

February 29

Then Manasseh knew that the LORD was God.
(2 Chronicles 33:13)

Manasseh's reign began when he was twelve years old. It ended when he was sixty-seven (696–641 B.C.). During his reign he undid everything his father, Hezekiah, had done (2 Kings 21:2). He built up the mounds upon which idols were placed; erected altars for Baal, made idols and put them in God's house; worshiped the host of heaven; made his own children pass through fire in sacrifice; practiced astrology; and used witchcraft.

Manasseh consulted mediums and spiritists; practiced sorcery; misled the people of Judah and the inhabitants of Jerusalem; and shed innocent blood, for through his tyranny the prophets of God were slain. He would not hear the Word of God from God's prophets.

The LORD became so incensed with the wickedness of this man that He said He was going to bring such evil on that nation that whosoever heard about it, his ears would tingle (2 Kings 21:12). More than any other man, Manasseh was responsible for the destruction of Judah.

Sure enough, God's patience ran out; the Assyrians came and took Manasseh bound with bronze chains, with hooks or thongs put through his nose, and carried him away to Babylon.

Even such a wicked man as Manasseh can be reached by God. "When he was in affliction, he implored the LORD his God, and humbled himself greatly before the God of his fathers" (2 Chronicles 33:12). After fifty-five years of evil, he repented. It was too late to save the nation, yet he removed the foreign gods and altars, and the idol from God's house, and restored worship of the true God. What mercy! It brings tears to my eyes every time I think of what God did in the life of that man. Surely He is plenteous in mercy.

March 1

Therefore we His servants will arise and build, but you have no heritage or right or memorial in Jerusalem. (Nehemiah 2:20)

The righteous have no business having intimate business with the unrighteous. The servants of Jehovah can have no true fellowship with Satan's slaves. Sanballat the Horonite, Tobiah the Ammonite official, and Geshem the Arab, when they learned about Nehemiah's desire to rebuild the walls of Jerusalem, scoffed openly. And, being outsiders, they began to agitate. They would not offer their help, for they knew that Nehemiah would never accept a minute of their labor or a penny in coin from such as them.

Some Christians make the mistake of seeking help from the world in order to accomplish the work God called the Christian to do. We seek the help of the unsaved, ungodly, unscrupulous, uncouth, unregenerate, unholy—*un* everything but *un*der the blood.

Some do not discern that you cannot run with the rabbit and also bark with the hound; you cannot serve in the courts of both David and Saul; you cannot curry favor with Jezebel and then call for fire with Elijah.

You cannot run with dogs and not catch fleas; nor can you plow with an ox and a jackass yoked together. Nehemiah knew that. He let those enemies of God know in no uncertain terms that they had no present share in the work—nor would they or their descendants have any in the future.

Said he: Our cause is just, our aim is noble, our purpose is right. Nothing you do can hinder us. The God of heaven is on our side, and He will prosper us. Therefore we, God's servants, will arise and build!

In like manner the Lord Jesus speaks to us today. We too are His servants. May we remember that whatever the Lord has given us to do, He will supply all we need to get the job done.

March 2

. . . for they perceived that this work was done by our God.
(Nehemiah 6:16)

Sanballat, Tobiah, and Geshem, along with their friends, did all they could to hinder the rebuilding of the walls of Jerusalem. Nehemiah and his people were laughed to scorn, despised, mocked, and scathingly ridiculed.

"What are these feeble Jews doing? Are they going to restore it for themselves? Can they offer sacrifices? Can they finish in a day? Can they revive the stones from the dusty rubble, even the burned ones? . . . Even what they are building—if a fox should jump on it, he would break their stone wall down!" (Nehemiah 4:2–3, NASB). Threats of physical violence were made (Nehemiah 4:8, 11); lies and false rumors were spread, to which Nehemiah replied that such things as they were saying had not been done, but they were inventing them in their own sick minds (Nehemiah 6:8).

In spite of all that the enemy did, Nehemiah would not let their attempts to strike fear into the hearts of the Jews succeed. Nor would he let their falsehoods upset his priority, prevent him from persevering, slow down his production, or wreck his program.

He maintained a fervent faith in spite of all the friction, fear, and falsehood. Within fifty-two days the wall was finished. That was proof that God was in the work. Success crowned Nehemiah's efforts. The wall of Jerusalem was finished to the glory of God.

Let us recognize that the work of Jesus Christ at Calvary was also wrought by God. For the Father who sent the Savior also raised Him from the dead to prove that our sins were gone. One day the world shall see you and me, the finished products of God's new creation; they will know that we too were wrought by God.

March 3

Do not sorrow, for the joy of the LORD is your strength.
(Nehemiah 8:10)

Having now returned to their beloved city, Jerusalem, the people requested that Ezra the scribe bring the Book of the Law of Moses and read it to them. When they learned what God's standards were, they began to weep. They recognized that they had fallen far short of God's will.

Clear exposition of God's Word—most likely portions of Deuteronomy—led to the conviction of sin. Then they were urged not to continue bringing forth tears of repentance but to rejoice. "It is a holy day. Be cheerful," they were told.

"Eat the fat"—considered by the people the most dainty morsel; "drink the sweet," that is, the new sweet wine (nonfermented). They were to share what they had with the poor. The idea is to celebrate now, rejoice this day in the LORD, and you will have strength for the future.

As far as restrictions are concerned, many things can restrict the joy of the believer. Sin may rob us. Fear also can rob us of our joy; so can ignorance.

God has provided a remedy, a cure for the lack of joy and for eliminating those things that would restrict our joy. The cure for sin is the shed blood of Jesus Christ. The cure for fear is found in the Word of God, who has not given us the spirit of fear (2 Timothy 1:7). Likewise ignorance can be cured by the God of the Bible, who would not have us to be ignorant.

As for reasons for rejoicing, we are commanded to rejoice. What God commands us to do, He enables us to do. Rejoice in Jesus Christ and discover that you will be strengthened to meet the testings of this day.

March 4

And if I perish, I perish! (Esther 4:16)

It was a rule that anyone going into the king's presence not having been invited could be killed. At Mordecai's insistence the young queen risked her life for her people. She told the messengers to inform Mordecai that she would tell the king about the conspiracy against the Jews to destroy them. ". . . so will I go to the king, which is against the law; and if I perish, I perish!" (Esther 4:16).

What Queen Esther was prepared to do did not happen; there was no need for her to die, for she found favor in the king's sight. Similarly, what Moses wanted to do—suffer death for his people (Exodus 32:32)—he could not. Recall, upon God's announced intention to destroy the people of Israel, that Moses interceded, "Oh, these people have sinned a great sin, and have made for themselves a god of gold! Yet now, if You will forgive their sin—but if not, I pray, blot me out of Your book which You have written."

How pathetic is the lament that consumes the heart of the distraught David over the death of his son. The memorable words once heard etch themselves upon the listener's soul: "O my son Absalom—my son, my son Absalom—if only I had died in your place! O Absalom, my son, my son!" (2 Samuel 18:33).

What the apostle Paul said was likewise admirable. He wanted so much that his people, the Jews, would accept Jesus as the Messiah. "For I could wish that I myself were accursed from Christ for my brethren, my countrymen according to the flesh"—if it meant they would believe and be saved (Romans 9:3).

What Esther feared could happen and did not; what Moses wanted to do and could not; what David desired but could not do; and what Paul longed for but which was impossible, Jesus Christ accomplished! For "while we were still sinners, Christ died for us" (Romans 5:8).

March 5

There was a man in the land of Uz, whose name was Job; and that man was blameless and upright. . . . (Job 1:1)

Just as depravity swerves from the appointed course, so uprightness, or rectitude, keeps to a straight and even line. The upright then are just; they are straightforward, righteous, unswerving in their direction.

David said God saves the upright in heart (Psalm 7:10), even though the wicked shoot at the upright secretly (Psalm 11:2) and seek to slay such as are upright in their manner of life (Psalm 37:14). God's countenance beholds the upright (Psalm 11:7).

To the upright God does good (Psalm 125:4); his future is peace (Psalm 37:37); he shall exult (Psalm 64:10); and for him gladness is sown (Psalm 97:11). The generation of the upright shall be blessed and for him there arises light in the darkness (Psalm 112:2, 4); he shall dwell in God's presence (Psalm 140:13), for the LORD knows the days of the upright and their inheritance shall be forever (Psalm 37:18).

Proverbs says that the integrity of the upright shall guide them (11:3); their righteousness shall deliver them (11:6); their tabernacle shall flourish (14:11). The highway of the upright is to depart from evil (16:17); wisdom is his shield (2:7).

Micah said that God's words do good to those who walk uprightly (2:7). And Isaiah pointed out that the way of the just is uprightness (26:7). No wonder David pleaded: "Lead me in the land of uprightness" (Psalm 143:10).

Of course, man of himself and by himself is downright *un*right, not *up*right at all. There is by birth *none* righteous. At that point Christ comes into the picture. Because of Calvary men can be declared perfect and upright. We can be characterized as was Job of old. Though many afflictions may befall us, nothing can undo what God has declared already done.

March 6

The LORD gave, and the LORD has taken away; blessed be the name of the LORD. (Job 1:21)

A group of men were discussing the statement "Money can buy anything." A wealthy businessman, it is said, went so far as to offer $4,000 to anyone who could convincingly name four desirable things that money could not buy. He was so positive that no one could meet the challenge that he smiled skeptically when one of the men took out a pad and a pencil. The man wrote four short lines and passed the note to the challenger.

He glanced at it carelessly at first, then gave it a more studied look, and without a word got out his checkbook and made good on his promise. The list of four things money cannot buy was: a baby's smile, youth after it is gone, the love of a good woman, and entrance into heaven. Indeed, the best things in life are free.

In fact, everything we have was given to us, for we came into this world with nothing. Job understood that. He knew that his God was sovereign and had the absolute right to do as He pleased.

Job lost houses, sheep, camels, oxen, donkeys, and most of his servants. His seven sons and three daughters were killed. His own body was afflicted with painful boils. With deep insight into the meaning of grace, he cried out, "Naked came I from my mother's womb, and naked shall I return there."

In other words, Job said: "I didn't have anything to begin with. Only by the grace of God was I permitted to get, own, possess, and enjoy anything. The God who gave me all things when I deserved nothing also has the right to take away all things." Surely that is a wonderful way to look at the grace of our loving Father.

March 7

Now when Job's three friends heard. . . . (Job 2:11)

A man has to be careful about the kinds of friends he chooses. If he is a rich man he will be suspicious, for he will recognize that wealth makes many friends (Proverbs 14:20; 19:4). Some friends are political, like the friendship produced when Pilate sent the Lord Jesus Christ to Herod (Luke 23:12). The writer of Proverbs warns us to not make friends with folk who are quick-tempered or desire to be with evil people (22:24; 24:1).

"Friends" named Eliphaz, Bildad, and Zophar made an appointment to come together to mourn with Job and comfort him. Those three friends insisted Job's suffering was due to secret sin. "My friends scorn me . . ." said Job (Job 16:20). They believed Job was a hypocrite—outwardly sanctimonious but secretly wicked. From their point of view the LORD would not allow a righteous man to suffer so much. No wonder Job cried out, "Have pity on me, have pity on me, O you my friends, for the hand of God has struck me!" (Job 19:21).

Then there are treacherous friends like Judas. He intended to give Jesus a kiss to identify Him as the one to be taken and arrested. Before he was able to complete his dastardly deed, the Lord blunted the thrust of his treachery with the words, "Judas, are you betraying the Son of Man with a kiss?" (Luke 22:48).

After Judas kissed Him, Christ said, "Friend, why have you come?" (Matthew 26:50). The word rendered *friend* here means "mate, companion, comrade, partner, fellow, associate," and is used only by Matthew. Judas broke that mutually binding relationship.

Thank God today for genuine friends. They are gifts from the Lord. Above all, thank God for Jesus Christ, a friend indeed.

> What a Friend we have in Jesus,
>> All our sins and griefs to bear!
> What a privilege to carry
>> Everything to God in prayer!
>>> *Joseph M. Scriven*

March 8

In whose hand is the life of every living thing, and the breath of all mankind? (Job 12:10)

Job took as much as he could from his three friends. When Zophar, one of the three, finished his presumptuous and legalistic argument, Job gave his rebuttal. Basically, Job pointed out that far too often the wicked are not immediately punished. The fact that robbers and evildoers were prospering while Job, a righteous man, was treated like a criminal contradicts the theory of Job's counselors.

With scornful sarcasm, Job turned upon them and said, "I realize you men know everything! Doubtless all wisdom will die with you. Well, I know a few things myself—you are no better than I am. In fact, who does not know the things you have been saying?"

Job's point was that their doctrine of the majestic wisdom of God is common knowledge. "Even birds and animals have much they could teach you. Ask the creatures of earth and sea for their wisdom. All of them know that the LORD's hand made them. So tell me something I don't know. Tell me something the birds and beasts don't know," Job argued.

Who does not know that in God's hand is the life of every living creature and the breath of all mankind? That is a fact abundantly taught in the Bible. Said the psalmist (Psalm 104:29): "You hide your face, they are troubled; You take away their breath, they die and return to their dust."

May we say to Jesus Christ, in whose hand our soul and breath are found:

> Then shall my latest breath
>   Whisper Thy praise;
> This be the parting cry
>   My heart shall raise;
> This still its prayer shall be:
>   More love, O Christ, to Thee,
> More love to Thee,
>   More love to Thee!

Elizabeth P. Prentiss

March 9

Man who is born of woman is of few days and full of trouble.
(Job 14:1)

God speaks through troubled circumstances; through open doors that none can shut; through closed doors that none can open; through accidents, sickness, unemployment, the evil deeds of men and of Satan. He speaks through heartbreak, anguish, frustration, even death.

I attended the funeral of an eighty-year-old father last week. As I sat there I wondered about his four sons.

The oldest boy had been a very close friend of mine. We met in junior high school back in 1940. We used to go on double dates. In an argument with the next oldest brother he was shot to death and was buried August 25, 1955.

The boy that killed him was committed to a prison for the criminally insane. The third oldest boy's mind has gone bad, although he has a college degree.

While I sat talking to the third son several days after the funeral in that filthy, vermin-infested home and watched him mash out cigarettes with his heel, the youngest boy came in. I had seen the youngest son at the funeral, but he was so ravaged by alcohol and scarred by sin that I did not at first recognize him. Now he entered, saw me, and handed me a half-filled pint bottle of whiskey. Then he sat at the open window, tossed out trash, ranted, and jumped from one subject to another. Evidently his brain was affected by alcohol.

I left, unable to get their attention long enough to pray. I asked God, "Why?"—four talented sons and their lives wasted. As I get older and experience troubled days, I am increasingly impressed with and convinced of the goodness of God's grace to me.

March 10

For now You number my steps, but do not watch over my sin.
(Job 14:16)

In his low moments Job believed that God was dogging his heels—that an unfriendly, unforgiving God walked behind him, counting every step he took, watching every move, taking account of every mistake, every failure.

I was looking at the attempt of a baby to walk last Sunday. Church service was over, and one of the members had her granddaughters with her as she came to speak with me. Whereas the older girl could walk, the younger one was struggling to maintain her balance. One leg seemed stronger than the other, for although the left stepped out, the right leg tended to drag.

How old were you when you stopped crawling and could stand on your own two feet and walk unaided, no one holding your hand? How many steps have you taken since those early days?

For God to number your steps means that your life span is set already. Your days are determined. The number of months you are going to live is already programmed, and you cannot pass beyond those bounds (Job 14:5).

Knowing that should teach a man to number his days and apply his heart to wisdom. A man ought to say, "My steps are numbered, and after I take my last step, then what?"

For God to number your steps means also that He has got His eyes on you. "For the ways of man are before the eyes of the LORD, and He ponders all his paths" (Proverbs 5:21). He knows your sitting down and your rising up (Psalm 139:2). "For His eyes are on the ways of man, and He sees all his steps" (Job 34:21). That is cause for rejoicing, because it means the LORD will guide and protect you.

March 11

For I know that my Redeemer lives. (Job 19:25)

The words *redeem* and *redemption* have in them basically the idea of "loose, deliver, set free." We read that God redeemed Israel from Egypt, delivered the Israelites from captivity. Job speaks of God's extricating him from all difficulties.

Sometimes the release is by payment of a ransom price or by buying out of the marketplace. In general, redemption may be considered as deliverance, but keep in mind that there is an intimate relationship between the redeemer and the redeemed. It is not as mechanical as going into the pawn shop to redeem your watch or to some redemption center to turn in eight books of stamps for a table lamp.

Redemption may be physical deliverance from disease, enemies, traps, or death. It may be deliverance from legal, caste, class, racial, or sex barriers. Of course it is also moral or spiritual deliverance from the power of evil in our hearts or the effects of that evil before God.

The very plain message of the Bible is that Christ, our Redeemer, paid the penalty of sin so we would not eternally die. There is therefore now no condemnation. However, salvation is not cheap, though it is free. It cost Christ His home.

He who was already in heaven voluntarily left His Father's house to come here to earth. Second, it cost Him His honor. His motives were impugned; He was mocked, ridiculed, blasphemed, and slain between two criminals.

Third, He himself was personally involved; His body was the price paid (Galatians 2:20). Realizing such cost, no Christian should ever feel he is a nobody. We are precious in God's sight, having been bought with blood more precious than silver or gold.

March 12

For what is the hope of the hypocrite, though he may gain much, if God takes away his life? (Job 27:8)

The word *hypocrisy* means literally "to answer or speak under, separate gradually, as speakers on a stage; thus, to play a part on a stage." From that a *hypocrite* came to be one who feigns or pretends to be, have, or feel what he is not, does not have, and does not feel.

The Lord Jesus did not hesitate to denounce hypocrisy. He considered hypocrisy a leaven that easily leavens the whole lump (Luke 12:1). A reading of the Gospels, especially Matthew, convinces us of our Lord's emphatic denouncement of that sin.

In the book of Matthew Jesus defined hypocrites as people who do good works to be seen of men (6:2), pray to be heard of men (6:5), fast to be noticed by men (6:16), and see toothpicks in other people's eyes but miss the telephone poles in their own eyes (7:5).

Hypocrites draw near to God with their lips, but their hearts are far away (15:7–8); they teach the traditions of men (15:9), but not the things of the Lord. They can discern the weather, but not the signs of the times (16:3); they test God (22:18).

Their spiritual shabbiness stops others from coming to God (23:13); they devour widows' houses and for a pretense make long prayers (23:14); they go through much ritual and ceremony, but omit the weightier things of life like justice and the love of God (23:23).

They love the chief seats and positions of authority and prominence, high-sounding titles (Luke 11:43); they whitewash the outside when rottenness is on the inside (Matthew 23:27). Let us then be sensitive to any semblance of hypocrisy in our lives and seek by being genuine and guileless to please God.

March 13

For God may speak in one way, or in another, yet man does not perceive it. (Job 33:14)

Although the Lord repeatedly speaks to us, most humans do not pay attention to what He says. Why is that? Since sin is deeply rooted, our brains are affected; our will, logic, reason—all are affected. Sin makes men hardheaded. God must work on our recalcitrant hearts to make out of us what He wants us to be.

How? By reproof, rebuke for faults and misdeeds; by reprimand, by correction, by chastisement. Most of us do not like to be reproved or rebuked or criticized—especially in front of other folks. Proverbs 12:1 says: "But he who hates correction is stupid."

Sometimes the people who reprove us need to be taught a lesson themselves. Some are right in what they say, but wrong in the way they say it—their attitudes and motives are bad. Some are ignorant and do not know what they are talking about.

How often has God spoken to you? In how many different ways and times? Perhaps He has spoken through accidents, disappointments, heartbreaks, prosperity and good times, sickness, a new baby, fire in the home, time spent in the hospital, a new friend, conscience, a teacher, pastor, purse-snatcher, smashed-up automobile, and so on. You can see that the possibilities are endless.

As the Lord speaks to your heart today, pray that you will perceive and respond. If He did not love us, He would not speak to us at all. He who has an ear to hear, let him hear what God speaks!

March 14

For His eyes are on the ways of man, and He sees all his steps.
(Job 34:21)

Sometimes you hear folks say, "He's got a long way to go and a tough row to hoe." Or: "He gave me a hard way to go." Or: "He has funny ways." Well, it means his behavior is strange. Your ways are your thoughts, deeds, speech, your entire manner; your lifestyle. Naturally, the Bible has much to say about man's ways, especially if the man is wicked.

There are the ways of darkness (Proverbs 2:13; 4:19), the way of lying (Psalm 119:29), the broad way of destruction (Matthew 7:13), the way of folly (Psalm 49:13) and grief (Psalm 10:5); the evil way, the false way (Psalm 119:101, 104, 128), the crooked way (Proverbs 2:15), and the corrupt way (Genesis 6:12).

Furthermore, the prostitute's house is the way to hell (Proverbs 7:27); and "the way of a fool is right in his own eyes . . ." (Proverbs 12:15). There is a way that seems right but its end is death (Proverbs 14:12). The way of the wicked is devious and strange, an abomination unto the LORD (Proverbs 15:9; 21:8), a way without peace, only destruction and misery (Romans 3:16–17). There is the way of Cain, religion without salvation (Jude 11); the way of Balaam, religion without integrity (2 Peter 2:15). A double-minded man is unstable in all his ways (James 1:8). Yes, ". . . we have turned, every one, to his own way" (Isaiah 53:6).

Is it any wonder God pleads with men: "Let the wicked forsake his way" (Isaiah 55:7); turn from your wicked ways (2 Chronicles 7:14); cleanse your ways (Psalm 119:9); stand not in the way of sinners (Psalm 1:1). You see that the Bible has much to say about man's ways. Praise God that you know the way of righteousness is *life* (Proverbs 12:28), and that Jesus Christ is *the* way!

March 15

No purpose of Yours can be withheld from You. (Job 42:2)

It is a fact that man, with all of his brilliance, cannot read the minds of other men. Only the spirit within a man can know that man's thoughts. Sometimes we betray our thoughts by our bodily movements—crossing of legs, folding of arms, and so on; or by our tone of voice, inflection, volume, pitch, or silence, and various facial expressions. Basically we cannot read minds.

God can read man's thoughts. That God does know the thoughts of man is made very clear in the Bible. In his charge to his son Solomon, David said: "The LORD searches all hearts and understands all the intent of the thoughts" (1 Chronicles 28:9). "You know my sitting down and my rising up; you understand my thought afar off" (Psalm 139:2).

On one occasion, after Christ forgave the paralyzed man of his sins, certain scribes said within themselves, "This man blasphemes."

And Jesus, knowing their thoughts, said, "Why do you think evil in your hearts?" (Matthew 9:4).

Another time the Pharisees and scribes watched Him to see whether He would heal on the Sabbath day, that they might find an accusation against Him. "But He knew their thoughts" (Luke 6:8). Finally, when the disciples were reasoning among themselves about which of them should be greatest, "Jesus, perceiving the thought of their heart, took a little child and set him by Him" (Luke 9:47).

Seeing then that the Lord knows our very thoughts, may we this day strive to think only those things that please Him. May we this day indeed bring into captivity every thought to the obedience of Jesus Christ (2 Corinthians 10:5).

March 16

Blessed is the man who walks not in the counsel of the un-
godly, nor stands in the path of sinners, nor sits in the seat of
the scornful; but his delight is in the law of the LORD; and in
His law he meditates day and night. (Psalm 1:1–2)

Would you believe that minus three, plus two, equals
one prosperous, happy individual? God wants us to be
happy; He desires to bless us. True happiness comes only
through fellowship with God in Jesus Christ. No Christ,
no contentment.

All attempts to secure happiness outside of faith in the
Lamb of God fail. Men may put on a front, show off, even
boast or brag, but it is all emptiness. Without true faith in
the shed blood of Jesus Christ, what men enjoy is at best
hollow, fleeting, transient—here today and gone tomorrow. Without Christ in his life, a man's fun is folly, his songs
are the blues, his goal is vanity.

What then shall the believer do to be prosperous? The
saint who desires to be blessed does not (1) accept the principles of the ungodly or adopt their lifestyles, (2) partici-
pate in the practices of outright, notorious sinners, and (3)
deliberately associate with those who openly mock or ridicule that which is holy.

On the other hand, the Christian who desires to be
blessed (1) delights in God's Word and (2) meditates on
God's Word day and night. The three negatives heighten
the two positives; the three don'ts build up the two dos.

Make up your mind today that you want to be blessed,
and God's Word will bless you and prosper you. Delight
in reading the revealed mind and will of the LORD, and His
Word will become a sword to parry Satan's thrusts, a hammer to smash stumbling blocks, a fire to burn away sin, a
light to shine on life's pathway, food to grow on, and a
telescope that peers into the future. Spend more time in
the Bible today and see if minus three plus two does not
equal one happy you!

March 17

But know that the LORD has set apart for Himself him who is godly; the LORD will hear when I call to Him. (Psalm 4:3)

The godly man is the man who loves God and his fellow man. Because he is one of the LORD's "merciful ones" and exercises mercy toward others, he ably represents a merciful and beneficent God. The LORD will defend those who act like Him. That is a fact the believer should know.

However, David's question, "How long will you turn my glory to shame? How long will you love worthlessness and seek falsehood?" (v. 2), is directed to the "sons of men," leaders, influential men who are guilty of seeking to crush him. Their attention is called to the fact that the very person they slander and persecute is one whom God has set apart for Himself.

Carnal men do not see Christians as God sees us. The man who by his wits tries to make it cannot understand the child of God. Men who hook and crook to get their way are never deeply satisfied. They are always insecure, suspicious of others. They are afraid that the way they got in is the way somebody else will put them out.

The shady character sees everybody in a dull light. He thinks you got yours the way he got his. Therefore you will have to protect it the way he protects his. But the psalmist wants it known that he is different. He was set apart by the LORD.

What I have, says David, the LORD gave to me. By His appointment I am where I am, I have what I have. Whether or not that helps your enemies change their attitudes or stops them from persecuting you cannot be promised. But it is wonderful for the blood-bought child of God to know that he is not alone in life. In any emergency the saint is heard. God's frequency is not jammed. His lines are not cut. When the believer calls on Him, He answers.

March 18

My voice You shall hear in the morning, O LORD; in the morning I will direct it to You, and I will look up. (Psalm 5:3)

When I lay down last night, I had no guarantee that I would wake up this morning. But I did wake up; I found the blood still running warm in my veins. I opened my eyes and could see.

It was a new day to hear the birds chirping and singing—a new day to behold the golden rays of the sun and to feel its warmth. A new day to let Jesus Christ live His life in me. A new day to feel the Holy Spirit moving in my heart. A new day to bid a prodigal son leave the pig pen of life and return to the Father. A new day to straighten out what I left crooked the day before. A new day to apologize for the wrong I committed.

A new day to witness for Christ, whereas the day before I was ashamed and kept quiet. A new day to keep my mouth shut whereas I talked too much yesterday.

David says to start your day right, talk with the LORD. It is important to begin the day with prayer. Some folks are not much good in the morning until they have had that cup of coffee. But what about prayer?

I saw a sign on a saloon advertising an "early-bird special." It read: "Come in and get your eye-opener!"

David said, "Make your prayer your early-bird special." I know from experience that that is good advice.

Sometimes I get an early morning phone call or get involved in something that causes me to put off my morning devotions for a few minutes. The minutes grow into hours. The day is almost over before I remember that I did not start the day right. The morning represents freshness, reprieve, opportunity, renewal, and we must see the importance of beginning right so that we can end right.

March 19

LORD, who may abide in Your tabernacle? Who may dwell in Your holy hill? (Psalm 15:1)

Have you ever dropped in to visit somebody and it felt like you had stepped into a refrigerator? The dog growled at you; the goldfish hid under the rocks in the tank; the cat scratched you for sitting in its favorite chair; the children did not even look up at you, let alone speak; the television was kept on, and you attempted to talk over it.

Trying to engage in conversation was like trying to hear a whisper at Niagara Falls. In short, you got the distinct impression that you were not welcome. You sensed the host saying later as you left, "Sorry you came; glad you're gone!"

The psalmist opens by asking, "Who can be a guest in Your tent? Who may dwell on Your sacred hill? What sort of person shall abide in God's pavilion? What kind of people spend time in His presence? What are the characteristics of the person allowed to be blessed as a guest in the house of the LORD?"

We come to recognize that God too has a standard. If a man is to be a guest in God's house, he must meet God's requirements. That is the thrust of David's message here. It is to remind us that if we are to be blessed while in the LORD's house, we must behave as He demands His guests conduct themselves: walk uprightly, work righteousness, speak the truth in our hearts.

What a wonderful thought that we pieces of mortal clay can be the guests of God! To think that He desires our company, seeks it, even enjoys it—amazes me. But I am glad, for "blessed are those who dwell in Your house" (Psalm 84:4). To be a guest in God's house is the desire of my soul.

> O Thou, in whose presence my soul takes delight,
> On whom in affliction, I call.
> My comfort by day and my song in the night,
> My hope, my salvation, my all.
>
> *Joseph Swain*

March 20

You will show me the path of life; in Your presence is fullness of joy; at Your right hand are pleasures forevermore. (Psalm 16:11)

The path of life that leads to the very presence of God also provides pleasures forevermore. The psalmist believed that. He was convinced that the future held even better things. Living in a day of apostasy and idolatry, David contrasted the lot of those steeped in heathenism with his own situation, one blessed of the Lord.

The joy we experience here below is not to be buried with our bones. If in this lowland of sorrow God grants mountaintop experiences, if in this "waste howling wilderness" (Deuteronomy 32:10) there is an oasis; if in these stormy seas there is a haven of rest—what must it be in that land where faith shall be sight?

A little boy refused to help himself to some cherries, even though the proprietor instructed him to grab a handful. Urged again to do so, the boy still refused. Finally the grocer himself picked up a handful and gave them to the boy. Later the mother of the boy asked him why he had not helped himself. "Mommy," replied the boy, "his hand was bigger than mine."

Surely, God's hand—His right hand—is a good hand, a big hand, with illimitable, inexhaustible resources, able to supply whatever you need, whenever you need it.

What are the pleasures to be found at His right hand? There is joy, delight, sweetness, peace, love, goodness, shining light, knowledge, salvation, deliverance, healing, life eternal, and life abundant! All those things may be found at the right hand of Jesus Christ our Lord.

March 21

As for me, I will see Your face in righteousness; I shall be satisfied when I awake in Your likeness. (Psalm 17:15)

Contrast. "As for me. . . ." Those words indicate a contrast. You can do as you please, but as for me. . . . For some people the highest good is material, temporal, physical. They delight in what they can see and in what the world has to offer. But as for me, said the psalmist, "Your commandments are my delights" (Psalm 119:143); "I delight to do Your will, O my God" (Psalm 40:8).

Communion. "I will see Your face. . . ." To behold God's face means to have fellowship with God, to commune with Him, to enjoy His favor. One who sees God's face is blessed, as was Moses (Numbers 12:8). The Bible says, "Blessed are the pure in heart, for they shall see God" (Matthew 5:8). And again, "Follow peace with all men, and holiness, without which no one will see the Lord" (Hebrews 12:14).

Completion. "I shall be . . . when. . . ." One interpretation suggests the psalmist bemoans his present condition: anxiety, war, oppression, sorrow, and so on, but joy comes in the morning. Tomorrow will be a better day! No matter how hard the times, how hot the fiery darts, how dark the night, how bitter the pill, how difficult the situation, when I wake up in the morning everything will be all right. On the other hand, the writer's hope may be not just vindication in this life, but a looking to the future when he shall awaken out of the sleep of death to be delivered once for all. Either way, here and now or there and later, the hope remains: "We shall be like Him" (1 John 3:2).

March 22

He leads me in the paths of righteousness for His name's sake.
(Psalm 23:3)

A *path* in Bible language means "a course of life or action." It is figurative. The path of righteousness is rugged, stony, narrow, cross-laden, beset with hidden snares, traps, ambush, tears, anguish, and agonizing travail.

Obviously, men do not need any extra help when it comes to walking in the wrong paths. On that point we are like sheep. Like it or not, a sheep is a stupid animal, easily led astray; on his own he does not know which way to take. Men resent that; they believe they know what is the right path.

Because of sin we do not know. As we are, as we come into this world, we do not know what paths to take. We must agree with Jeremiah 10:23: "O LORD, I know the way of man is not in himself; it is not in man who walks to direct his own steps."

"All we like sheep have gone astray; we have turned, every one, to his own way" (Isaiah 53:6). "There is a way which seems right to a man, but its end is the way of death" (Proverbs 14:12).

The truth of the matter is, we need someone to guide us and lead us in paths of righteousness. According to the Bible the only one who can do this is Jesus Christ, the Good Shepherd. Have you discovered this?

Following the Lord and walking in paths of righteousness cannot fail. Why? Because God's honor is at stake. He must lead in right paths in order to maintain the honor of His name. He must prove Himself to be what He declares Himself to be. You cannot go wrong today if you let Him lead.

*Yea, though I walk through the valley of the shadow of death,
I will fear no evil.* (Psalm 23:4)

The word *yea* means "in addition to" or "moreover," and refers us back to the first three verses of this psalm. The writer states that the LORD is his Shepherd, supplies all his needs, makes him lie down in green pastures, leads him beside still waters, refreshes his soul, and leads him in right paths.

What more could anybody ask for? In addition to all that, He takes away fear. Defined as a painful emotion marked by alarm, dread, and disquietude, *fear* is a passion implanted in nature that causes flight from an approaching evil, whether that evil is real or imaginary.

Whenever men are faced with a new situation and find themselves unable to make adequate adjustment, fear enters. A number of physiological reactions may occur: hair stands on end, eyes bulge, skin color changes, one breaks out in a cold sweat, knees knock, blood pressure increases, the heart pounds, teeth chatter, one trembles, gets sick to his stomach—those are some of the ways men show that they are scared.

We are suggesting that fear of evil is basically due to the rejection of Jesus Christ, remembering that *evil* here means "calamity, catastrophe." Perfect love casts out fear. If sinful men reject that perfect love as God has shown it in Jesus Christ, then what can they expect?

The psalmist David had the key to the whole problem of the fear of death. Without God, men are lifelong slaves to the fear of death. David knew that and was able to cry out, "Yea, though I walk through the valley of the shadow of death, I will fear no evil: for You are with me; Your rod and Your staff, they comfort me" (Psalm 23:4).

March 24

You prepare a table before me in the presence of my enemies.
(Psalm 23:5)

We have many enemies, including the world and the
devil, but the last enemy to be destroyed is death (1
Corinthians 15:26). Death shocks with its suddenness. It
disrupts family life, makes widows and orphans, stills the
voices of loved ones, dissolves friendships, upsets the best-
laid plans, breaks hearts, causes pain and sorrow, immo-
bilizes bodies, disarticulates speech, mystifies and strikes
terror into the hearts of many.

Yet God prepares a table before us in the presence of
Death. That is an act of judgment! By the table the world is
judged. In witnessing His grace to us, God condemns the
world's work. What the world needs is supplied by God
alone through faith in the shed blood of Christ.

By the table Satan is judged. He is taught that men love
the Lord because of who He is and what He did at Calvary. Finally, to Death comes the message: "See, you no
longer strike fear into the hearts of all men. Your power is
limited; your days are drawing to a close. Your influence
is waning. Your sting has been removed; your destruction
is near. My guests have no slavish fear of you!"

How true, for when Christ arose from the grave He had
all power in His hands—even the keys of death, hell and
the grave. Surely goodness and mercy shall follow the
Christian all the days of his life, and he will dwell in God's
house forever.

If death is permitted to enter this earthly tabernacle—
and death will come if the Lord Jesus tarries—God the
Father will but transfer us to a heavenly mansion to continue the feast at a table presently beyond our ability to
describe.

March 25

The humble He guides in justice, and the humble He teaches His way. (Psalm 25:9)

There are many reasons why we should desire and practice humility. According to the Bible humility is a quality to be sought (Zephaniah 2:3), and its counterpart, gentleness, is one of the fruits of the Holy Spirit (Galatians 5:23). Humility is to be worn like a coat, put on like a garment (Colossians 3:12). "Pursue gentleness," exhorted Paul to Timothy (1 Timothy 6:11). Humility is an attribute of Christ; it is an element of Christlikeness (Matthew 11:29; 2 Corinthians 10:1).

Many promises are made to the humble and gentle: (1) they shall eat and be satisfied (Psalm 22:26); (2) they shall inherit the earth and shall delight themselves in the abundance of peace (Psalm 37:11); (3) the LORD lifts up the humble and beautifies them with salvation (Psalm 147:6; 149:4); (4) they also shall increase their joy in the LORD (Isaiah 29:19).

Humility enables you to hear the voice of God. Intimate fellowship with the LORD is needed so you can hear Him direct you, teach you, warn, exhort, admonish, and guide you. The true scholars of the LORD are the humble, the lowly in heart. They are the teachable ones.

Come to the LORD in humility, said David, and be assured He will guide you aright. Humility is submission to God's will, a sincere desire to learn from Him. Because God is good and true, He is sure to offer that which is just and right.

He forgets not the cry of the humble (Psalm 9:12). We Christians have the assurance that, washed in the blood of Jesus Christ, we can be truly humble. We can come to the LORD knowing that He will guide us and teach us His way.

March 26

LORD, I have loved the habitation of Your house, and the place where Your glory dwells. (Psalm 26:8)

Perhaps the phrase *house of God* sounds strange to those who believe in an omnipresent God who dwells not in temples made with hands (Acts 17:24). Actually, the term *house* includes more than the physical structure itself, be it a tent, stone building, fortress, cave, tabernacle, or temple.

Where God's presence dwelt in Shekinah glory, that was God's house; where sacrifices were offered to Him and priests ministered before Him under the theocracy in Israel, there dwelt the glory of God, the honor of the LORD; there was God's house.

The psalmist had much to say about the house of the LORD, for he desired to dwell there forever (Psalm 23:6), all the days of his life (27:4). Said David: "They are abundantly satisfied with the fullness of Your house" (36:8). "We shall be satisfied with the goodness of Your house" (65:4). "Blessed are those who dwell in Your house; they will still be praising You . . . I would rather be a doorkeeper in the house of my God, than dwell in the tents of wickedness" (84:4, 10).

"Those who are planted in the house of the LORD shall flourish in the courts of our God" (92:13). "Holiness adorns Your house" (93:5). "I was glad when they said to me, 'Let us go into the house of the LORD'" (122:1).

In the New Testament the Church is also called God's house. Christians, people with faith in the shed blood of Jesus Christ, constitute the house of God. Simon Peter said that the time is come that judgment must begin at the house of God in persecution. Paul desired that Christians know how to behave themselves in the house of God (1 Timothy 3:15). Keep in mind that your body is the temple of the Holy Spirit, the place where God's honor dwells. Rejoice that God lives in you.

March 27

Hear, O LORD, when I cry with my voice! Have mercy also upon me, and answer me. (Psalm 27:7)

You must be on good standing and speaking terms with the LORD if you expect Him to hear you when you cry. We all know that God hears everything. He heard the moans of the Israelites groaning in slavery there in Egypt, and the LORD raised up Moses to deliver them.

He heard the secret war plans of the King of Syria and revealed them to His prophet Elisha. He heard Nebuchadnezzar boast and took away the monarch's mind. He heard Gehazi lie to Naaman and to Elisha and smote the greedy servant with leprosy.

Today He hears the curses of the angry mobs, the blasphemy of the wicked, the plans of the gangsters, the whispers of schemers, the epithets of racists, the lies of the ungodly liars, the sinful songs of men made silly and simple by bottled spirits. David's request is that of a believer, a request desired in every Christian's heart: LORD, hear me!

The prayers of the saint are legitimate. All who have faith in the shed blood of Christ have access to the Father. Through Christ we can come boldly to the throne of grace. God knows our voices, and when we cry out He hears.

So many factors combine to determine the quality and character of your voice that no two voices are alike. But rest assured, the LORD who made you a unique individual knows your voice when He hears it. Do not hesitate to call on Him today in praise or petition. Call, and He will answer.

March 28

Wait on the LORD; be of good courage, and He shall strengthen your heart; wait, I say, on the LORD! (Psalm 27:14)

I remember when we were boys and someone said, "Wait!" we would answer, "Weight broke the wagon down!" I often wondered if that expression was made up to teach us how to spell the two different words.

We live in such an age of hustle-bustle. There is instant coffee, push-button machines, fast-food restaurants, and instant-on television. I am just old enough to remember having to crank up my father's car and almost getting an arm knocked off in the process. Today we turn the ignition key and that is it—most of the time.

Slow driving motorists and red lights that are too long irritate us. Such are the times in which we live. Some things are too slow for us. Students just out of high school immediately want high-paying jobs. Newly licensed and ordained preachers immediately want big churches and salaries.

We need to heed God's Word and learn to wait on Him.

The Hebrew word used has the probable original meaning of "twist or stretch." There is the idea of tension, of enduring. Can you imagine a stretched rubber band *waiting* to snap back together again?

It is not an idle waiting or loafing, nor is it one of hopelessness. Rather, it is like a taut rope; there is eager looking for the LORD. From the depths of despair David called his own soul back to the patience needed to wait on the LORD. Faith to wait on Him encourages the heart; it strengthens and emboldens you. Wait on the LORD and find that that is true.

March 29

Weeping may endure for a night, but joy comes in the morning.
(Psalm 30:5)

I think a man ought to realize that he is going to die. He did not come here to stay. He is but a pilgrim, a sojourner, just passing through.

The thought does not mean one has to be morbid or melancholic; yet it is a realistic, sobering thought. From the Bible one learns that sorrow does not last always; a better day is coming.

Walk up and down the city streets. See the trash, poverty, unemployment, bars and saloons, purse-snatchers, criminals, and dope smokers. Watch television and tell me if you hear the message that weeping endures only for a night and joy comes in the morning. The films produced by Hollywood would never promote such information.

Read the headlines of your newspapers. Listen to the radio—its blues and its news—and tell me if there is such a message as this text gives. I think not.

The only valid and authentic record for such a statement is the Bible, the Word of God. The LORD is not a man that He should lie. Being omniscient, He makes no mistakes. Take Him at His Word. Weeping is but for a night; joy comes in the morning. Prepare for it by believing it even before it arrives, and your faith will make the morning even brighter.

March 30

Oh, taste, and see that the L<small>ORD</small> *is good. . . .* (Psalm 34:8)
. . . if indeed you have tasted that the Lord is gracious.
(1 Peter 2:3)

To *taste* means to enjoy, to partake, perceive, or experience, so that we take the command here figuratively, not literally. Actually, that verse is an appeal to exercise faith. The way to taste God is to trust God, to take refuge in Him.

Unbelief, on the other hand, has no desire to taste and see the goodness of God. Unbelief hears the roar of the lions and stops dead in its tracks. Unbelief feels the heat of the fiery furnace and prepares to bow down to the idol gods of this world.

Unbelief sees the boisterous waves, hears the howling of the tempestuous winds, and screams in terror. Unbelief trembles at the sight of Goliath the giant; unbelief despairs at hindrances, shrinks from dangers, gives up while languishing in prison.

Faith goes on in spite of appearances, feelings, persecutions, or adversities. Faith goes on to taste and to see that the L<small>ORD</small> God is good.

In short, the proof of the pudding is in the eating thereof. Only when we eat God's Word as meat or drink it as pure milk do we find it delicious. Only then do we grow.

Too often I hear professed Christians attempt to rationalize away the meaning of some passage in God's Word. They make themselves judges of the Bible rather than let the Word judge them.

Here is the thrust of those two verses: Step out on the authority of "thus says the Lord" and you will discover that the Lord is good, kind, gracious, and faithful. Do not be a malnourished Christian—weak, emaciated, and puny looking. Show some spiritual muscle. Do as Jeremiah did; eat God's Word. Today you will experience every blessing that the Lord desires to bestow upon you.

March 31

There is no want to those who fear Him . . . those who seek the
Lord shall not lack any good thing. (Psalm 34:9–10)

Some of us may have a problem defining "good thing."
What we deem good may not be good for us. Fried foods
sure taste good, but nutritionists suggest we cut them out.
We recognize that what others suggest is good for us may
indeed not be good at all.

We simply do not know always what is good for us. The
sin nature with which we were born has twisted our thinking and blinded our eyes, making us incapable of accu-
rately determining what is good for us. Our values are distorted by sin.

Sin makes some good things no good. If a man rejects
God's absolute standard, he is in trouble. He sets up his
own watered-down relative standard and mixes it with
delusion, deceit, self and folly, so that it becomes impossible for him to determine what is really good for him.

It is so easy to choose that which is bad, destructive,
and which leads down the path to hell. If it were not for
the Lord's stepping in and guiding our feet, lighting up
our pathway, directing us, and supplying what we need,
we surely would be in bad trouble.

Yes, it takes time for experience to back up or to cor-
roborate what faith already accepts as true. But the psalmist would say, "Believe God anyway!" Believe that He is
able to make all things work together for your good.

Such an attitude, belief, or philosophy of life brings joy,
eliminates murmuring and complaining, helps others,
pleases God, strengthens the church, influences sinners for
Christ, chases away the devil, and magnifies the name of
Jesus.

April 1

Seek peace, and pursue it.
(Psalm 34:14; see also 1 Peter 3:11)

That is a command. Seek peace, inquire for it, crave, go after, search for, strive for peace with all your heart. Make it your aim in life; run after it and grab it! Another writer has paraphrased this verse: "Search for peace as a thing hidden; pursue it as a thing fugitive."

On the other hand, there are some things men ought not to seek. Israel was warned not to seek after fortune-tellers. The wicked seek after falsehood; they seek to slay the righteous. Evil men seek only rebellion, mischief, and mixed wine. Christ said, "An evil and adulterous generation seeks after a sign" (Matthew 12:39).

What should men search after? David said, "Seek the LORD and His strength, seek His face evermore" (1 Chronicles 16:11). Solomon said to seek wisdom as silver, and search for her as for hidden treasures (Proverbs 2:4). Earnestly seek good (Proverbs 11:27).

Zephaniah exhorted: "Seek righteousness, seek humility" (2:3). Isaiah said: "Seek justice" (1:17). Amos said: "Seek good and not evil" (5:14). The Lord Jesus stated: "But seek first the kingdom of God and His righteousness" (Matthew 6:33).

The apostle Paul admonished: "Seek those things which are above" (Colossians 3:1). Finally, the author of Hebrews said believers have here on earth no continuing city, but seek the one to come (13:14).

Surely there is much for the Christian to do. There are many things to be sought after. The saint is one who has peace with God, and the peace of God is available. May that peace rule in your own heart today and enable you to "live peaceably with all men" (Romans 12:18). "Pursue the things which make for peace" (Romans 14:19). "Pursue peace with all people" (Hebrews 12:14).

April 2

God is our refuge and strength, a very present help in trouble.
Therefore we will not fear, even though the earth be removed,
and though the mountains be carried into the midst of the sea;
though its waters roar and be troubled, though the mountains
shake with its swelling. (Psalm 46:1–3)

Fear: Fear is defined as a painful emotion marked by alarm, dread, disquiet. It is caused by the expectation of danger, pain, disaster; fear is terror, apprehension; a passion that causes flight from approaching evil, whether real or imaginary.

Faith: Note the determination of the psalmist here, the determination of faith. We will not fear no matter what happens! The natural calamities described are tremendous. The firmest of all created objects—mountains—are used to paint a picture of horror.

Men climb mountains, fly over them, drive around them, tunnel through them. Men do not pick up mountains and cast them into the depths of the sea. No, man has no such power. Assuming men could stir up the waters of the ocean and cause them to roar so loud that the thundering of Niagara Falls pales into whispering insignificance, assuming men could shake mountains with the vehemence of volcanic power—even so, said the writer, we will not fear.

> A faith that shines more bright and clear
>> When tempests rage without;
> That when in danger knows no fear
>> In darkness feels no doubt.
> Lord, give me such a faith as this . .
>
> *William E. Bathurst*

Fortress: The faith that drives away fear is found only in the Fortress—the refuge and strength of Jesus Christ. He is my rock. Is He yours too? He is my shelter, my castle, my high tower, buckler, and shield; He is my refuge and strength, my "right now" help in "right now" trouble. His nearness now is a foretaste of what the future holds.

April 3

For this is God, our God forever and ever; He will be our guide even to death. (Psalm 48:14)

We need guidance because we were born blind. We cannot see the way we should go, the pathway we should walk upon, the road we ought to travel. We need guidance because our own hearts deceive us and play tricks on us. We have an incurable heart disease, and we are desperately sick with sin.

We need guidance because there is an evil, supernatural being, Satan, who constantly seeks to beguile, deceive, ensnare, and defeat us. We need guidance because there are so many confusing ways to go; and there are those ways that seem right but the end thereof is death (Proverbs 14:12).

We need guidance because we are earthly creatures with limited knowledge. We are ignorant of the future; we do not know what tomorrow will bring. Guidance comes from the eye of God who said, "I will instruct you . . . in the way you should go; I will guide you with My eye" (Psalm 32:8).

Guidance comes from the Word of God, for it is written, "Your word is a lamp to my feet and a light to my path" (Psalm 119:105). Guidance comes by the Holy Spirit, of whom it is written, ". . . He will guide you into all truth" (John 16:13).

With Jesus Christ as your pilot, your leader, there is nothing to fear along your pilgrim journey. There is no need to worry, for worry produces fear, fear brings doubt, and doubt dismisses faith. Without faith it is impossible to please God.

God's guidance is infallible; He makes no mistakes. The Christian is never deprived of the protecting presence of the holy angels of God, nor is he deprived of the marvelous guidance of the ever-present Holy Spirit.

April 4

Against You, You only, have I sinned, and done this evil in Your sight. (Psalm 51:4)

One night David arose from his bed, walked out upon the roof of his house, and saw a beautiful woman bathing herself in her purification ritual. Lusting after her, he inquired who she was. She was Bathsheba, wife of Uriah the Hittite.

Sending for her, David committed adultery with her. Uriah was ordered into the forefront of the battle against the Ammonites and was killed. David then married Bathsheba.

God sent the prophet Nathan to rebuke David. Psalm 51 tells of David's feelings at that point. David's sin, like all sin, had a frightful outreach; indeed, there was a five-fold ramification. First, David sinned against Bathsheba, even though her own ambition and moral laxity may have played a part in the matter. Second, he sinned against Uriah by taking his wife and then causing him to lose his life. Third, Israel, too, was affected; the Jews lost the battle in which Uriah was killed. Fourth, David sinned against himself and against his posterity, for the baby born to Bathsheba died. Furthermore, it was announced that the sword would never depart from David's house (2 Samuel 12:10).

But above and beyond all that, David's sin was against God: "You only" means "You *especially*." Here, David lined up with God against David. Here is the real meaning of *confess*—to speak the same thing as God says about our deeds. David was penitent, broken, contrite, humbled; in his heart he knew he was wrong, and he knew that God was right.

He knew that the LORD was a perfect judge whose justice would be vindicated. When we confess and condemn our sins, our action justifies God.

April 5

For You have delivered my soul from death. Have You not kept my feet from falling, that I may walk before God in the light of the living? (Psalm 56:13)

This psalm was written by David when he fled from Saul and the Philistines captured him in Gath. Fleeing from the wrath of the jealous king Saul, David went to a place called Gath (1 Samuel 21:10) as a solitary fugitive, hoping to escape notice in that enemy country. Imagine running from one enemy to hide in a country full of enemies!

That desperate expedient fell through; the servants of King Achish recognized David as the one who had killed their champion Goliath, and the one of whom the multitudes sang: "Saul has slain his thousands, and David his ten thousands." Following their suspicions, they took him. Fearing for his life, David pretended he was crazy.

"So he changed his behavior before them, pretended madness in their hands, scratched on the doors of the gate, and let his saliva fall down on his beard" (1 Samuel 21:13). Feigning madness, David escaped harm.

King Achish said to his servants: "Look, you see the man is insane. Why have you brought him to me?" So David was let loose and escaped. Because of that experience he was moved to write that God had delivered his soul from death, his feet from falling, so he could walk before God in the light of life.

Past deliverances ought to strengthen us now and move us to thank God for future deliverances. Past victories can point to future victories if we but let them. If you have trusted the Lord in the past and He brought you through, why not trust Him with the future?

April 6

My heart is steadfast, O God, my heart is steadfast.
(Psalm 57:7)

I teased one of our church members about making her rounds in the hospitals of Philadelphia. In October I visited her in the Metropolitan Hospital; in December the Jefferson Hospital. The following September I saw her again in the Metropolitan Hospital; then in November in the Misericordia Hospital.

When you have a heart condition, you do not always have a choice. Emergencies occur and you sometimes have to go where you are taken. Nevertheless, in such situations it is an advantage to have a fixed heart.

That member suffered a number of heart attacks so that physically she had a "bad heart." But spiritually she had a good heart—settled, steadfast, established, and cleansed by the blood of the Lord Jesus Christ. The way to keep the heart steady is to bind it to the Lord Jesus.

Perhaps you have seen some truck drivers stop on the highway, get out of their cabs, and proceed to tighten down their cargo. So it is that amid the howling winds of adversity, the tempestuous rolling sea, and the storms of life, you need someone to steady you.

You need to be tied down by the Holy Spirit to Jesus Christ, the only sure foundation. Joined to Him, the heart is steadfast; the fluttering, wayward, agitated heart is calmed.

Hear the Lord command even now: "Let not your heart be troubled; you believe in God, believe also in Me. . . . Peace I leave with you, My peace I give to you; not as the world gives do I give to you. Let not your heart be troubled, neither let it be afraid" (John 14:1, 27).

April 7

My soul, wait silently for God alone; for my expectation is from Him. (Psalm 62:5)

In the midst of treachery and double-faced behavior when the wicked are boldly flaunting their ungodliness, how can the Christian stay cool, calm, and collected? David suggests in this "alone" and "only" psalm (vv. 2, 4, 5–8): Wait on the LORD.

Surely a materialistic age finds it difficult not to put its trust in things or in people who promise to supply those things. To leave all quietly to God is deemed too passive. The world says God helps those who help themselves. The Bible teaches that God helps.

When we wait on Him in every circumstance, we can expect grace for every trial, a way out for every test, an answer for every problem. As the years come and go, our faith in Christ is confirmed. Things happen, events occur, that let us know we are on the right track.

Those who wait upon the LORD are blessed (Isaiah 30:18); they are not ashamed (Psalm 25:3); "they shall inherit the earth" (Psalm 37:9), have their hearts encouraged (Psalm 27:14), their cries heard (Psalm 40:1), their strength renewed, and are enabled to soar on eagles' wings, to run and not be weary, to walk and not faint (Isaiah 40:31).

Whatever happens to you this day, look to Jesus Christ who shed His precious blood for you. He alone is your hope, your only expectation, salvation, and deliverance. Wait, and you will see.

> Bear and forbear, and silent be
> Tell to no man thy misery:
> Yield not in trouble to dismay
> God can deliver any day.
> *Martin Luther*

April 8

Let their table become a snare. (Psalm 69:22)

The word *table* is a symbol of blessings, the provision of God. Your table is your welfare. That is easily seen in Psalm 78:19–20: "Can God prepare a table in the wilderness? Behold, He struck the rock, so that the waters gushed out, and the streams overflowed. Can He give bread also? Can He provide meat for His people?"

In Psalm 69:22 there is an imprecation, or curse. David calls down the wrath of God upon his enemies—who are also Israel's enemies and God's enemies. He is unable to restrain himself as he thinks of the intolerable acts committed against him.

He is hated without a cause (vv. 4, 14); his destruction is sought (v. 4); he is alienated by his own blood relatives (v. 8); he is reproached (v. 9); ridiculed and made the song of drunkards (v. 12); his enemies shame and dishonor him (v. 19).

David breaks out into imprecation that the Lord transform their table into a troublesome trap; that their enjoyments eventually become their end; that their riches be responded to with retribution; and that their blessings become curses (read vv. 22–28).

In this present-day church age, we Christians do not utter such curses. We have been commanded to bless those who persecute us—"bless and do not curse" (Romans 12:14).

We have no desire to see tables become traps, light become darkness, material wealth become spiritual poverty, or mental brilliance degenerate into moral buffoonery.

Let us pray that God will use us today to help turn men to the Christ who has so wonderfully provided every table.

April 9

For a day in Your courts is better than a thousand. I would
rather be a doorkeeper in the house of my God than dwell in
the tents of wickedness. (Psalm 84:10)

I thank God for all who take delight in being in the house
of God. Strange as it may seem, there are those who may
be found in God's house but who do not delight in it. That
is a contradiction. In the very presence of God is fullness
of joy; at His right hand there are pleasures forevermore.

To be in God's house and not to be delighted shows that
something is amiss. Something is wrong—not with God
but with man. To go to a jeweler and not find a diamond
ring; to attend the circus and not see a clown; to go to the
supermarket and come out with an empty shopping cart—
something is wrong.

To go to a party and fall asleep; to go to the zoo and not
watch the peacock preen, the monkeys swing, or hear the
roar of the lions or the trumpeting of the elephants—what
a waste of time! Worse still is it to go to church and not be
delighted.

It is true that some people do not find the Lord's tabernacles amiable; their souls do not yearn for God's presence. That is because their motives are improper, their purposes not spiritual. Some are ignorant of the will of God
for His church. Still others, who know that will, do not
submit themselves to it.

The psalmist does find God's tabernacles amiable; his
soul longs for the courts of the LORD; his heart and flesh
cry out for the presence of the living God.

For him, just to sit at the threshold of God's house was
better than being bedded down resting in the air-condi-
tioned, wall-to-wall carpeted room of the wicked.

April 10

No good thing will He withhold from those who walk up-rightly. (Psalm 84:11)

God has no pleasure in withholding any blessing from mankind, but He has His own standards, criteria, and time schedule. He sets His own conditions. That is why David first confessed that he had done what the LORD wanted and then cried, "Do not withhold Your tender mercies from me, O LORD" (Psalm 40:11).

In other words, obedience, or walking uprightly, is tied in with receiving good things from the hand of the LORD. Our sins hide God's face from us; our iniquities come between us and our God (Isaiah 59:2). Jeremiah put it bluntly: "Your iniquities have turned these things away, and your sins have withheld good from you" (Jeremiah 5:25).

How often in life we have yearned after that which glittered and glowed, only to discover it was not gold. How often we have been deceived by the swindlers of this world who seem to think: *Everything good you have, I will take away!*

It takes faith to believe God's promises for all who walk uprightly. Surely things happen in life that cause us to wonder—debilitating diseases, crippling accidents, loss of loved ones, destruction of property, dissolution of marriages, and waywardness of children.

Such events give us cause to wonder what life is all about. Somehow the Christian comes to believe that God knows what He is doing. Armed with such assurance, you can face successfully the difficulties of life, whatever they are. Imagine going along life's highway saying, "No good thing will the Lord hold back from me!" Such an attitude, such a philosophy will revolutionize your entire life.

April 11

I will hear what God the LORD will speak, for He will speak peace to His people and to His saints. (Psalm 85:8)

Through faith in the shed blood of Jesus Christ, Christians have peace with God. Such peace *with* God makes available to us the peace *of* God. It is that latter peace the psalmist has in mind. That peace is a wholeness of heart, a completeness of character; a togetherness of the body, soul, and spirit; the prosperity of the personality. It is a calm, cool, collected Christian spirit.

Now God speaks at different times and in various ways. Sometimes He speaks in the midnight hour; sometimes early in the morning. Sometimes He speaks through a donkey or from a burning bush that does not consume away.

If necessary, the very stones, rocks, hills, and mountains would cry out. He speaks through angels; He speaks through men, whether they be prophets, preachers, paupers, princes, or peasants. He speaks through women, as He did with the Samaritan woman at the well.

Sometimes He thunders as with fire and smoke at Mount Sinai; sometimes He whispers in a still, small voice. Sometimes He speaks to us at home in our secret closets or when we are flat on our backs convalescing in the hospital. Sometimes no voice at all breaks the silence of the heavens. Instead there is something within that we cannot explain; something in the waiting soul jars us, and somehow we know.

But wherever and whenever, states the psalmist, He will speak peace to His people. I like that, don't you? The God we serve is not silent when we need Him. In the slavery of Egypt He speaks peace. In the fiery furnace of idolatry He speaks peace. In the den of lions He speaks peace. On the stormy seas of life, to the howling winds and frothy whitecaps of a restless sea, He speaks, "Peace, be still" (Mark 4:39).

April 12

We finish our years like a sigh. (Psalm 90:9)

In the later months of the last year of Israel's wandering in the wilderness, day by day Moses saw those who had left Egypt when they were twenty years old and older falter on the journey, stop, and drop dead. Condemned to find graves in the wilderness, Israel's days rapidly declined.

The morning dawn quickly vanishes as mist before the sun when the darkness of the night softly fades away before the breaking day. But once again, the promise of a new day—one made bright by the rising of the sun—wanes swiftly and gives way to the inevitable, inexorable gloom of evening, whose shadowy fingers begin to write their mournful message across the sky: Day is done.

However long we live, whatever the number of years we put in, the assessment remains: We spend our years as a tale that is told. When the pharaoh of Egypt asked Jacob how old he was, Joseph's father replied: "The days of the years of my pilgrimage are one hundred and thirty years; few and evil have been the days of the years of my life" (Genesis 47:9).

Compared with God's eternal presence, our years are but a sigh or a whisper, scarcely heard and soon forgotten. We sing our song on the stage of life and pass off the scene. Our years are brought to an end like a sigh, the expression of sorrow and weariness; life is over like a fleeting sound, a moan, a mere murmur.

Thank God, in Jesus Christ, that the story is not over, the tale is not finished, the sigh is not the signal that all is ended. In Christ we have life eternal, and death is but the prelude to a continuous symphony of life.

April 13

So teach us to number our days, that we may gain a heart of wisdom. (Psalm 90:12)

A man dropped two pennies on the floor of a department store as he pulled out his wallet to make a purchase. He stooped to hunt the two cents and left his wallet lying on the counter. When he straightened up, the billfold was gone; it had contained fifty dollars. Some of us are penny-wise and dollar-foolish. But worse, some are time-wise and eternity-foolish.

We recognize that life is but a fleeting shadow. We are but clay and dirt and dust. At best life is a leaf trembling in the wind, a flower all too soon fading and dropping its petals softly to the ground. Life is but a blade of green grass wet with the morning dew, soon to be withered by the scorching rays of the noonday sun.

Death is part of God's program, calculated to make us feel the urgency of the need for repentance and to value each day rather than squander it in frivolous pursuits, ignorance, and lack of purpose.

To number one's days is to recognize that death is a reality. It is to accept Job's statement that "man that is born of a woman is of few days." Our days are determined, the number of months set, the bounds of the years appointed, and we cannot pass beyond. To number our days is to realize that we did not come here to stay.

April 14

He who dwells in the secret place of the Most High shall abide under the shadow of the Almighty. (Psalm 91:1)

Today men are very security conscious in their insecurity. There is increased use of watchdogs, windows are barred, gun sales have risen, tear gas repellents are advertised and sold, and alarm and security system installation has become a booming business.

We really do not wonder at the phenomenon; it is a sign of the times. For these are days of burglary, rape, robbery, and murder. Probably you have been affected directly or indirectly by the rising tide of crime.

However, we can put too much emphasis on our own efforts to protect ourselves and thereby fail to realize that we have a God who is in the protection business! Whether we are threatened by the trapper's snare or the deadly pestilence, He watches over us. Whether our assailant be the terror by night or the arrow that flies by day, He watches. Whether it be the disease that stalks in darkness or the destruction that lays waste at noon, He watches. Whatever and wherever the evil or distress—danger, disease, destruction, or death—the LORD is our refuge and our fortress, our God in whom we trust.

However, the secret place of security is only for those who believe in the shed blood of Jesus Christ. All others are in trouble. Without Jesus Christ a man supports himself on a broken cane. Without Christ a man leans on a cracked crutch. Without Christ he stands on sinking sand. Without Christ he is like the straw that the wind drives away. "Unless the LORD guards the city, the watchman stays awake in vain" (Psalm 127:1).

April 15

He shall call upon Me, and I will answer him; I will be with him in trouble; I will deliver him and honor him. (Psalm 91:15)

The writer of this psalm knew that life was rough; it was no bed of roses. Exposed to dangers, toils, and hardships, he had much to say about the trapper's snare, the deadly pestilence, the terror of the night, the arrow that flies by day, evil that stalks in darkness, and destruction that lays waste at noonday. He spoke of poisonous snakes, wild beasts, and disastrous plagues.

Note the value of *prayer*, simply defined as calling upon the LORD. Second, those who trust the LORD are *promised* something: "I will answer him," said the LORD. Those who trust God in prayer also have the promise of God's *presence*, even in the midst of trouble.

Finally, see in this verse *preservation*: "I will deliver him and honor him." There is no promise that the Christian will not get into trouble. After all, we are but strangers and pilgrims here, living in a world system ruled by the devil.

But with Jesus Christ as your traveling companion you can make it. Evil may come your way, but it can never touch the sacred core of true life that is hid with Christ in God. The LORD will take care of you, through every day, o'er all the way.

Whether in the lions' den with Daniel; in the fiery furnace with the Hebrew boys; or in the muddy dungeon with Jeremiah; on the ash pile with Job; whether downtrodden slaves in Egypt or exiles in a strange land with the Israelites; in Caesar's palace with certain early Christians; in exile on Patmos with John; in a pit with Joseph; on the stormy sea with the disciples; or in prison with Paul and Silas— trust God!

Trust in the LORD; He will deliver you. He will answer your prayer; He will give you His presence; He has promised that in time of trouble, He will preserve you. Trust Him today.

April 16

Your thoughts are very deep. (Psalm 92:5)

Since man's thoughts are unknown to men, obviously the thoughts of God are unknown to men. God must reveal His mind, and He has done that in the Bible.

We learn that God's thoughts are *incomparable*. Divine thoughts do not compare with human thoughts. "'For my thoughts are not your thoughts, nor are your ways my ways,' says the LORD. 'For as the heavens are higher than the earth, so are My ways higher than your ways, and My thoughts than your thoughts'" (Isaiah 55:8–9).

God's thoughts are *innumerable*. Divine thoughts baffle human ability to count them. "Many, O LORD, my God, are Your wonderful works which You have done; and Your thoughts toward us . . . are more than can be numbered" (Psalm 40:5). "How great is the sum of them! If I should count them, they would be more in number than the sand" (Psalm 139:17–18).

God's thoughts are *unsearchable*. Divine thoughts are profound, God's designs unsearchable. William Cowper, in a time of despair, rode through London looking for the river into which he planned to plunge and commit suicide. The fog was so thick that night that he rode in the horse-drawn cab for an hour or more. For him life had been hopeless, without meaning. He desired to end it all. But where was the river? Rebuking the cab driver for taking so long to find the riverbank, Cowper thrust open the cab door only to discover that he was right back at his own doorstep. Later he would write:

> God moves in a mysterious way
> His wonders to perform;
> He plants His footsteps in the sea,
> And rides upon the storm.

April 17

For He knows our frame; He remembers that we are dust.
(Psalm 103:14)

Man's frailty and the brevity of life are recurrent themes in the Old Testament. We are dirt (Genesis 2:7); the chemicals that compose our bodies are worth less than ten dollars. However, man could never put those ingredients together and create another man. God alone is Creator.

Man is dust; man is like grass; man is like a flower of the field. Said Job: "He comes forth like a flower and fades away; he flees like a shadow and does not continue" (Job 14:2). Adds David: "The wind passes over it"—the scorching, withering south wind—"and it is gone, and its place remembers it no more" (Psalm 103:16).

Add to the scriptures that speak of man as dust, grass, and a flower, other verses that describe him as a leaf, a handspan, a shadow, a puff of steam, an earthen vessel, a clay pot. Recognize that the words we hear intoned over someone else by the preacher at the cemetery—"earth to earth, ashes to ashes, dust to dust"—may soon be spoken over you and me.

While man's stay is short, his life brief, his strength weakness, his frame feeble, his form frail, his power puny, his body clay—God's mercy endures forever. That is the point the psalmist makes. It is a contrast between man and God. Men may pass away, but the lovingkindness of the LORD is from everlasting to everlasting upon all who revere Him and keep His commandments.

It is precisely there that the blood-washed child of God cries, "Thank you, Jesus!" For we believe God is mindful of us; He knows our frame. He knows just how much we can bear. Our weakness appeals to His compassion. Mindful of the brittle, fragile material He works with, God in love sent Christ to die on Calvary. Now the eternal Holy Spirit dwells in our bodies of dust, and creatures of time possess eternal life right now. Soon the trumpet shall sound, and we shall receive bodies of glory like that of our Lord. Keep looking up!

April 18

Let the redeemed of the LORD say so. (Psalm 107:2)

Men are not mind readers. No man knows what is in the heart of another man. Your own spirit in you knows what you are thinking, and God knows, for He is a discerner of hearts. Because men cannot read your mind, it is necessary for you to reveal your relationship with God. If you are a Christian, you are required by the Lord to make known to others where you stand.

In other words, you should boldly confess that Jesus is Lord. Some people say, "You don't have to talk it, just live it." Yet there is no Bible support or sanction for such silence of the saints. "I believed, therefore I spoke" (Psalm 116:10). "Therefore whoever confesses Me before men, him I will also confess before My Father who is in heaven" (Matthew 10:32).

Christians need to let the world know about Jesus Christ. It is our duty. We need to confess Him in order to counteract anti-Christian propaganda. Confession that Jesus Christ is Lord is a foil to the works of Satan. Confession that Jesus is Lord encourages the hearts of other believers.

Confession that Jesus is Lord is an opportunity to gain rewards to be enjoyed when this life is over. It is not enough just to "live it." The fact that some who are great talkers are also loose livers is not an excuse for sincere believers to remain silent.

No genuine Christian knowingly, willingly refuses to confess Jesus as Lord (Romans 10:9). Confession is the external expression of an inner conviction.

Speak to someone today about the Lord Jesus Christ.

April 19

*Oh, that men would give thanks to the LORD for His good-
ness, and for His wonderful works to the children of men!*
(Psalm 107:8)

Jesus Christ is wonderful in His *conception*. It was announced by an angel, first to Mary, then to Joseph; He was
conceived of the Holy Spirit in the womb of a virgin.

Jesus Christ is wonderful in His *birth*. He was named
before He arrived; a special star called "His star" heralded
His birth. Wise men came to worship Him.

Jesus Christ is wonderful in His *life*. He was tempted
but did not and could not sin. He preached and taught. He
performed miracles—made the sick well, the weak strong,
the dumb speak, the blind see, the deaf hear, the lame walk,
the hungry satisfied, forgave sinners, exorcised demons,
and raised the dead.

So wonderful was His life that the Father spoke from
heaven His approval: "This is My beloved Son, in whom I
am well pleased" (Matthew 3:17). Surely you can see how
nothing but wonderful works would be expected of such
a wonderful Savior.

Jesus Christ is wonderful in *death*. While wicked men
with evil hands nailed Him to the cross, He actually laid
down His life Himself. There was love at Calvary and
forgiveness there where His blood was shed for our sins.

Yes, Jesus Christ is wonderful in death, for the sun refused to shine; darkness covered the land; the earth did
quake; the veil of the Temple was torn in two; rocks were
split; and graves were opened.

Jesus Christ is wonderful in His *resurrection*. He kept
His word; death could not hold Him down. He rose from
the grave with all power in His hands.

I repeat, surely such a wonderful Savior can do nothing
but *wonderful* works. Praise Him!

April 20

For He satisfies the longing soul, and fills the hungry soul with goodness. (Psalm 107:9)

All of us come into this world with an emptiness. We try to hide it; we put on a front; we pretend. But the emptiness remains. We try to fill it with all kinds of things. We keep busy. However, when our efforts fail and the front wears thin, we are right back where we started.

Why? Because only He who made us can fill the void. There is chaos in our lives until we find order in God. There is darkness until we find Him who is Light. There is no rest unless we find it in Him who said, "Come to Me, all you who labor and are heavy laden, and I will give you rest" (Matthew 11:28).

There is war until we discover the Prince of Peace. There is hunger until we eat the Bread of Life. There is thirst until we drink of that fountain that never shall run dry. There is hopelessness until we build our hope on things eternal.

There is helplessness until we lean on the everlasting arms. There is death until we find life abundant and eternal in Christ Jesus.

Only God can satisfy the longing soul; only God can fill the hungry soul with goodness. The first step toward fulfilling your purpose in life is to accept Jesus Christ who loved you, shed His own blood on Calvary for you, and was buried but rose again from the dead.

April 21

The LORD is high above all nations, and His glory above the heavens. (Psalm 113:4)

I am reminded of a reporter who interviewed a man celebrating his one-hundredth birthday.

"To what do you attribute your great age?"

He answered, "To clean living. I never drank, smoked, overate, or stayed up past nine o'clock."

The reporter objected, "But my grandfather did the same and he only lived to be eighty-two."

Then came the calm explanation by the old man, "His trouble was that he didn't keep it up long enough."

Some years ago atheistic Russian astronauts probed space, returned to earth, and arrogantly announced they had found no such place as heaven up there. Lunar landings did not get past God's big toe. In other words, the astronauts did not go far enough. Spiritually speaking, "Unless one is born again, he cannot see the kingdom of God" (John 3:3).

The moon is just a satellite, a relatively small body orbiting the earth. The moon is the "lesser light to rule the night" (Genesis 1:15–16) by giving light upon the earth. The earth is God's footstool.

"The LORD is high above all nations" (Psalm 113:4). He rises to supreme heights when He sits on His heavenly throne. "For You, LORD, are most high above all the earth; You are exalted far above all gods" (Psalm 97:9). Thus the title Most High or Most High God stresses transcendence, a rising above.

Nothing man does or says can in reality bring down the Most High God who possesses heaven and earth, who places the nations where He so desires, who exercises authority in both heaven and earth. No man can really demean the majesty of Him who is enthroned on high. He enjoys an inconceivable loftiness, so high that the highest heavens are far beneath Him.

April 22

Who is like the LORD our God, who dwells on high, who humbles Himself to behold the things that are in the heavens and in the earth? (Psalm 113:5–6)

Now the amazing thing about our God who sits so high is that He looks so low. His loftiness cannot be measured adequately unless His stooping down is also considered. Have an idea of the loftiness, or highness, and you can better appreciate the complemental condescension.

The verb rendered *humble* means "to be or become low, be abased." It is used in Proverbs 29:23: "A man's pride will bring him low; but the humble in spirit will retain honor." And again: "Every valley shall be exalted, and every mountain and hill brought low" (Isaiah 40:4).

God, the Most High, stoops to look at the sun, moon, stars, and the planets. He stoops to look at the angels, the seraphim and cherubim of heaven. He stoops to look at the earth, His eyes running to and fro upon its mundane shores.

"Though the LORD is on high, yet He regards the lowly" (Psalm 138:6). He stoops low to behold mankind—to talk with Adam, to question Cain, to walk with Enoch, to save Noah, to call Abram, to wrestle with Jacob, to interpret for Joseph, to raise up Moses, to warn Balaam, to fight for Joshua, to judge for Gideon, to rule for David, and to deliver Jeremiah.

Surely the greatest act of humility was when, in the fullness of time, the LORD who was high above all nations came down to be born of a Jewish virgin. He who owned the silver and the gold and the cattle upon a thousand hills came down to a manger, no crib for His head. He who was rich became poor. He who holds the worlds in His hands let men drive spikes through those hands. He humbled Himself and became obedient unto death, even the death of the cross.

April 23

For You have delivered my soul from death, my eyes from tears, and my feet from falling. (Psalm 116:8)

The God who cares for our souls, which are very valuable, also cares for our eyes and for our feet. Man's soul is his inner life. One of the most important questions in the world is, "For what profit is it to a man if he gains the whole world, and loses his own soul? Or what will a man give in exchange for his soul?" (Matthew 16:26).

The soul has to do with our awareness of our environment. C. I. Scofield says it is the seat of the affections, desires, emotions, and the will of man. Since the word *soul* represents the entire inner life and therefore life in general, *The Amplified Bible* puts it: "You have delivered my life from death."

The real you is not just the external. There is more to you than meets the eye. Eyes represent intelligence; with them we see, we learn. The eyegate is a tremendous door to knowledge.

The eyes also reflect the soul. Some experiences in life move us to tears of sorrow and grief. We hear the lament by Jeremiah for Israel: "Oh, that my head were waters, and my eyes a fountain of tears, that I might weep day and night for the slain of the daughter of my people!" (Jeremiah 9:1).

Next are the feet. With our feet we walk, so they represent action, conduct, behavior. Thus the writer could say that God hates "feet that are swift in running to evil" (Proverbs 6:18).

In life's uneven and treacherous journey we sometimes stumble. Falling feet point to mistakes, traps, hidden snares, and errors. In this psalm of gratitude the writer expresses thanks for God's keeping power of his total being. He extols the goodness, grace, and answered prayers granted him by his God.

April 24

In my distress I cried to the LORD, and He heard me.
(Psalm 120:1)

We had just finished a 1,400-mile trip through the states of Pennsylvania, Ohio, Indiana, and Michigan. We passed by many cemeteries. Some were well-kept with freshly manicured lawns, newly-laid wreaths, fresh flowers, and expensive headstones. Others looked ancient, their markers weather-worn, their names and dates barely legible.

As I thought of the multitudes of people who have died throughout the centuries and of the fact that even now more than six billion people live upon the earth, a question entered my mind: With so many people coming and going, can there be a personal God? Does God really care about each person who walks these mundane shores? Is there a purpose in life for so many people? If not, what is the alternative?

Then it occurred to me that nobody else in the world looks exactly like me in every detail, not even if I had an identical twin brother. Each voice pattern is unique; each footprint and fingerprint pattern is especially designed by God, the master programmer.

When the LORD created you, He then broke the mold and destroyed the pattern. Such uniqueness has a purpose—a purpose not to be lost in the crowd or wasted in the masses. God is concerned about you. Your individuality is part of the LORD's program. As He is concerned, so ought you to be about yourself.

You should be able to say, "In *my* distress *I* cried unto the LORD, and He heard *me*." You matter to God; that is why He made only one you. For you He sent His Son. Christ died for you. There is nothing in the world more important than your personal relationship with Him.

April 25

I will lift up my eyes to the hills—from whence comes my help? My help comes from the LORD, who made heaven and earth. (Psalm 121:1–2)

See the crowd on their way to Jerusalem to worship. Looking up to the sacred mountains of Jerusalem where Jehovah dwells, one of the pilgrims asks, "From whence comes my help?" The question is not one of doubt or despondency. The pilgrim is not perplexed.

Rather, there is expectation, for the question becomes an opportunity for someone else to answer, to affirm that whatever the challenges that lie ahead, his help is in Jehovah the Creator.

From whence does my help come in these last days of such terrific challenges? From God the Creator who spoke and it happened. Creation came by the word of God. He spoke the creative word and matter came into existence. God said, "Let there be!" and there was. "'Let there be light'; and there was light" (Genesis 1:3).

"By the word of the LORD the heavens were made, and all the host of them by the breath of His mouth. For He spoke, and it was done; He commanded, and it stood fast" (Psalm 33:6, 9). "He commanded and they were created" (Psalm 148:5). "The worlds were framed by the word of God . . ." (Hebrews 11:3).

Our help comes not from temporal man, but from an eternal God; not from man the polluter, but from Him who is pure; not from man whose computers break down, but from God, who is all-wise, whose resources have no limits, whose help is inexhaustible, and never fails.

Our help does not come from the mountains, but from Him who made the mountains. Our help does not come from the foolishness of astrology and horoscopes, but from Him who created the stars and every planet—not from the creature but from the Creator.

April 26

How precious also are Your thoughts to me, O God!
(Psalm 139:17)

That which is precious is of high cost or worth, valuable, rare, weighty. *Precious* here could also mean "overwhelming" and "incomprehensible." Thus the thought came to my mind: "How did David know God's very thoughts?" The answer is: In a number of ways.

There is the possibility of direct contact with the LORD. When David once inquired of God whether to go up into any of the cities of Judah, the LORD said, "Go up . . . to Hebron" (2 Samuel 2:1).

There was also the work of the Holy Spirit in David's life. When Samuel anointed David king in the midst of his brethren, the Spirit of the LORD came upon David from that day onward (1 Samuel 16:13).

Then there are circumstances. Sometimes things happen in life, and you just know God is in control. You know what He wants; you see His hand opening and closing doors. David gave God the credit for delivering him from the paw of the lion and out of the paw of the bear while he kept his father's sheep.

God also spoke through the prophet Nathan with respect to David's sin with Bathsheba and again in the matter of building a house for the LORD. David knew something of the mind of God. In spite of his faults, David was blessed with an inner desire to please God, to know God's thoughts.

No Christian can be a good Christian who ignores the thoughts of God revealed in the Bible. The LORD wants us to think His thoughts, see things His way. Tradition, race, culture, politics—those things must not be allowed to blot out God's thoughts. When we follow David's footsteps in a matter, we will find, as he did, that God's thoughts are indeed precious.

April 27

The LORD opens the eyes of the blind. (Psalm 146:8)

I remember one of our members who had been blind for more than twenty years before her death. Sometimes she was despondent and believed some people were taking advantage of her or neglecting her because of her handicap. She would then dismiss such fears with, "I'm depending on my Jesus."

Like the rest of us her eyes were first opened when she came into this world as a baby. We often take so much for granted. You may recall that Fanny Crosby was born with normal eyesight, but by mistake someone put the wrong solution into her eyes, and she was blinded.

However, God gave Fanny Crosby spiritual eyes and that wonderful woman, who lived some ninety-five years, wrote the words to such favorite hymns as: "Jesus Keep Me Near the Cross"; "Rescue the Perishing"; "All the Way My Savior Leads Me"; "Pass Me Not, O Gentle Savior"; "Blessed Assurance"; "Savior, More than Life to Me"; "I Am Thine, O Lord"; and many others.

The sister who was a member of our church had her eyes opened a second time when the Holy Spirit opened them. She saw Jesus Christ and believed that He died for her. In this way the Lord opened her spiritual eyes.

Finally, her eyes were opened a third time—when death closed them here on earth. At her funeral I remarked that her eyes, closed on earth, were opened in heaven; she beheld the face of Jesus Christ. What a joy to see Him and to see loved ones gone on before—to be in that land where there is no night, no pain, just peace, joy, love, and eternal life in the presence of Him who opens the eyes of the blind.

April 28

Let everything that has breath praise the LORD. Praise the LORD! (Psalm 150:6)

Do insects "breathe?" Yes. Said F. B. Meyer: "Let the gnats make music with the vibration of their wings!" When the Israelites disobeyed God and hoarded the manna, it bred worms. A God-prepared worm ate the roots of the gourd that provided shade for Jonah (Jonah 4:7).

Worms ate up King Herod Agrippa I (Acts 12:23). And what of the filthy flies and nasty gnats that plagued the land of Egypt at the command of God's servants Moses and Aaron (Exodus 8:16–24)?

Do animals breathe? Of course. We think then of the quails that fell in the wilderness and provided food for the Jews (Exodus 16:13). What about the donkey that spoke to Balaam (Numbers 22:28)? And the ravens who brought food to the prophet Elijah (1 Kings 17:4–6)? Or the lions who offered their manes as pillows to Daniel in the den (Daniel 6:22)? Or the great fish that swallowed Jonah and three days later spat him out on dry land (Jonah 2:10)?

Do humans breathe? Certainly (Genesis 2:7; Job 33:4). Man was created for God's praise and glory. The failure to praise God is an indication of ingratitude, willfulness, stubbornness, and sin. Men who fail to praise God have missed their purpose in life.

How is God praised? First by believing that the Father sent His only begotten Son, Jesus Christ, to die on the cross for our redemption. Praise Him through prayer, study of the Bible, clean living, witnessing, and service. Let every step of the way to heaven be hallowed with a shout of "Hallelujah! Praise the LORD!"

April 29

Turn at my rebuke; surely I will pour out my spirit on you; I will make my words known to you. (Proverbs 1:23)

These words in Proverbs are a portion of "The Call of Wisdom"—Wisdom here being personified and speaking for God.

When God rebukes us you can bet He knows what He is doing. He has no ulterior motives; He makes no mistakes. His purpose is good.

Yet how hardheaded we are. Even when it is God Himself who tries to straighten us up, we balk. He has to knock us on the head just to get our attention. What is our problem? Why must the Lord's approach be one of reproach and reproof? Why must He so often come with a strap in hand? Because sin is so deeply rooted in our hearts. When self is enthroned we seek to run our lives without interference from anyone.

How sensitive have you been to the rebukes of God? That is a key question in the life of the believer. You will not get far in this life if the Lord has to spend all of His time spanking you, trying to get you to straighten up.

When God reprimands you and you repent, the Lord will reward and bless you. He will make known to you His words, His thoughts, His heart. He will share His knowledge with you.

He will teach you to number your days and to apply your heart unto wisdom. Behold, the fear of the Lord is the beginning of wisdom. Any man who has Jesus Christ in his heart is a wise man.

~

April 30

Keep your heart with all diligence, for out of it spring the issues of life. (Proverbs 4:23)

At first reading we are prone to believe the word *it* refers to the heart. So the verse would declare: "Keep your heart with all diligence, for out of your *heart* are the issues of life." But a better way is to see the word *it* as referring to the act of *keeping*. Thus, "Keep your heart with all diligence; for out of *keeping the heart in wisdom* proceeds life."

Condition: The condition of the human heart is not good. It is diseased, suffering from atheism (Psalm 14:1), arteriosclerosis (Exodus 8:15), and arrogance (Proverbs 16:5). Man's heart is devilish (Mark 7:21–23) and deceitful (Jeremiah 17:9).

Concern: Are you concerned about your heart's condition? You should be. Your heart is the fountain of action, and whatever comes out of it colors your entire life.

Cure: The change of the human heart is supernatural. It is not man-made. Some attempts to change the heart are ludicrous and futile. Going off to a convent or a monastery does not necessarily help. A murderer cut off his hand that held the pistol that killed a man. A forger induced blindness by withdrawing fluid from his eyes. Such "cures," however are foolish and inadequate.

Only through faith in the shed blood of Jesus Christ can a man receive a new heart. Wise, diligent keeping and preserving come by the love of God poured abroad in our hearts by the Holy Spirit (Romans 5:5). Christ is the cure!

> O to grace how great a debtor
> > Daily I'm constrained to be!
> Let Thy goodness, like a fetter,
> > Bind my wandering heart to Thee:
> Prone to wander—Lord, I feel it—
> > Prone to leave the God I love;
> Here's my heart, O take and seal it;
> > Seal it for Thy courts above.
> > > *Robert Robinson*

May 1

Go to the ant, you sluggard! Consider her ways and be wise.
. . . How long will you slumber, O sluggard? When will you
rise from your sleep? A little sleep, a little slumber, a little
folding of the hands to sleep—so shall your poverty come on
you like a prowler, and your need like an armed man. (Proverbs 6:6, 9–11)

What is on your agenda for today? Perhaps you do as I
have done daily for many years. Each morning I make out
a list of things I hope to accomplish before the day's end.
Seldom do I complete every item on the schedule, for time
seems to fly and before I know it, day is done.

Yet how I thank God for good health, for strength, for a
desire to keep busy serving Him and seeking to bring glory
to His name. Laziness is not a virtue. It is interesting to
note how busy the people were that the Lord called to do
His business. Not an idle one was in the lot.

Moses was busy keeping the flock of Jethro, his father-
in-law, when God spoke to him from the burning bush.
When David was called, he was busy minding his father's
sheep. Gideon was busy threshing wheat; Amos was following after the flock; Matthew was collecting taxes. Peter
and certain other future disciples were either fishing or
mending their nets. Even Paul was busy traveling on the
road to Damascus to do more evil when the Lord Jesus
intercepted him!

What are your plans for today? If you have prayed over
each item and have gotten God's O.K., then go to it! Keep
busy in His will, and you will discover the joy of serving
Jesus Christ, the One who gave Himself for you. Remember that you can do all things through Christ who strengthens you (Philippians 4:13). May that knowledge motivate
you until the Lord returns.

May 2

These six things the LORD hates, yes, seven are an abomination to Him: A proud look, a lying tongue, hands that shed innocent blood, a heart that devises wicked plans, feet that are swift in running to evil, a false witness who speaks lies, and one who sows discord among brethren. (Proverbs 6:16–19)

Knowing that God hates the seven things mentioned above, what can we do? Let the spotlight of God's Word filter through our souls. The Bible will reveal to us the presence of any such devilish evils as are mentioned in today's text.

Once the spotlight shows them up, we must admit our wrong, confess our sin, and rely fully upon the blessed Holy Spirit. Our text is a mirror set before the human heart; and what it reflects is monstrous. We are brought face to face with the holiness of God, whose hatred is directed against such evils.

Knowing what God hates helps us to understand what He loves. Because we love Him we try to avoid what He hates and we try to do what He loves. Christ alone is able to exorcise such evils, and we need just such a Savior.

Before Him the demons of haughty eyes, lying tongues, murderous hands, wicked hearts, mischievous feet, false witnessing, and spreading dissension will cringe and cry out, "We know who You are, Jesus, Son of God! Have You come here to torment us before the time?"

With a sweep of His nail-pierced hand, those hateful demons will be consigned to the pit. I am so glad that I serve a Savior who has all power in His hands and who will work on us and in us to make us just like Him.

May 3

Write them on the tablet of your heart. (Proverbs 7:3)

"The heart is the one center in man to which God turns, in which the religious life is rooted, which determines moral conduct" (Gerhard Kittel). Likened unto a tablet, upon which may be written that which is good or bad, the heart is variously described as hard, strong, new, deceitful, fleshy, and so on. Jeremiah said: "The sin of Judah is written with a pen of iron; with the point of a diamond it is written on the tablet of their heart" (Jeremiah 17:1).

The Israelites' sin was permanently, indelibly etched upon their hard hearts. Their only salvation was to have their petrified hearts removed. The promise was made: "I will put my law in their minds, and write it on their hearts" (Jeremiah 31:33). "I will take the stony heart out of their flesh, and give them a heart of flesh" (Ezekiel 11:19). The promise was made that one day the Jews as a nation will have their eyes opened and recognize that Jesus is indeed the Christ. Now just as evil may be written upon the tablets of the heart, so may that which is good. "Let not mercy and truth forsake you; bind them around your neck, write them on the tablet of your heart" (Proverbs 3:3). An outward binding up is a good reminder, but mercy and truth must be written upon our hearts, in our very minds.

"Bind them [God's law, words, commandments] on your fingers; write them on the tablet of your heart" (Proverbs 7:3). Outward, external acceptance is not enough. God's Word and godly virtues of mercy and truth must be received in the mind and become a part of your nature.

The ideal is to be and thus to do. Do because you are. Inner renewal is to show itself in outward obedience.

May 4

There is one who makes himself rich, yet has nothing; and one who makes himself poor, yet has great riches. (Proverbs 13:7)

One interpretation of this verse makes it a condemnation of bad attitudes toward wealth. In other words, some, having nothing, pretend to be rich; and others, being wealthy, pretend to be poor. Either way, the writer condemns pretense.

Neither the foolish love of display (showing off what you own) nor foolish miserliness is pleasing to the Lord. God wants men to be honest, unpretentious, without sham —to be just what they are.

It is no sin to be poor. In fact, the Lord often warned those who were rich that their wealth could make it difficult for them to enter into the kingdom of God. This present church age that has concerned itself more with things than with people is warned by the Lord of the church:

"Because you say, 'I am rich, have become wealthy, and have need of nothing'—and do not know that you are wretched, miserable, poor, blind, and naked—I counsel you to buy from Me gold refined in the fire, that you may be rich" (Revelation 3:17–18).

True riches are found only in Jesus Christ. The Christian must see the reality of his wealth, for we live in a highly materialistic age; advertisements bombard our senses, and our values easily become warped. We look, we see, we desire; we take steps to obtain.

We need to learn to be content with such things as we have, remembering that the Lord Jesus promised never to leave us alone (Hebrews 13:5). Let us keep in mind too that we possess in Christ incomparable wealth—eternal salvation, abundant life, joy, inner peace, and the power to live victoriously. Yes, we are rich. We need not pretend anything—just live.

May 5

A sound heart is life to the body, but envy is rottenness to the bones. (Proverbs 14:30)

A calm, tranquil, undisturbed, composed, healthy heart or mind is the life of the entire body and being. The question then comes, How is that sound heart obtained? Basically, it is the gift of God to all who believe in Jesus Christ. If you are a Christian, how do you maintain a sound heart? Three things are suggested:

Envy. Guard against envy because envy leads to other passions like anger, wrath, jealousy. In other words, people who are envious of others are sick and open to more sickness. Envy is bad on the heart.

Exercise. Physical exercise does profit a little (1 Timothy 4:8). Spiritual exercise—religious discipline, piety—they are profitable. With the Holy Spirit manifesting Himself in love, joy, peace, patience, goodness, gentleness, meekness, and faith, the Christian is able to develop a healthy, normal outlook on life.

Eating. What you eat has to some degree an effect on your heart. We need to feast on the Word of God and learn more about Jesus Christ. We need to learn that the words that proceed out of God's mouth are real soul food.

Said the psalmist: "How sweet are Your words to my taste, sweeter than honey to my mouth!" (Psalm 119:103; see also John 6:27 and 1 Peter 2:2). Surely Christians who read, study, memorize, digest, and assimilate God's Word are eating good food and supplying that which will help them maintain a healthy, sound heart.

May 6

But the righteous has a refuge in his death.
(Proverbs 14:32)

A minister was called to aid a church member who was in great distress upon his deathbed. Attempting to console him, the preacher said, "You mustn't carry on like this. Really, there is nothing so terrifying about dying. It's simply a matter of going home."

The failing man reached out and grabbed the preacher and said, "That's just it. It's going home for you, but it's leaving home for me. This earth is the only home I know. I'm worried. I don't know anything about a home over there. I'm dying, and I don't know where I'm going."

The minister realized that here was a church member who had never been born again. He was dying without Christ and without hope. Turning to the Bible, passage after passage was read and explained. At last the terrified man came to know Jesus Christ and put his trust in Him. Finally looking into the preacher's eyes, the man said, "It's all right now. I'm going home."

That is as it should be. Every Christian should know what his end is, where he is going. God wants you to know; it is not a matter of being presumptuous, as some think. The fact that some people abuse whatever they do is no reason for throwing out the thing they abuse.

The Christian has a hope after death. Here is a real witness to hope in eternity. Somehow knowing just a little of what lies ahead enables us to live better right here and now. God has so made us that only when we keep the future clearly in mind are we better people here and now on this earth.

May 7

A merry heart makes a cheerful countenance.
(Proverbs 15:13)

When we were children we rolled our eyes, puffed out our cheeks, stuck out our tongues, wrinkled our noses, and otherwise showed our displeasure and anger. We were warned, "Keep it up and you'll look like that when you grow up—if you live to grow up!"

Now that we are adults we look back and laugh at the faces we made. But we have learned something about the face. It may well tell what is on your mind and mirror your thoughts; indeed, your face can be a dead giveaway.

The fallen countenance of Cain (Genesis 4:5–6); the shining face of Moses (Exodus 34:30); the painted face of Jezebel (2 Kings 9:30); the changed countenance of Belshazzar (Daniel 5:6, 9); the scowling face of the hypocrite (Matthew 6:16); the battered, spittle-bespattered, bloodied face of Jesus Christ (Isaiah 52:14; Matthew 26:67; 27:30)—those all tell a story.

Surely, if anybody should rejoice, it is the Christian. We should have cheerful faces. "For . . . God who commanded light to shine out of darkness . . . has shone in our hearts to give the light of the knowledge of the glory of God in the face of Jesus Christ" (2 Corinthians 4:6).

You don't have to tell how you live each day,
    You don't have to say if you work or you play.
A tried, true barometer serves in the place;
    However you live, it will show in your face.

The false, the deceit that you bear in your heart
    Will not stay inside where it first got a start;
For sinew and blood are a thin veil of lace;
    What you wear in your heart, you wear in your face.

If your life is unselfish, if for others you live,
    For not what you get, but for how much you can give;
If you live close to God in His infinite grace,
    You don't have to tell it: it shows in your face.

Author Unknown

May 8

He hears the prayer of the righteous. (Proverbs 15:29)

This verse indicates that God's delight is expressed by His answering what He hears. What then happens when *you* pray?

Thank God that He hears the prayers of the righteous. Jacob prayed; the angel with whom he wrestled blessed him. Joseph prayed; he was delivered from a pit and from a prison and put into a palace. Moses prayed, and Israel triumphed over the enemy.

Joshua prayed, the sun stood still, and God gave the victory. Hannah prayed; the baby boy Samuel was born and her reproach removed. Elijah prayed; fire fell down from heaven.

Hezekiah prayed; he lived fifteen years longer. Esther prayed; Mordecai was exalted, Haman was hanged, and Israel saved. The disciples prayed, and while they prayed the Holy Spirit fell upon them.

The church prayed; Simon Peter was delivered from prison. Paul and Silas prayed; the prison shook, their bonds fell off, and the prison doors opened. God is pleased with the prayers of the upright. Keep on praying. When praying days are over, you will drop this robe of flesh, rise to seize the everlasting prize, and join the Church triumphant in the skies.

May 9

And before honor is humility. (Proverbs 15:33; 18:12)

The words *humility* and *humbleness* come from the Latin *humus*, the word for "ground, soil." Humility stresses lack of pride, pretense, or assertiveness. It is the reverent attitude toward God as supreme and holy ruler. It means gentleness, affliction, or to be bowed down.

Humility is one of the loveliest flowers in the garden of the born-again heart. The appeal is made to each Christian: "In lowliness of mind let each esteem others better than himself" (Philippians 2:3).

The story is told of a Christian young man who said, "I am willing to be third." When pressed to explain he said: "My mother taught me to put Christ first, others second, and self last. So I'm willing to be third."

The verse points out that humility is the way to honor. In this text *honor* means "weight, or heaviness." Other Hebrew and Greek words translated *honor* mean "glory, fame, beauty, preciousness," and so on. But here it is to make heavy, weighty. That is close to the Greek word rendered "worthy."

When the psalmist says, "How precious also are Your thoughts to me, O God!" (Psalm 139:17), *precious* means weighty, hard to grasp. To honor is to appraise as heavy, weighty, to determine worth. An abundant crop is a heavy crop and indicates prosperity and blessing.

Honor is the reward the Lord bestows upon those who fear (reverence) Him and obey Him. The fear of God is wisdom; without it, man is a fool. Said the writer in Proverbs 26:1: "As snow in summer and rain in harvest, so honor is not fitting for a fool."

True honor comes then not from man but from God. He gives grace to the humble (1 Peter 5:5), and honor shall uphold the humble in spirit (Proverbs 29:23).

May 10

Commit your works to the LORD, and your thoughts will be established. (Proverbs 16:3)

Man has evil thoughts; that is part of his nature. Man needs to be born again—given a new nature. If any man be in Christ he is a new creation (2 Corinthians 5:17), but the old man is still there. Christians are still capable of thinking thoughts they should not think.

In my prayer life I tell the Lord about the thoughts that enter my head. Such confession helps restrain me from carrying out the thoughts. I tell Him what is on my mind because I know He knows already (Job 42:2; Psalm 139:2; Luke 5:22; 6:8; Hebrews 4:12; and so on).

To *commit* means to roll, like rolling a stone from the mouth of a well or cave. Isaiah spoke of the heavens rolling up like a scroll. Amos said, "But let justice run down like water" (Amos 5:24).

Roll your deeds on the Lord. God will work with you and cause your thoughts to become agreeable to His will. In that way your thoughts or plans will succeed, and be established. Roll them on Him, and discover that He is ever ready to take charge, to complete them. Roll them on Him, and discover that no work is too big, too broad, too large, too heavy for His shoulders.

Roll yourself upon the Lord. That is what Christ did at Calvary. "Father, into Your hands I commit My spirit . . ." (Luke 23:46). And the Father raised Him up on the third day. If you too allow the Lord to establish your deeds, He will also establish your thoughts.

May 11

The LORD has made all for Himself: yes, even the wicked for the day of doom. (Proverbs 16:4)

This verse has caused trouble in some theological circles. Some men interpret it to mean God *created* wicked people. However, the Lord did not create the devil; He created Lucifer, who became puffed up with pride and decided he wanted to be God.

Adam and Eve were created in innocence; they willingly sinned and fell. The fact that God foreknew those things and that He permitted them to happen does not make Him responsible for evil. Said the writer of Ecclesiastes: "Truly, this only I have found: that God made man upright, but they have sought out many schemes" (7:29).

But some men seem unwilling that God's holiness should be thus vindicated. "Because God made us capable of sinning, why does He find fault with us?" they ask. "If God's purposes are fulfilled by an evil man, why condemn the man?" Such talk is rebuked by the prophets (Isaiah 45:9–10; Jeremiah 18:6) and by the apostle Paul (Romans 9:20–24).

After all, shall the piece of clay say to the potter, "Why did you make me the way I am?" Shall the thing formed say to the Creator, "Why have You made me like this?"

God is sovereign. Said King Nebuchadnezzar when his mind was restored, "He [the Most High God] does according to His will in the army of heaven and among the inhabitants of the earth. No one can restrain His hand or say to Him, 'What have You done?'" (Daniel 4:35).

Today's verse suggests, as one writer put it, "There are ultimately no loose ends in God's world." God has a plan. It is that everything has its own end, including the punishment of the wicked. Christians can be certain that God is justified in His judgments (Psalm 51:4; Romans 3:19). We can rest assured that the LORD is in charge. Righteousness will triumph.

~

May 12

*Everyone proud in heart is an abomination to the LORD; though
they join forces, none will go unpunished.* (Proverbs 16:5)

By pride I do not mean self-respect or a sense of one's
own proper dignity or value. Rather, pride here is conceit,
haughtiness, arrogance, exaggerated self-importance—an
excessively high opinion of oneself.

What is wrong with that pride? It causes a man to think
he is self-sufficient and does not need God. At that point
he is akin to the fool who says in his heart, "There is no
God" (Psalm 14:1). It blinds a man to the fact that everything he has was given to him. Unmindful that he has received all things, he is not thankful. Ingratitude is one of
the first steps to idolatry (Romans 1:21).

Pride is not realistic. A proud man's estimate of himself
is incorrect. When he thinks too highly of himself, his values become twisted. His dream world, of which he is at
dead center, cannot cope with reality.

Pride moves men to despise other men created by God
and for whom Jesus Christ died. If you think low, you will
look low, and act low. One root of man's inhumanity to
man is pride. War, racism, murder, crime—all are rooted
in pride.

Pride renders a man ignorant of grace. His heart is filled
with works that he himself has achieved. "Pride goes before destruction, and a haughty spirit before a fall" (Proverbs 16:18). "Before destruction the heart of man is
haughty" (Proverbs 18:12). "A man's pride will bring him
low" (Proverbs 29:23).

A proud man is spiritually related to the devil, whose
beauty and power and wisdom went to his head (Isaiah
14:13–14; 1 Timothy 3:6). Is it any wonder that God hates
pride and resists it? (James 4:6, 10).

May 13

When a man's ways please the LORD, He makes even his enemies to be at peace with him. (Proverbs 16:7)

There are many blessings for the man who pleases God. The number one way to please God is to believe on Him whom God has sent. "He who does not believe God has made Him a liar, because he has not believed the testimony that God has given of His Son" (1 John 5:10).

You cannot possibly please God without faith in the shed blood of Jesus Christ. Once you have settled that matter as a saved, heaven-bound, blood-washed creature, there are available to you many blessings. Note that I said *available*. That means that even as a Christian there are some conditions you must meet in order to receive what the Lord has to offer.

The text talks about your ways—they must be pleasing to the Lord if you are to receive a special blessing. Please the Lord in your ways, and He will raise up friends for you. He gave Aaron to Moses; Jonathan to David; Pharaoh to Joseph; Ruth to Naomi; Elisha to Elijah; Ebedmelech to Jeremiah; Zacchaeus had a lot of enemies, but found in Jesus a friend that sticks closer than a brother; and God gave Luke and Timothy to Paul.

All hearts are in God's hands. He alone has access to our spirits; He alone has power over our souls. One blessing of pleasing God is that God reconciles even your enemies and can turn them into friends.

We ourselves were at one time enemies of God—hateful, walking in darkness, dead in sin, fighting God every step of the way, without Christ, "having no hope, and without God in the world" (Ephesians 2:12).

One day the Holy Spirit touched our hearts, and the blood of Calvary cleansed us. Hearts of stone were melted, and we became friends of God. If God could change us, He can change anybody.

May 14

The name of the LORD is a strong tower; the righteous run to it and are safe. (Proverbs 18:10)

The name of the LORD is excellent in all the earth (Psalm 8:1); it is holy and awesome (Psalm 111:9). God's name is great (Psalm 76:1), eternal (Psalm 72:17), enduring forever.

His name is glorious (Psalm 72:19); His name is salvation, for whoever calls on the name of the LORD shall be saved (Romans 10:13).

Had you lived in a city with a high wall around it, this text would be more meaningful to you. For the high towers, placed at strategic points, overlooked all other buildings. From them the soldiers could look out, spot the enemy, warn the inhabitants, and prepare for battle.

From those prominent towers archers could shoot and spears could be thrown. Thus David could say, "For You have been a shelter for me, a strong tower from the enemy" (Psalm 61:3).

One of the blessings of being a Christian is to learn the secret of true safety. We learn not to try to fight life's battles on our own. We are too puny, too weak to try to be self-sufficient against the forces of evil.

The saint must stay on the alert, wear the whole armor of God, endure hardships, remain in prayer, study the Bible, and stick with the Lord. Be careful of taking advice from unsaved folks, or even carnal Christians, who depend upon their experiences rather than upon the Word of God.

Do not run out of the high tower looking for any better protection. For all that God our Strong Tower is, all that He has, He uses to keep us safe and bring us to Himself at last.

May 15

Death and life are in the power of the tongue.
(Proverbs 18:21)

Many men are afflicted by the besetting sins of speech and the misuse of the tongue. Some of the most difficult sins to avoid are those of the tongue. With the tongue we flatter (Psalm 5:9); backbite (Psalm 15:3); deceive (Psalm 50:19); devise mischief (Psalm 52:2); curse (Psalm 59:12); and tell lies (Psalm 109:2).

Though it is but a small organ in the body, it is capable of doing great things. Just as it takes but one match to burn down a thousand acres of tall timber, so the tongue, small as it is, can cause a holocaust.

So manifold are the evils of an uncontrolled tongue that James (ch. 3) likens it to a world of mischief. A dirty tongue makes the whole body dirty. Furthermore, like an untamable beast, the tongue is a restless evil, full of death-bearing venom.

James goes on to warn that even the proper use of the tongue today is no guarantee against misuse tomorrow. Some of the same people who bless God will, at the least provocation, curse human beings who were made in God's image.

Even though we are fallen creatures and need to be restored to that image through faith in Jesus Christ, nonetheless our value in God's sight is not lessened.

We learn then that when the tongue is out of control, when we are angry and "lose our heads," then we are liable to curse others, men for whom the Lord Jesus Christ died.

Surely the ability to control our tongues is much needed these days. "Whoever guards his mouth and tongue keeps his soul from troubles" (Proverbs 21:23). May we say as did David, "I will guard my ways, lest I sin with my tongue" (Psalm 39:1).

May 16

But there is a friend who sticks closer than a brother.
(Proverbs 18:24).

The Bible says, "A friend loves at all times" (Proverbs 17:17)—*all* times, not just when things are going well. The writer in Proverbs offered this observation also: "The poor man is hated even by his own neighbor, but the rich has many friends" (Proverbs 14:20). And again: "Wealth makes many friends . . . and every man is a friend to one who gives gifts" (Proverbs 19:4, 6).

The Bible says: "Faithful are the wounds of a friend" (Proverbs 27:6). When a true friend sees something wrong, he reproves; but even his sharpest rebukes come from a heart of love. The true friend is one we can trust; we believe that he has our best welfare at heart. Though what he says thrusts home painfully, we can take it because we believe in and depend upon the sincerity of his motive.

Not everyone who takes you to task when you do wrong or make a mistake is your friend. Some people just want to show off their authority, get under your skin, or get revenge. Some are mean and evil. Others are hypocrites, guilty of the very thing they condemn in you. But not so the friend here described in the Bible.

Who qualifies as your best friend? Surely it is Jesus Christ. He alone loves you at all times. His reproof is always beneficial, "for whom the LORD loves He chastens" (Hebrews 12:6). It is He who sticks, clings, cleaves, keeps closer to you than a brother, demonstrating His loyalty and affection.

Earthly friends die and leave us, reminding us of our own mortality. The best that earth can afford by way of friendship and joy is fleeting, transitory. But Jesus Christ said: "I will never leave you nor forsake you" (Hebrews 13:5).

May 17

For as he thinks in his heart, so is he. (Proverbs 23:7)

Unfortunately this scripture is often taken out of context. The Bible does not teach: *Think* good and you *are* good. No. From God's point of view you cannot be good until you accept the shed blood of the Christ of Calvary. Until then all of a man's thoughts are but evil continually.

It will help if you keep in mind that verse 7 is a part of verse 6: "Do not eat the bread of a miser [him that hath an evil eye, KJV], nor desire his delicacies; for as he thinks"—as the one with the evil eye thinks—"so is he." This context is all too often ignored.

One definition of *evil eye* is: a look or stare superstitiously believed to cause injury or misfortune to others. However, the Bible has nothing to say about giving the "double whammy."

In the Bible the human eye is the index of the mind, and an evil eye speaks of envy (Matthew 20:15), having a grudge (Deuteronomy 15:9), and not of some magical eye used in enchantment by witches.

It is the product of a bad heart (Mark 7:21, 22). As the bountiful or generous eye (Proverbs 22:9) deals with that which is kindly, so the evil eye speaks of a grudging spirit. A man with an evil eye is ill-natured, greedy, inhospitable.

He is hypocritical too, for while he bids you eat of his food, he secretly hopes you will choke on it! As he deals with himself, so he deals with you. He is stingy, *a miser*, and so he regards others with the same eye—an evil eye, hard and resentful.

Covetousness is seen here also. Those with the "gitmo's" (get-mores) are warned: "A man with an evil eye hastens after riches, and does not consider that poverty will come upon him" (Proverbs 28:22). Thank God today that you are the apple of His eye.

May 18

Do not boast about tomorrow, for you do not know what a day may bring forth. (Proverbs 27:1)

You do not know what will happen tomorrow. (James 4:14)

Man's desire to know what a day may bring forth has caused him to act in disobedience to God's command. Adam and Eve's desire to be wise led to their downfall. Behind the building of the tower of Babel was the desire to practice divination; it led to confusion. Still today there are those who dabble in witchcraft, seances, fortune telling, spiritism, horoscopes, and so on.

It is not that God wants to keep men in ignorance. He is the God who states through His apostle: "But I do not want you to be ignorant" (1 Thessalonians 4:13). But He wants us to know what *He* wants us to know, not necessarily what *we* would like to know.

It is therefore foolish to brag about what we shall do. Jezebel boasted of her intention to kill Elijah. In the end she was trampled underfoot and eaten by scavenging dogs. The rich man in Luke 12 boasted of his wealth and intent to become even wealthier, but in the end died a fool.

Because death can be sudden and destruction can come without warning and without remedy, it behooves us to make sure that we are grounded in God through faith in the shed blood of Jesus Christ.

Not knowing what a day may bring forth moves us to depend upon Christ. We learn to trust Him who holds the future. Our ignorance of things to come gives us an opportunity to exercise faith, an opportunity to believe that God is faithful and will finish whatever He has started.

Finally, not knowing what shall happen on the next day teaches us to number our days that we might apply our hearts to wisdom.

May 19

The heart of the wise is in the house of mourning. (Ecclesiastes 7:4)

These are the words of a writer whose point of view is that of a man under the sun. He expresses a natural wisdom; as far as man can see, under the sun all is vanity, futility, and emptiness. However, we who are Christians have a point of view that is above the sun. In other words, we see through the eyes of God, and so in Christ we have a hope. All is not vanity.

We have no argument with this text. The mind or heart of the wise *is* in the house of mourning; a wise man *does* think about death. It is not that we are to be morbid, down in the dumps, melancholy. Human beings have a way of bouncing back from adversities, a way of returning from the burial of a loved one at the cemetery with a desire to live on and somehow make it in life. The writer would say that a man who does not pay attention when God speaks is a fool.

If hurricanes grab our attention, thunderbolts are heard, lightning flashes are seen, earthquakes shake our very souls, and floods strike fear, surely then death too has a message. The point is that adversity, sorrow, and death can lead to a wise philosophy of life. You cannot see life properly unless you take death into account. Death is not a sleeping dog we can pass by on tiptoe.

So if you would be wise, then lay to heart the matter of death. Integrate the fact of death with your philosophy of life. You will get a proper appreciation of life when you have a sympathetic understanding of trouble, sorrow, and death. Moses put it this way: "So teach us to number our days, that we may gain a heart of wisdom" (Psalm 90:12).

May 20

And His name will be called . . . Mighty God. . . . (Isaiah 9:6)

This title definitely stresses the deity of the Messiah. This Child born—this Son given—is God Himself. *El* is used always in Isaiah as a name of God. Whereas *Elohim* (pl.) may or may not refer to the supreme being, *El* is never used of gods or lesser beings. (See Isaiah 36:18–20 for the use of *Elohim* for "gods.")

Now the word *mighty* modifies or describes the word God. It is a very broad term meaning not only mighty but strong (Proverbs 30:30), powerful; it may be used of counsel, deeds, miracles, and so on. The miracles wrought in Egypt are said to be the results of a mighty power (Deuteronomy 4:37).

It took a mighty God to control rivers, frogs, gnats, flies, livestock, hail, fire, grasshoppers; to hide the sun for three days; to kill the firstborn of all who had no blood applied to their doorposts.

In other words, Jesus Christ, Mighty God, is someone you can depend on (Deuteronomy 10:17; Nehemiah 9:32; Isaiah 10:21; Jeremiah 32:18). He cannot be bribed or corrupted. No Watergate mess with Him!

Sometimes we view with alarm the temporary defeats suffered in some skirmishes. Surely all of us have had setbacks in life. We have lost money, property, jobs, friends, loved ones, relatives. We have been mistreated, disappointed, discouraged; our hearts have been made to bleed for some thoughtless word or deed. Poor health, aches and pains remind us that we do not have long to stay here.

If we love God and have been called according to His plan and purpose, we know that all these things work together for our good. Our Savior is the Mighty God.

May 21

His name will be called Wonderful Counselor. (Isaiah 9:6)

Many scholars feel that there should be no comma between the words *Wonderful* and *Counselor*, such as we find in the King James Version. Omitting the comma fits in well with the other double titles: Mighty God, Everlasting Father, Prince of Peace. As *Mighty* modifies *God*, *Everlasting* distinguishes *Father*, and *Peace* qualifies *Prince*, so *Wonderful* describes *Counselor*.

A counselor is one who gives advice; he is a lawyer. *Wonderful* here means exceptional, extraordinary, marvelous, magnificent, surpassing, powerful, awesome, secret, incomprehensible. Jesus Christ is the wisdom of God. "Counsel is mine, and sound wisdom" said the writer of Proverbs (8:14), speaking of Christ. In Him are hidden all the treasures of wisdom and knowledge (Colossians 2:3).

His testimonies are wonderful (Psalm 119:129). The entrance of His words gives light. His word is truth. When He spoke, something happened.

"Be opened!" and deaf ears were unstopped. "Lazarus, come forth!" and the dead man was raised. "Be cleansed!" and lepers were made whole. "Go wash in the pool of Siloam," and blind eyes were opened. "Go, and sin no more," and an adulteress was forgiven. "Peace, be still," and turbulent winds and boisterous waves ceased their howling and roaring.

If you lack wisdom, ask of Him in faith; He gives to all liberally and without reproach. Problems? He can solve them. You do not know where to turn? He is the way. Frustrated and full of anxiety? Cast all your cares on Him!

May 22

His name will be called . . . Prince of Peace. (Isaiah 9:6)

We realize there are those who do not recognize Jesus Christ as prince, author, captain, or leader. In sin, men waged war against the Prince of Peace; in sin, men killed the Prince of Life. In sin, men falsely accused Christ the Prince of Righteousness of being in league with the prince of demons, Beelzebub (Matthew 9:34; 12:24).

In sin, Satan, the prince of this world system (John 12:31; 14:30; 16:11), tried to get Christ, the Prince of the kings of the earth, to bow down and worship him (Matthew 4). So it is sin that prevents men from knowing who Jesus Christ really is or moves them not to want to recognize and honor Him.

A prince is a leader, ruler, a chief; he furnishes the first cause or occasion. He sets the example; he is the predecessor in a matter. He is a commander. Whatever Christ is Prince of, He gives; it comes from Him, out of Him; He is its source. Peace comes from Him. He demonstrates it; He nurtures it or works it out in those to whom He gives it; He perfects it; what He starts He finishes.

As Prince of Peace He will cause wars to cease. As Prince of Peace He provides peace with God. We call it justification, a foundational aspect of salvation (Romans 5:1). As Prince of Peace He provides the peace of God; it is available to all who love the Lord Jesus.

Is He your Prince of Peace? Are you a whole person? Does your soul prosper? Is your personality integrated? Are you in harmony with Christ? Have you let Him remove all peace disturbers from your life? Surely the peace He gives to you the world cannot take away.

May 23

I will be like the Most High. (Isaiah 14:14)

When Satan tempted Adam it was his hope that Adam would swear allegiance to him. The devil knew that all had been created for God's glory. However, his perverted mind sought to usurp the authority of God. Satan said in his rebellious heart: "I will ascend into heaven, I will exalt my throne . . . I will also sit . . . I will ascend above the heights of the clouds; I will be like the Most High" (Isaiah 14:13–14).

There are three wills in the world evident in the drama there in the Garden of Eden. God had made known His will to Adam and to Eve. The devil came and expressed his will. The first human beings demonstrated they too had their own wills.

God's will was disobeyed when Adam and Eve ate of the fruit of the tree. Satan's will was stymied for the time being when the first pair would not submit further to him. Even so, Adam's expression of self-will was devastating.

Although Satan's primary goal was not reached, he is content in the one fact that anything done apart from God's will is sin. Since Satan has no love in his cold heart for man, he strives to push men to follow the dictates of their own hearts. We discover that Satan is extremely active in the battle for the minds of men.

Indeed, it is a vicious struggle. Satan's ignoble and profane purpose is to get men to center their thoughts upon everything but God. It is written, "The wicked in his proud countenance does not seek God; God is in none of his thoughts" (Psalm 10:4). Knowing all these things, may it be yours to say to the Lord, "Not my will, Master, but Thine be done in my life today!"

May 24

Therefore thus says the Lord GOD: "Behold, I lay in Zion a stone for a foundation, a tried stone, a precious cornerstone, a sure foundation; whoever believes will not act hastily." (Isaiah 28:16)

Isaiah fearlessly predicted the fall of the Northern Kingdom at the hands of the Assyrians. Judah too, he preached, was headed for captivity. You can understand why the prophet was considered a nuisance— "an intolerable moralist." People, princes, and priests mocked. "Listen to him: 'Line upon line ... command upon command ... rule upon rule ... lesson upon lesson ... verse upon verse ... precept upon precept ... here a little, there a little!' Why, it's the same monotonous refrain, and we are sick and tired of hearing it!

"Give us a nice liberal preacher who will tell us more and more about nothing until we know less and less about everything. Give us a psychological, political preacher who will puff us up with the profundity of his philosophical platitudes!

"Give us a slick-haired Dapper Dan who will meet our material needs, who will preach the pie out of the sky so we can eat it now. By and by when we die we will be carried through the sky in the chariot of our choice—a Rolls Royce!"

Judah believed Isaiah did not understand practical politics. But she had to learn that her only hope was in the LORD, who is an unmovable foundation. Egypt will come and go; Assyria will come and go; and their armies disappear. Their chariots will come to a halt; their horses will break their legs; their swords become dull; their arrows will snap; and their spears fall to the ground—but God has placed a solid stone in Zion.

That stone is Jesus Christ—tried, proved, precious. Can you truthfully say these words from the pen of Edward Mote?

> On Christ the solid Rock, I stand;
> All other ground is sinking sand.
> *Edward Mote*

May 25

For thus says the Lord GOD, the Holy One of Israel: "In re-turning and rest you shall be saved; in quietness and confi-dence shall be your strength." But you would not. (Isaiah 30:15)

Sennacherib, King of Assyria, was on the march. The Israelites were afraid—it was fear born out of disobedi-ence. Repeatedly Isaiah had warned them of the coming destruction if they fought. Their only hope was to turn to God, and He would preserve them. But no, they hastened to make an alliance with Egypt against Assyria. Their act indicated bad religion had led them to play bad politics.

Their dependence upon Egypt was like leaning on a bro-ken cane that might snap at any time and pierce the hand. Egyptian politics were full of wind and bluster. Always promising, seldom ever to deliver, Egypt's reputation for effectively helping others was bad.

The believer must take to heart the fact that "but those who wait on the LORD shall renew their strength" (Isaiah 40:31). Christians must believe that the LORD shall fight for them. Take hold of the promise and see how God calms the disturbed heart. Here is the test of good religion: What do you do when trouble comes your way? How do you react?

God commands the Christian to wait on Him. Wait for His help with quiet disposition. Is Sennacherib breathing hot fire down your neck? Play it cool! God will take care of you.

The world walks by sight, and its wisdom would dic-tate a course of action that depends upon an outside show of strength. It would choose bombs instead of the Bible, chariots instead of Christ, alliances but not the Lord's arm. True strength is found only in Jesus Christ. He is our strength in time of trouble (Psalm 37:39).

May 26

The work of righteousness will be peace, and the effect of righteousness, quietness and assurance forever. (Isaiah 32:17)

One of the blessings of righteousness is *peace*—wholeness, soundness, completeness, prosperity, or well-being.

Quietness is another blessing of righteousness. "When He [God] gives quietness, who then can make trouble?" (Job 34:29). Said the writer of Ecclesiastes (4:6), "Better a handful with quietness than both hands full, together with toil and grasping for the wind." Of the wicked, Zophar told Job, "He knows no quietness in his heart" (Job 20:20). In Proverbs 17:1 we read: "Better is a dry morsel with quietness, than a house full of feasting with strife."

A third blessing of righteousness is *assurance*. Whereas unrighteousness produces cowards, righteousness promotes confidence and security.

"Let us draw near with a true heart in full assurance of faith" said the writer of Hebrews (10:22). The God of the Bible is He who delights to give assurance to the righteous. He wants us to know and to know that we know.

To that end He gave us the Holy Spirit (1 John 3:24). The Bible was written to give us confidence. "These things I have written to you who believe in the name of the Son of God, that you may know that you have eternal life" (1 John 5:13).

If the gospel came not unto you in word only, but also in power, and in the holy Spirit, and in much assurance (1 Thessalonians 1:5), then you have every right to sing with meaning and to sing from the very depths of your heart:

> Blessed assurance, Jesus is mine!
>
> O, what a foretaste of glory divine!
>
> Heir of salvation, purchase of God,
>
> Born of His Spirit, washed in His blood.
>
> *Fanny Crosby*

May 27

He feeds on ashes; a deceived heart has turned him aside; and he cannot deliver his soul, nor say, "Is there not a lie in my right hand?" (Isaiah 44:20)

God made man for Himself, there is no doubt about that. Man's purpose in life is to worship and glorify God. Man was made for that end, and by nature he must worship. It is foolish to talk about eliminating religion; it simply cannot be done. Those who try to wipe out religion soon discover that they themselves have a new religion—the religion of trying to wipe out religion.

Communists have called religion the opiate of the people, but they fail to see that Communism is another religion itself. Even the so-called atheist has a god; his god is "No-God."

The hunger in man's soul is a natural thing; it is part of his constitutional makeup. It distinguishes him from the dog on the street, the cat in the alley, the monkey in the zoo, and the lion in the jungle. From time to time I meet men who do not know those facts or know and will not accept them.

Ignorant of human nature, they resent me because they think I have some man-made pull or gimmick that keeps people coming to church each Sunday.

Man *must* worship somebody or something; he cannot help it. If he does not worship the one true God, the God and Father of Jesus Christ, the God of the Bible, then he will worship the creature; he will worship some homemade image as a god. He will exchange the Creator for the creature.

That is idolatry. The object made or used as an image or representation of a deity is worshiped as an idol. Unfortunately, the idolater is deceived and does not realize that the idol he has created is nothing, vanity, a lie. Only the true and living God is able to deliver.

May 28

When You make His soul an offering for sin. (Isaiah 53:10)

"You crucified Him!" was Simon Peter's message to the Jews (Acts 2:23). The apostle charged that they had slain the Prince of Life (Acts 3:15). Yet Christ said: "I lay down My life. . . . No one takes it from Me, but I lay it down of Myself . . ." (John 10:17–18). The fact that both assertions are true is what we call a paradox.

Another dimension is added by Isaiah's statement that God the Father was responsible for the death of His Son. Christ was "smitten by God [Isaiah 53:4], and afflicted . . . yet it pleased the LORD to bruise Him, He has put Him to grief."

Note that it pleased Jehovah to bruise Him—"when *You* make His soul an offering" (Isaiah 53:10). Had not Christ volunteered, had not God the Father so willed it, Calvary never would have occurred. It was not in man's power to kill Life, crush the Rock of Ages, extinguish the Light of the World, or eclipse the Sun of Righteousness. Mere man could not depose the King of Kings, court-martial the Captain of Salvation, bury the Resurrection, or pull down the Bright and Morning Star.

No, that was God's prerogative, who alone could appoint Christ's life an offering for sin. We learn that the suffering servant was to be instrumental in removing the burden of sin and guilt. How? By dying. The LORD laid upon Him the iniquity of us all. He was innocent, without blemish, without spot, holy; but He became an offering and gave His life as a guilt offering, a trespass offering, for our sin.

Therefore, God's will was done, not man's. It never would have entered man's head that God the Son should become a man and die, but God willed it. He did it for you and for me, that many might be brought to righteousness and be given a right to the tree of life.

~

May 29

For truth is fallen in the street. (Isaiah 59:14).

The story is told of a French artist whose family had gathered around his deathbed and sought to create an atmosphere of assurance of recovery. "You're looking much better," his wife assured him.

"The color has returned to your cheeks," said his son.

"You're breathing easier, Father," his daughter managed to say.

The father smiled weakly. "Thank you," he whispered. "I'm going to die cured."

Is there really ever a situation so bad, so hopeless that we must lie?

Must we perjure ourselves? Must we tell lies in order to soften the blow, rectify injustice, redress wrong, banish grief, eliminate peril, spare pain, or escape death?

The God of the Bible unequivocally says no. Truth in the inward parts is desired by the God of truth. He bids us to buy the truth and speak the truth in love, every man to his neighbor. To that end He has sent the Spirit of truth to guide us into all truth. He has established the church, which is the pillar and ground of the truth; He has given us the Bible, His Word, which is truth.

Jeremiah said: "Truth has perished and has been cut off from their mouth" (Jeremiah 7:28). One fears we are now in just such an age, for multitudes believe there are times when we are justified in telling falsehoods.

However, as followers of Him who is the Truth, we buck the trend of the times. For we know that in the end, truth will win out. God's truth will march on to victory.

May 30

For He has clothed me with the garments of salvation, He has
covered me with the robe of righteousness. (Isaiah 61:10)

You may recall that some years ago it was a fad to
streak—go running naked in public. *Time* magazine called
it an epidermis epidemic. A newspaper supplement called
it running in the raw. Since so many college students were
involved, I called it educated exhibitionism.

At any rate, it was demonic (Luke 8:27; Acts 19:13–20);
it was displeasing to the Lord, a cause for shame (Genesis
3:7, 10), and degrading (Exodus 32:25; 2 Samuel 10:4; Isaiah
20:3–4; Nahum 3:5).

What are you wearing right now? Of the virtuous
woman God said, "Strength and honor are her clothing"
(Proverbs 31:25). He exhorted the saints at Ephesus: "Put
off . . . the old man . . . put on the new man, which was
created according to God, in true righteousness and holiness" (Ephesians 4:22–24). "Yes, all of you be submissive
to one another, and be clothed with humility," said God
through Simon Peter (1 Peter 5:5).

I am glad God clothed me—not in the robe of my self-
righteousness and so-called good deeds, but He clothed
me in that *one* good deed done at Calvary and robed me in
the righteousness of Jesus Christ.

As you travel along life's highway today may you recall the words of the old spiritual:

> I got a robe, you got a robe,
>   All o' God's chillun got a robe . . .

Rejoice, if you too can say,

> I know my robes gwinter fit me well—
>   I tried it on at de gates of Hell!

May 31

In all their affliction He was afflicted. (Isaiah 63:9)

Those words are part of a prayer of the prophet Isaiah. He looked back to the days of Moses and Joshua, to a time when Israel had not yet betrayed God's confidence in her and had not yet disappointed Him and gone whoring after idol gods.

In those days Jehovah continuously had shown His lovingkindness. As their deliverer He bore them safely through their many dangers, trials, toils, troubles, and snares.

It is difficult to grasp the idea that when those things happen to the children of God they happen to God also. Imagine the Creator of heaven and earth, the one only true and living God—all-powerful, all-knowing, everywhere present—imagine Him having the ability to feel what His creatures feel and to suffer along with them.

The text is saying that in all their distress, He was distressed. He felt what they felt. Their sufferings were His sufferings. He could not, He did not, remain unaffected. Their afflictions were reflected in His own being. He was moved inwardly.

I rejoice in that, for as a blood-bought child of God, I have someone who knows and cares. The knowledge that Jesus Christ is affected when I am afflicted is a soft pillow for my weary head and helps dispel heartbreak and sorrow.

May it be yours to remember this day: "Many are the afflictions of the righteous, but the LORD delivers him out of them all" (Psalm 34:19).

Whatever your experiences today may be, the Lord Jesus Christ knows and He cares. He is a high priest who can be touched with the feeling of our infirmities (Hebrews 4:15).

June 1

For My people have committed two evils: they have forsaken Me, the fountain of living waters, and hewn themselves cisterns—broken cisterns that can hold no water. (Jeremiah 2:13)

The plaintive words pour forth from the lips of a heart-broken God. "My people" refers not to the ignorant, unenlightened heathen who would not change their own gods (v. 11), but to those who have known Jehovah.

What thirsty Israel needed could be found only in their God; He alone was the reservoir of fresh water, ceaselessly flowing. But Israel had forsaken Him. In the attempt to satisfy their thirst, the Jews built their own wells. If a man does not drink the living water from the fountain of life, the only alternative is to construct his own cistern. But the very fact it is man-made suggests its inferiority; it is cracked by sin.

Men have nothing but sin to cement the cracks. A cracked cistern cemented by sin is a cistern cracked still. Of what value is it? Like salt that is not salty, a cistern that will not hold water is good for nothing.

We Christians must not forget that we are the people of God. He has not saved us and left us on our own to fetch water as best we can from whatever source we please. We too must continue to drink at the fountain that never shall run dry. After all, the water I drank yesterday does not help my thirst today. This is another day; with it comes new trouble. There are new disappointments, sorrows, temptations. Let us continue to drink deeply from the well of God's Word.

June 2

The temple of the LORD, the temple of the LORD. . . .
(Jeremiah 7:4)

Men mistakenly put their trust in bow, sword, spear, chariots, horses, military alliances, pacts, wealth, and idol-gods. To that list Jeremiah added lying, or deceptive, words.

The prophet's Temple sermon was directed mainly at those religious people for whom the Temple had become a fetish, who were more interested in outside show than inner character.

They practiced injustice, oppressed strangers, shed innocent blood, committed adultery, murdered, stole, swore falsely, burned incense unto Baal, walked after other gods; but then on the Sabbath day they went to the Temple, stood before Jehovah, and acted out their religion.

With lying words the false prophets encouraged the people in their folly, maintaining that because the Temple was located there, the LORD would take care of them. He would protect Jerusalem.

How tragic it is for a man to think he can see when he is blind, to think he can hear when in actuality he is stone deaf, to find that while he has a song on his lips there is no real melody in his heart, to discover that the symphony of his soul is all phony, to think that he is a solid citizen of heaven when he is on his way to hell. How sad! Jeremiah said: "Behold, you trust in lying words that cannot profit" (7:8).

Thank God that your faith is not based upon the local assembly you attend. It is not the building or the service rendered there that gives security; it is not the denomination or preacher. It is Jesus Christ who now is seated in heaven making intercession for all whose bodies are the temple of God through the presence of the indwelling Holy Spirit.

June 3

Set your heart toward the highway. (Jeremiah 31:21)

This glorious chapter in Jeremiah deals with the restoration and joy of Israel when the nation finally returns to Jehovah through faith in Jesus her Messiah. When that time comes in the life of this people, there shall be taking up of tambourines, the dancing of the merrymakers, planting and reaping, singing and shouting for gladness, and their mourning will be turned into joy.

Jehovah said that because He would surely have mercy upon Israel, He wanted the nation to set up signposts, place for herself landmarks, and direct her mind to the highway, the way by which she went.

The Christian has chosen the highway to heaven. For the saint "the highway of the upright is to depart from evil" (Proverbs 16:17). The highway to heaven is not without potholes and pitfalls. Heartaches, disappointments, mistakes, discouragements, pain, sorrow, sickness, and disease—all come to the Christian on the highway to heaven as well as to the unbeliever on the road to hell.

The difference is where the road leads, its ultimate stopping place. The Christian can endure pain now, because there is healing at the end of the road. Believers can put up with weeping at midnight because there is joy coming in the morning.

On this highway we are hard-pressed, yet not crushed; perplexed, but not in despair; persecuted, but not forsaken; struck down, but not destroyed (2 Corinthians 4:8–9).

We can walk because there is someone walking beside us who has been our way before, having set His heart toward the highway to Calvary.

June 4

Then Jeremiah said, "False! I am not defecting to the Chaldeans!" (Jeremiah 37:14)

Fearful of the Egyptian army, the Babylonian soldiers withdrew from their siege of Jerusalem. In the interim Jeremiah left the city to go to the land of Benjamin to his own native village. Possibly it was to negotiate some business concerning family property that he had purchased from his cousin Hanamel, son of his Uncle Shallum (Jeremiah 32:7).

As Jeremiah was at the gate of Benjamin, a guard by the name of Irijah grabbed Jeremiah and said, "You're deserting to the Chaldeans!"

The prophet responded: "That's a lie! I'm not going over to the Chaldeans!"

But Irijah would not listen; he had the prophet arrested. The officials in anger beat Jeremiah and threw him into prison.

A twelve-year-old boy, an important witness in a lawsuit, was severely cross-examined. Said the lawyer, "Your father has been telling you how to testify, hasn't he?"

"Yes," said the boy.

"Now," said the lawyer, "just tell us how your father told you to testify."

"Well," said the boy modestly, "Father told me that the lawyers would try to tangle me in my testimony; but if I would just be careful and tell the truth, I could tell the same thing every time."

Rest assured it still pays to tell the truth. Jeremiah suffered for telling the truth, but he pleased God. The head of the church is Jesus Christ who said, "I am . . . the truth." Though in many areas truth has been sacrificed, walk uprightly today in the name of Jesus.

June 5

Is there any word from the LORD? (Jeremiah 37:17)

Jeremiah was in jail, having been arrested and charged with treason. Then King Zedekiah sent and took Jeremiah out, and in the palace the king secretly, timidly asked, "Is there any word from the LORD?" The king was sincere. He was anxious to know and probably meant well, but was too weak to put the good advice into action.

Jeremiah did not flinch. He did not change his tune because he was in jail or because he stood before royalty. He stuck with his prophecy of judgment. "You shall be delivered into the hand of the king of Babylon!" The message had not changed. Jeremiah was no magician-preacher-prophet, pulling out of different pockets that which different audiences at different times desired to hear.

Today there are folks who want to be massaged, not given a message; they look for entertainment, not edification; syncopation, not sanctification. We have spectator saints instead of witnessing workers. Programs producing pecuniary profits are preferable to prayer and preaching.

Jeremiah would not compromise. His message from God warned that leaning on Egypt would prove to be leaning upon a broken cane that would pierce the hand.

Thank God for another word—the word of forgiveness. In Christ Jesus our sins were judged. The word from the Lord who is the Word made flesh is that whoever believes in Him shall not perish. Rejoice in the word from heaven from a God who keeps His word.

June 6

*You have made us an offscouring and refuse in the midst of
the peoples. All our enemies have opened their mouths against
us.* (Lamentations 3:45–46; 1 Corinthians 4:13)

Lamentations is the work of the prophet Jeremiah, and
here he laments, or cries, for the people of Israel. The sorrows they suffer are because of their sin. Daily weeping
over Zion, the seer shows them that their misery is but the
inevitable effect of backsliding and forgetting God.

The nation was warned many times through Moses
(Deuteronomy 28:37), Solomon (1 Kings 9:7), the psalmist
(Psalm 44:13–14), Jeremiah (Jeremiah 24:9), and Ezekiel
(Ezekiel 22:4).

Israel was defeated in battle, humbled, humiliated, cut
off; cast out, carried into slavery, driven, removed, and
dispersed. Thus it was that in disobedience Israel became
an astonishment, a byword, a curse, a derision, a mocking,
a laughingstock, a proverb, a reproach, a scorn, a shaking
of the head, and a taunt.

In short, Israel disobeyed God and was reckoned as dirt
by the nations of the world. It remains true today that anti-
Semitism dogs the footsteps of the Jew, and hatred seeks
to destroy the nation.

Such destruction will never occur; her enemies will never
succeed. Jehovah has promised that when the sun stops
shining by day and the moon and stars refuse to give light
by night, only then will the seed of Israel cease from being
a nation before Him forever (Jeremiah 31:35–37).

Whatever headlines the nation of Israel may make in
today's newspapers, remember this: God keeps His word.
You can look forward to that day when Jerusalem shall be
the world's capital, and you will be reigning with the King
of kings and Lord of lords.

June 7

Yet they will know that a prophet has been among them.
(Ezekiel 2:5)

Ezekiel had been sent to preach among a people described by God as rebellious. Theirs was a shamelessness that springs from the hardness of the heart. They were stiff-necked, openly disputing with God, contentious. Said John Calvin: "The Jews were not only rebellious against God and puffed up with proud contempt, but their impiety was so desperate that they opposed themselves to God without disguise."

Perhaps you wonder why the people bothered even to hear the messenger, for Ezekiel was not really popular. Since his earlier prophecies concerning Jerusalem had been fulfilled, that gave him an entrance; they would at least come and listen.

One thing is sure: they would know Ezekiel was God's prophet. Even today we can know God's messenger. First, we need to examine the life of the prophet; he must practice what he preaches. A second test is truth. "When a prophet speaks in the name of the LORD, if the thing does not happen or come to pass, that is the thing which the LORD has not spoken; the prophet has spoken it presumptuously" (Deuteronomy 18:22).

A third test is God's Word; it is our only standard, or yardstick, by which to measure the preacher's message. By these tests we may know God's prophet is among us. Ezekiel's message was not to change. Whether the audience was pleased or displeased, he was to preach the same message that God gave him. God's word was put forth, not Ezekiel's; it was an absolute standard, not a relative one.

June 8

And He said to me, "Son of man, can these bones live?"
(Ezekiel 37:3)

Even in captivity the Jews persisted in their wickedness, indicating that punishment is not often successful in the rehabilitation of men. The situation appeared hopeless, and the whole house of Israel was saying, "Our bones are dry."

To them it was as if their soldiers had been slain in battle by the sword, their bodies unburied, and their bones picked clean by the buzzards, bleached by the noonday sun, made smooth by the blasting sand driven by the wind.

Then one day God visited Ezekiel, lifted him up and carried him to the midst of the valley, set him down among the bones, and said, "Son of man, can these bones live?" God already knew the answer, and Ezekiel knew that the Lord knew. He realized that what seems impossible to men is possible with God; Jehovah had the solution in His hands.

Ezekiel was correct. No matter how hopeless a situation may look, the Lord has the answer. God used Ezekiel to combat the spirit of gloom that had befallen the captives. Although the fulfillment of this vision is still future, and we await the time when Israel will assume the center of the world's spotlight, there is right now a message for you.

All about us lie men dead in trespasses and sins. Their bones can be made alive only by faith in the shed blood of Jesus Christ. Bringing one to life is the work of the blessed Holy Spirit, who indwells all true believers. Today as you walk about at home, work, or play and hear the shaking and rattling, pray that your heavenly Father will use you to prophesy to the bones and that the Holy Spirit will do a regenerating work.

June 9

Nebuchadnezzar the king made an image of gold. (Daniel 3:1)

From the time of Cain to the time of Nebuchadnezzar idolatry had increased tremendously. Babylon was indeed full of gods and goddesses. What King Nebuchadnezzar did was not strange. He was a pagan. Though undoubtedly he respected Daniel's wisdom and appreciated Daniel's God (2:47), his heart was unregenerate.

Idolatry is *dumb*; it is intellectually stupid, irrational, one manifestation of the insanity of sin (read Isaiah 44:8–20). In Acts 17 Paul shows its absurdity. If a man has a mind to think, ears to hear, eyes to see, and a mouth with which to speak, is it not foolishness to make an idol that can do none of those things and still claim that that idol is one's god?

Idolatry is not only dumb, but it is also *degrading*; it is morally destructive, debasing. Note that the king made an image, and it was the image of a man. The deification of man is the first step in the downward trek of the soul, an essential ingredient of idolatry.

Idolatry is *dear*; it is expensive, costly. Note that Nebuchadnezzar made an image of gold; idolaters will spare nothing in the worship of their gods. Millions of Americans spend billions of dollars in the collection plates of their gods—nicotine, alchohol, and music.

Look at the fabulous salaries paid certain athletes, movie stars, musicians, and night club entertainers, that are grossly out of proportion to any moral, tangible, permanent, and constructive good those people do. Above and beyond the material cost there is the damage done to the soul, man's most precious possession.

Like the idol Nebuchadnezzar made, every idol is headed for destruction. "Little children, keep yourselves from idols" (1 John 5:21).

June 10

Is not this great Babylon, that I have built for a royal dwelling by my mighty power and for the honor of my majesty?
(Daniel 4:30)

There has been no prouder age than the one in which we now live. Pride, arrogance, haughtiness, self-seeking, and conceit are seen everywhere. Men are mad, mean, and miserable. Pride is a sign of the times and has even reared its ugly head in the church. Some churches have prospered materially and have become no longer concerned with the poor in their communities. For many the church has become just a status symbol.

Even Bible school students have become puffed up with their knowledge. We have forgotten what we were when Jesus Christ found us—slaves in the marketplace of sin.

Arrogant pride is an awful thing. Unbridled, it makes animals out of men. It incapacitates. It blinds men to justice and is vengeful, belligerent.

Pride makes men supersensitive to the least slight. It makes fools out of men who become proud of their folly. Men become proud of culture gaps and boast of their ancestry, skin color, race, and IQ.

Rockers look down on classical music. Liquor drinkers think they are sophisticated superiors to those who do not indulge. Women proud of their painted beauty make ridiculous efforts to stem the process of aging. Men proud of their intellect and genius have become fools in their rejection of Jesus Christ and the Bible.

In his arrogance and pride, Nebuchadnezzar lost his mind. God took it away from him in order to teach him that the Most High God rules in the kingdom of men. Insane for seven years, he later was restored. May we remember this day not to think more highly of ourselves than we ought to think (Romans 12:3).

June 11

Go, take yourself a wife of harlotry and children of harlotry.
(Hosea 1:2)

Hosea, a northerner, was a contemporary of Amos, Isaiah, and Micah. His ministry was to Israel and his message was for Israel, because Israel was in a morass of immorality. A quick study of Hosea reveals the one prominent evil of idolatry—the worship of heathen gods and goddesses.

Once the Jews rejected Jehovah they left themselves open to the adoption of the evil practices of the pagans surrounding them. That led to their political and moral downfall. Some of their sins mentioned are swearing, lying, killing, stealing, adultery, and the rejection of the knowledge of God.

By far, harlotry was the overriding iniquity. In fact, Hosea learned through personal, bitter experience the meaning of Israel's idolatry—her turning away from a loving God. Ordered to marry Gomer, whom God knew ahead of time would turn out to be a whore, the prophet obeyed. In time Gomer deserted Hosea and took up living with other men. Yet Hosea was commanded to take her back, love her, and forgive her. Hosea's tragic married life is a picture of Israel's relationship with God.

I could not help but marvel at Hosea's submissiveness to Jehovah. In a world system that is operated by the devil—one that hates Christ, Christians, and the church—there is much work to be done. What has the Lord called you to do? What sacrifices have you made? Have you been submissive to the will of the Lord, enabling Him to show His love for others through you?

June 12

Therefore people who do not understand will be trampled.
(Hosea 4:14)

The *"mis"* family is a large one, made up of such members as misconstrue, misinterpret, misjudge, miscalculate, and misapprehend. Misunderstanding is one member of this family that affects many Christians. To be misunderstood is the penalty we suffer for being different. Christians are different because Christ lives in them.

If you live a clean and disciplined life, one free of immorality and destructive habits, then prepare to be misunderstood. People will say you think you are better than they.

Some folks misunderstand because their hearing is not good. The gospel may be plain as ABC, but some people are "DEF." They are talking when they should be listening.

Prejudice leads to misunderstandings also. Some minds are closed by jealousy, covetousness, and greed. Some folks do not want to understand because there is hatred in their hearts. Sometimes misunderstanding is the result of ignorance.

Whatever the reasons for misunderstanding, the saint must remain Christlike when misunderstood. We must strive to understand those who do not understand us.

That way they may take notice of us, that we have been with Jesus Christ (Acts 4:13). Do not become discouraged. Turn your eyes to Calvary.

June 13

Ephraim has mixed himself among the peoples; Ephraim is a cake unturned. (Hosea 7:8)

Mixture. Ephraim stands for the ten-tribe kingdom of Israel and is a title used some thirty-seven times in the book of Hosea. Note first of all that Ephraim mixed himself among the peoples. That means he courted favor first of one country, then another. When Ephraim let go of the only true help, the LORD God, where else was there to turn? (Hebrews 10:26).

Joined to idols (Hosea 4:17), Ephraim turned first to Egypt, then to Assyria (Hosea 7:11): "Come, help us to fight our enemy; and then when you need help, we'll come to you." Jehovah is a jealous God; He had warned the Israelites against such mingling, but they disobeyed Him (Psalm 106:34–36).

Mess. Ephraim not only mixed himself with the immoral, but he was a cake not turned, a half-baked loaf of bread.

Cooked on hot stones, the pancake had to be turned at the right moment. Otherwise it would be badly burned and black on one side and rough, doughy, gooey on the other side—a distasteful and unappetizing concoction.

Such a pancake is of no value; you cannot eat it. A very graphic description of Israel (Ephraim), the half-baked cake was used by God to demonstrate Israel's inconsistencies, weaknesses of character, twisted values, and pursuit after worthless goals.

Message. God is looking for separated saints (consistent Christians). Let the Holy Spirit have His way, and you will not turn out to be a half-baked pancake, done on one side and undone on the other. For what God does, He does well; what He starts, He finishes. In Christ we are complete.

June 14

Aliens have devoured his strength, but he does not know it; yes, gray hairs are here and there on him, yet he does not know it. (Hosea 7:9).

Why was Ephraim ignorant? What was it that Ephraim did not know? Ephraim had become weak, because he had turned his back upon his soul's sole source of strength, Jehovah. When men turn their backs on the sun they walk in darkness. When they reject God they reject wisdom; their end is stupidity. When they reject God they reject power; their end is weakness. When they reject God they reject wealth; their end is poverty. When they reject God they reject heaven; their end is hell.

Without God in his life, Ephraim became spiritually ignorant, and that is the worst type of ignorance. Without God to help, Ephraim sought the help of other nations: Syria, Assyria, Philistia, Egypt. Hosea calls them aliens, strangers. By relying upon foreign nations who knew not God, Ephraim weakened himself. He did not know that reliance upon foreigners robbed him of his strength.

When you are out of God's will, you will seek the help of non-believers. But you not only do not help yourself, you also hurt yourself. The devil never meant anybody any good. Associate yourself with the wrong people and they will tear you down. If you are being torn down and do not know it, you are in the same shape Ephraim was.

The thing to do today is make up your mind to wholly rely upon the Lord. Let Him be your strength, and discover that He is able to turn ignorance into knowledge. Your gray hairs will only prove that you are becoming more like Jesus Christ, the Ancient of Days (Daniel 7:22; Revelation 1:14).

June 15

So I will restore to you the years that the swarming locust has eaten. (Joel 2:25)

Blessed in every way possible, the Jews still failed. They fell into idolatry or spiritual whoredom, and the wrath of God was visited upon them. There were from time to time temporary revivals, and the Lord gave respite; but repentance did not last long.

Because of their rebellions, rain was withheld, causing drought and failure of crops. Swarms of locusts were sent; God's great army chewed up everything in sight that was chewable. Combined with enemy soldiers besieging their cities, starvation, cannibalism, and death became their lot.

The grass withered; their cattle, oxen, sheep, donkeys, and camels died. Beasts of prey stalked the land. Cruel soldiers raped their women and crushed their men. The nation suffered slavery. They were spoiled of their iron, copper, silver, gold, cedars of Lebanon, wine, and olive oil. Misery was their lot.

Then Joel preached and exhorted, "Israel, straighten up! Turn to Jehovah. Go to Him with all your being. Tear your heart, not your clothing. And He will open up the heavens again. The drought will end. The locusts will disappear. The harvest will return in abundance.

"The LORD's presence will be realized; peace will be established. Prosperity will be yours. Even at this late hour further disaster can be averted. For the LORD is merciful."

Be it known this day that we serve a gracious Lord who is full of lovingkindness. Walk today in the knowledge that we serve the God who restores our souls as well as the years.

June 16

Surely the Lord GOD does nothing, unless He reveals His secret to His servants the prophets. (Amos 3:7)

On Wednesday, July 13, 1977, about 9:30 P.M., lightning struck a major transformer in New York's power system. Practically the entire city and some of its suburbs were blacked out. People were trapped in elevators and on subway cars. Trains were delayed. Televisions and air conditioners shut off.

Clocks and traffic lights stopped. Looters and pickpockets took advantage of the blackout. Theaters were evacuated. Saloons were emptied, although some stayed and sipped cocktails by candlelight. Millions were left in the dark. The thought occurred to me: *Will anyone see the hand of God in all this?*

Surely there is no effect without a cause. Centuries earlier Moses had warned Israel of the consequences of disobedience and concluded: "The secret things belong to the LORD our God, but those things which are revealed belong to us and to our children forever, that we may do all the words of this law" (Deuteronomy 29:29).

Now Amos encountered a similar problem: the people failed to realize there is a connection between cause and effect. Amos preached judgment. The people asked, "Amos, who made you a prophet of doom, a preacher of gloom? Who gave you the right; what authority do you have for predicting that God will punish us?"

It did not dawn upon them that there is no effect without a cause. In other words, there would be no Amos without a Jehovah God. Israel's sins called forth judgment. Our sins called forth God's judgment too; Christ who became our sin was smitten. Today we who believe are able to say to the world:

> It is no secret what God can do;
> What He's done for others, He'll do for you!

Stuart Hamblen

June 17

Then Haggai, the LORD's messenger, spoke the LORD's message to the people saying, "I am with you, says the LORD." (Haggai 1:13)

The Babylonians were overthrown by the Medo-Persians, who were much more favorable to the Jews and permitted them to return to Jerusalem. Once there, the Jews found that their houses, the walls, and the Temple had been smashed, the land left desolate, and there was much work to be done. Haggai's message was one of encouragement to continue building the Temple.

Short and sweet, still the prophet's words were strengthening. The very power of heaven was wrapped up in the four words "I am with you"; they expressed exactly what Jehovah wanted the Israelites to know as they proceeded to rebuild.

We can take God at His word. But the words of men cannot always be trusted. When things get too thick some men will thin out; even after promising to stick with you to the end, the end comes all too soon. Men forget to keep appointments, get sick, and change their minds.

If you take God at His word you will discover that He is with you; when you have His word, you have Him. He is His word. His presence is tied up with the observance of His word. To obey Him is to know He is with you.

Throughout the Bible we hear this wonderful refrain: "I am with you!" For Jacob it meant the guarantee of the fulfillment of God's promise (Genesis 28:15). For Moses those words gave him courage to stand before the pharaoh of Egypt (Exodus 3:12). For Gideon those words meant victory in battle (Judges 6:16). For Jeremiah there was boldness to preach (Jeremiah 1:8). For Israel God's promise meant rest, confidence in war, and strength to be delivered (Exodus 33:14; Deuteronomy 20:1; Isaiah 41:10, 43:2). Hear Him say to you today, "I am with *you!*"

June 18

This is the word of the LORD to Zerubbabel: "Not by might nor by power, but by My Spirit," says the LORD of hosts. (Zechariah 4:6)

After seventy years of captivity in Babylon, the Jews were allowed to return to their homeland. Their country had been left in ruins by the cruel Chaldeans, and yet there was no great push to rebuild God's Temple or restore the city walls.

In part, laziness was responsible. Then, too, there was opposition from others living there. In part, selfishness was the cause: the self-centered returnees put their own interests first and rebuilt beautiful homes, letting God's house remain in ruins.

So God sent the prophets Haggai, Zechariah, and Malachi to exhort the people. Ezra stressed rebuilding the Temple; and Nehemiah pushed the rebuilding of the walls of Jerusalem.

Zerubbabel too was one whose zealous desire to finish rebuilding the Temple was commendable, but in the face of such formidable foes it would be folly not to recognize his own utter helplessness. He needed to hear what God told Jeremiah on one occasion, "'For I am with you,' says the LORD, 'to deliver you'" (Jeremiah 1:19).

Zerubbabel needed to be told that the battle is the LORD's and He will prevail. Faced with the tremendous task of rebuilding the ruined Temple, he could not succeed on his own, but he was assured of success for divine help was available.

If you want to build a spiritual community, a holy temple, a Christian church, a beautiful home, a sanctified life, then remember—it is not by your might, or by your power, but by the Holy Spirit.

> Holy Spirit, all divine,
>> Dwell within this heart of mine;
> Cast down every idol throne,
>> Reign supreme, and reign alone.

Andrew Reed

~

June 19

And you shall call His name JESUS. (Matthew 1:21)

So commanded the angel and Joseph obeyed. The virgin Mary had been told the same thing by Gabriel (Luke 1:31). Months before Jesus was born, it was *predicted* that He would come and would be named Jesus. No human father was to determine His name, for that was the personal *prerogative* of His heavenly Father.

See here not only the prediction and prerogative but also the *purpose* of His name. *Jesus* was a rather common Jewish name at the time.

It is the Greek rendering of the Hebrew name *Joshua*, which is a contraction of Jehoshua. The name means "Jehovah saves" or "Jehovah helps" or "Jehovah is salvation."

Thus the name predicted is also a name of purpose; He shall save His people from their sins. Christ came to save sinners. Unfortunately, most people today do not know that. They fail to see beyond the office parties, the liquor, gifts, mistletoe, eggnog, bonuses, and Santa Claus.

Finally, recognize that there is *power* in His name. In that name the Holy Spirit was sent, converts were baptized, and the lame healed. In that name God the Father answered prayer. Indeed, "there is no other name under heaven given among men by which we must be saved" (Acts 4:12). "For whoever calls on the name of the LORD shall be saved" (Romans 10:13). In the future, at the name of Jesus every knee shall bow.

> Jesus! the name that charms our fears,
>> That bids our sorrows cease,
> 'Tis music in the sinners' ears,
>> 'Tis life, and health, and peace.
>>> *Charles Wesley*

June 20

Where is He who has been born King of the Jews?
(Matthew 2:2)

The wise men from the East asked this question some months after the birth of the Lord Jesus. Indeed the inquiry could have been made up to two years after His birth. God had impressed their hungry hearts, and we see first of all that they sought a *place*.

Of course, Micah 5:2 predicted some 700 years earlier that the ruler of Israel would come forth out of Bethlehem Ephratah. But to get the wise men started, God caused a star, "His star," to be seen possibly only by themselves.

There is no record that anyone else saw it. They saw it in the East. They did not follow it, but knew by their calculations that it appeared over Jerusalem.

Second, they looked for a *person*. "Where is He who has been born King of the Jews? For we have seen His star in the East and have come to worship Him."

Third, they had a *purpose*. They wanted to worship Him.

Children look at parents, students at teachers, neighbors at neighbors, fellow workers and church visitors at their peers. They are looking and asking, "Where is He?"

We ought to be able to tell them and show them that we know who and where He is, because one day the Holy Spirit found us and pointed us to Calvary. Where is He? He is no longer in a manger or on His mother's lap or in Joseph's arms.

He is no longer on the cross or buried in a tomb. He is the resurrected, ascended, seated-in-heaven, soon returning King of kings and Lord of lords! Where is He? He is in my *head*, teaching me facts about God. Where is He? He is in my *hands*, that I may do right. He is in my *feet*, that I may walk right. He is in my *mouth*, so that I will talk right. He is in my *heart*, so that I may become more like Him day by day.

June 21

You are the salt of the earth; but if the salt loses its flavor, how shall it be seasoned? It is then good for nothing but to be thrown out and trampled underfoot by men. (Matthew 5:13)

Salt is a very common substance. However, it is still one of the most precious and useful mineral compounds. Some things are precious because they are rare; salt is precious because of its usefulness. Salt preserves that which once had life but now is dead and in time will rot completely.

As salt, Christians are to slow up corruption. Salt arrests the spread of corruption. The Christian prevents society from going to hell in a supersonic Concorde jet. We keep the world from going to pieces, disintegrating more rapidly than it would otherwise.

As we live for Christ, our lives are like a pinch of salt, slowing up the corruption and rottenness of the world. Because we are salt, we cannot blend in, tie up with, associate intimately with, keep up with all that goes on in a Christless world. Then salt begins to lose its taste. Salt that has no taste is useless.

Ask yourself this: Am I salt that is salty? There really is no other kind, since any change in its chemical constitution or any loss of its chemical qualities means it is no longer salt. The question really is: What kind of an investment am I to the Lord? Have I been a profitable servant?

God paid dearly for you and for me; with blood more precious than silver or gold, Christ bought us out of the slave market. He has watched over us through many dangers, toils, and snares.

A salty Christian is one ready for suffering, sacrifice, and service. At school, in the neighborhood, on the job, at home, wherever you are, be an influence for Jesus Christ.

June 22

I did not come to bring peace but a sword. (Matthew 10:34)

Jesus Christ could not avoid trouble. His very coming into the world caused trouble. Of lowly birth, He was cradled in a manger. The news of His coming stirred an evil king who sought to do away with Him by slaying many innocent children there in Bethlehem. For more than 2,000 years wicked men, supported by the devil, have sought to wipe out Christ's influence and to destroy His name.

It was the preaching of Christ that evoked such bitter response. If He had kept quiet it would have been a different story. But Christ's sermons, preaching, and teaching brought not peace but a sword.

He split families, turned mothers against daughters and sons against fathers, set men at variance with one another, polarized attitudes, pricked hearts, changed minds, convicted consciences, caused divisions, deflated egos, and stirred up the old natures of wicked men.

Christ preached about hell. He was a judgment preacher. Such preaching was despised then, and it is still despised today. Self-righteous folks hate it, humanists do not believe it, materialists and lovers of luxury do not want to hear it.

Christ preached against hypocrisy.

Christ preached holiness. As He demonstrated, clean, separated living backs up one's witness.

There was a purpose in preaching about hell, hypocrisy, and holiness. It was calculated to lead Jesus Christ to Calvary. He knew that, but it did not stop Him from preaching. Calvary was the goal. He had come to die. Because He had you and me in mind, He kept on preaching.

And he who does not take his cross and follow after Me is not worthy of Me. (Matthew 10:38)

Here is the first mention of a cross in the New Testament. The cross is a symbol of death and all that leads to death. Christ knew full well the method by which He would be put to death. The Jews had seen condemned criminals carrying their crosses to the place of execution and fully understood the imagery.

Discipleship may well include death. To carry your cross is an acknowledgment or proof that you know what is happening and that you are willing and ready if need be to persevere, to accept whatever you have to endure. The word *his* is emphatic; you are not called upon to carry somebody else's cross—just your own. There are some things other folks cannot do for you; you have to do them for yourself. *Your* cross is *your* cross.

It includes all you may suffer because of your stand for Jesus Christ—all the hardships, heartaches, humiliation, and pain. Note that I said because of your stand for Christ. Your cross is not the ordinary adversities of life that even unbelievers experience. After all, man that is born of a woman is of few days and full of trouble (Job 14:1).

Whatever troubles we Christians get into as a result of being out of God's will and doing wrong do not come under the heading of crossbearing. A disciple of Christ bears the cross that represents the hostility of the wicked. Discipleship is a matter of being worthy, having weight because of our connection with Christ.

Imagine the Creator using such an expression for the creature. Worthy? Yes, but not because of education, race, knowledge, nationality, or intellect, but because our faith is in Him alone, empty of everything but Jesus Christ.

June 24

Come to Me, all you who labor and are heavy laden, and I will give you rest. (Matthew 11:28)

The God of the Bible is very gracious; He is kind. "I am the LORD, exercising lovingkindness . . . in the earth" (Jeremiah 9:24). His invitations to mankind are marvelous examples of grace. If that were not true, how would we explain a holy God inviting sinners to have fellowship with Him?

What explanation could we give for an omnipotent God inviting weak, helpless men to come to Him; a God of light seeking after men who love darkness; a God of love loving the unlovable; a God of life quickening the dead? How can that be?

Well, I cannot explain it; I can only proclaim it. It is a fact. The God of the Bible is gracious, and He extends an invitation to you and to me. This characteristic of God is manifest from Genesis to Revelation. To Noah came the invitation: "Come into the ark, you and all your household, because I have seen that you are righteous before Me in this generation" (Genesis 7:1).

In Isaiah we read: "'Come now, and let us reason together,' says the LORD; 'though your sins are like scarlet, they shall be as white as snow; though they are red like crimson, they shall be as wool'" (1:18).

Revelation 22:17 reads: "And the Spirit and the bride say, 'Come!' . . . And let him who thirsts *come*. Whoever desires, let him take the water of life freely." God pleads with men and begs them to accept His invitation.

Our attention is drawn to the words of Christ. The Lord had come unto His own—His own land, His own people—but the nation as a whole rejected Him. Even His own brothers did not believe in Him. Here He turns to those who seek help. When Christ extends an invitation to you, He means business. When He says, "Come to Me," He means it.

June 25

An enemy bas done this. (Matthew 13:28)

You have heard that certain people in high places have what is called an "enemy list." Christians also have such a list. First, sin is our enemy. The penalty of sin is death. The first step in defeating that enemy is to believe in the shed blood of Jesus Christ, who paid the penalty at Calvary.

Second, the devil is an enemy. He is a liar, a slanderer, an accuser of the brethren, and a deceiver of the nations. I do not blame Satan for every evil that befalls me as some people do by their flip expression "The devil made me do it!", but he is an enemy nonetheless (Matthew 13:39).

Third, the world is an enemy (John 15:18–19). Since the devil is the prince of the cosmos, or world system, that is understandable. It is a fact—unbelievers hate genuine Christians (1 John 3:13), and we need to be reminded that friendship with the world system is unhealthy and unwise.

Fourth, death is an enemy. It breaks family circles and ties of friendship; it makes widows and orphans, bereaves, disrupts, intrudes, robs, and mystifies.

Death is the last enemy to be destroyed (1 Corinthians 15:26). That destruction is guaranteed by the Lord Jesus Christ who, after dying on the cross for our sins, rose from the grave with all power in His hands, holding the keys of Hades and of death (Revelation 1:18).

It is good for you to know who your enemies are, but there is no need to be worried about them. He that is in you is greater than all your foes combined, and He prepares a table of blessing for you in their presence (Psalm 23:5).

June 26

But the boat was now in the middle of the sea, tossed by the waves, for the wind was contrary. (Matthew 14:24)

Like Simon Peter and the other disciples, we find ourselves in the midst of a troubled sea. Beneath us lurk unknown denizens of the deep, devilish and demonic. Terrible creatures hide under the briny foam of hypocrisy, greed, and rebellion. Against the sides of the ship beat the frothy white-capped waves of turmoil, racism, immorality, crime, and war.

Tossed with the waves, the old ship of life dips and rises, rocks, rolls, and reels. The boisterous winds of adversity, inflation, unemployment, political corruption, and sickness all flow with the fury and power of a devastating hurricane. We are in trouble, at sea in a storm.

Now here comes someone walking on the water. Who is it? It is Jesus Christ, walking over life's tempestuous sea. It is He from whom came chart and compass; He who can, if He will, hush the wild ocean. He says to you and me, "Be of good cheer! It is I; do not be afraid."

Is it your heart's desire to walk with Christ today? Then keep your eyes upon the Lord Jesus. Do not let your bad circumstances make you take your eyes off Him, for if you look at your environment and troubles you will sink in despair and despondency.

Keep your eyes on Christ today. When the waves of chaos and confusion roar, He will give you peace. When the ocean slime of ugliness would discourage you, He provides beauty that encourages. When fear would paralyze you, He gives hope to stimulate. When sorrow would break your heart, He gives joy to heal. When Satan would drown you, He sees to it that the Holy Spirit is your lifeguard. So walk with Him on the waters of the stormy sea of life. Fear not. He will be with you. Soon the storms of life will all be over. Hallelujah!

June 27

The gates of Hades shall not prevail against it.
(Matthew 16:18)

Decisions. First of all, the phrase "gates of Hades" suggests the decisions of the wicked. People came to the gates of the city for judgment of family, business, and religious matters. There the elders met to give counsel and make decisions (Deuteronomy 21:19; 25:7). Taken as evil decisions, "gates of Hades" here stands for the wisdom, stratagems, plans, plots, and schemes of the unrighteous.

Deeds. Second, the phrase "gates of Hades" refers to the deeds of evildoers. A gate signifies going out and coming in, exit and entrance. Therefore, behavior or deeds are meant. No other institution in the world has been more violently assaulted than the Church.

There are not just heresy and doctrinal assaults on the outside, but there are the deeds of wickedness perpetrated by those on the inside. Paul warned the saints at Ephesus: "Also from among yourselves men will rise up, speaking perverse things, to draw the away the disciples after themselves" (Acts 20:30).

Death. Third, the "gates of Hades" may be seen as death. For a gate represents the power to keep in or to keep out, thus to confine, control, shut up. If any one place is able to do that, it is the grave. Once in the grave no man has the power to break out; only God can redeem him.

Today, praise God for the Church, the Body of Christ, the Bride of Christ. Rejoice that the Lord has placed you in the Church, protected you from the decisions and deeds of evil, and removed the fear of death. The victory is yours through Jesus Christ.

June 28

For what profit is it to a man if he gains the whole world, and loses his own soul? (Matthew 16:26)

Businessmen are much concerned about making a profit. I can understand that. When a person invests money, time, expertise and energy, he expects a return. God has said that the laborer is worthy of his hire. In the parable of the talents a man gave one servant five coins; another, two; and another, one coin. To each man was given according to his ability.

The five- and two-talent men traded and made a profit. The one-talent man hid the money and gave it back when the master returned from his trip. The master said that the servant should have deposited his money with the bankers so that, when he returned, he could have received his money with interest (Matthew 25:27).

"In all labor there is profit" (Proverbs 14:23). Some men are greedy. They want to make a killing, become millionaires overnight. In their love for money they cut corners, falsify weights, defraud, use inferior materials, lie, cheat, and steal. Such practices indicate those people may not be saved.

The question the Lord asks could be applied even to the man who is a legitimate businessman working honestly. One of the paradoxes, the seemingly contradictory thing about being a Christian, is this: When you believe in the shed blood of Jesus Christ and your soul is saved, it is also true that you gain the whole world.

"For all things are yours . . . the world or life or death, or things present or things to come—all are yours" (1 Corinthians 3:21–22). We are heirs of God and joint heirs of Christ. How do you like *that* for profit—all that and heaven too!

June 29

Grant that these two sons of mine may sit, one on Your right hand and the other on the left, in Your kingdom. (Matthew 20:21)

The mother of James and John came to the Lord Jesus and requested that her two sons be given prominent positions at His side in the kingdom. Although she was the prime mover, the sons supported her request; according to Mark 10:35, the sons made this desire known also.

They were not rebuked by the Lord. Their desire was noble. They were sincere. Furthermore, she came worshiping Him. But their request angered the other disciples. Perhaps jealousy had a part in the anger inasmuch as James and John, along with Simon Peter, constituted the inner circle. Imagine making such a request and leaving out Simon Peter altogether!

What they desired had serious implications of which they were totally unaware. "You do not know what you ask," said the Lord. The request was based upon a wrong concept of the kingdom (Acts 1:6). Despite all the Lord taught them, the disciples had in mind an earthly kingdom, one similar to the days of David and Solomon, one that would liberate them from the heel of the Roman soldiers.

We learn that though the request was sincere it caused others to be angry, and those who made it were ignorant of what it involved. The basic fault of their desire was that it was based upon a false concept of the kingdom that Christ had come to set up at that particular time.

The lesson He wanted to teach the disciples concerned true greatness. But they must understand first that it is a spiritual kingdom, not a physical one. Willingness to serve others is the mark of spiritual greatness. Christ illustrated that in His own life, for "even the Son of Man did not come to be served, but to serve, and to give His life a ransom for many" (Mark 10:45).

June 30

So Jesus had compassion and touched their eyes. And imme-diately their eyes received sight, and they followed Him. (Matthew 20:34)

God touched Adam and Eve, clothing them with animal skins after their disobedience (Genesis 3:21). Jacob wrestled with the Angel of the LORD, who touched the socket of Jacob's hip and crippled him (Genesis 32:25). Elijah, fleeing the wrath of Jezebel, became tired, sat down under a juniper tree, and prayed that he might die. As he lay and slept there, behold, an angel touched him and said, "Arise and eat" (1 Kings 19:7).

Granted the privilege of being in the presence of God, Isaiah was made aware of his own uncleanness. Then one of the seraphim put a live coal from the altar upon the prophet's mouth, saying: "Behold, this has touched your lips; your iniquity is taken away" (Isaiah 6:7).

Jeremiah protested the call of Jehovah, and God put forth His hand, touched Jeremiah's mouth, and said, "Behold, I have put My words in your mouth" (Jeremiah 1:6, 9). When Simon Peter's mother-in-law lay sick of the fever, the Lord touched her hand and the fever left her (Matthew 8:15).

Likewise He touched the eyes of two blind men who followed Him (Matthew 9:27–29). A deaf man with an impediment of speech was brought to the Lord; Christ touched him and the man's ears were opened, his tongue loosed (Mark 7:33–34).

All those people and others, were they present, could attest: "He touched me and made me whole!" The physical touching was but a picture, a foreshadowing, of the spiritual touching. Today sin-sick souls need spiritual healing.

No matter how hopeless and helpless your situation may seem to be, call on Jesus Christ for the touch of His hand.

July 1

All of you will be made to stumble because of Me this night, for it is written: "I will strike the Shepherd, and the sheep of the flock will be scattered." But after I have been raised, I will go before you to Galilee. (Matthew 26:31–32)

Repeatedly the disciples were told to expect the worst to happen to their Master (Matthew 12:40, 16:21). Yet when the time came, the disciples ran away. How true to form! You can be told a thing and know it is going to happen, yet when it does occur you are caught off guard, totally surprised.

A young lady who recently buried her stepmother said to me, "She was very sick for a long time and had wasted away to under seventy pounds. I knew she was dying. Yet when the call came that she had passed, I was unprepared, shocked."

Sometimes it takes a crisis to show up our true colors, to reveal where our treasures are. When everything is peaches and cream, some of us act like angels. But what happens when the winds of adversity blow and the waves of trouble roll?

In the case of the disciples, the limitation of their faith was shown. We learn from them that what counts most is not how long we have been associated with Christ or how courageous we think we are. It is not sophistication or education. What counts is what Christ has done in us and with us.

Unable to stand the test, the disciples soon went to their homes, separated from Christ and each other. All cohesion disintegrated; the Savior was abandoned; fellowship was temporarily disrupted; the sheep were scattered.

"Indeed the hour is coming, yes, has now come, that you will be scattered, each to his own, and will leave Me alone. And yet I am not alone, because the Father is with Me" (John 16:32). May Christ's confidence be yours to realize in those moments of loneliness that you are *not* alone.

July 2

Watch and pray, lest you enter into temptation. The spirit indeed is willing, but the flesh is weak. (Matthew 26:41)

Each time I hear those words I am reminded of one of the deacons in my first pastorate. Whenever called upon to pray, he would stand and talk to the Lord, but always with both eyes wide open. When I questioned him about it, he replied: "The Bible says watch and pray, and, Reverend, you have to keep your eyes on these people!"

In His Olivet discourse, Christ described the Tribulation and said, "Watch therefore, and pray always that you may be counted worthy to escape all these things" (Luke 21:36). In 1 Peter 4:7, the apostle said: "But the end of all things is at hand; therefore be serious and watchful in your prayers."

Now we never know what will happen next in life. We do know that trouble is in the air we breathe, and that we are "rollin' through an unfriendly world." "Man who is born of woman is of few days and full of trouble" (Job 14:1). Tests and trials come and go; temptations and hidden snares often take us unaware.

Day and night—at home, in the streets, on the job, in church—there is trouble. Sometimes friends, sometimes enemies are involved; sometimes the family, at other times strangers. Problems of money, marriage, property, children, job, and health arise. We do not know where or when the test will come.

Christ knew what awaited the disciples. He wanted them to be prepared. God does not want any of us who belong to Him to enter into testing, trials, temptations, and tribulations unprepared, or get caught off guard or asleep.

He exhorts: Since trouble is headed your way, keep on watching, and keep on praying. Victory is won only through such vigilance and prayer.

July 3

"Which of the two do you want me to release to you?" They said, *"Barabbas!"* (Matthew 27:21)

Here is a picture of life itself, for daily we are confronted with the necessity of making decisions. Often there can be no compromise, neutrality, procrastination, or fence-straddling. We cannot be like the little boy who listened to the Sunday school lesson on Lazarus the beggar. When asked which of the two men he wanted to be he replied, "I want to be like the rich man while I'm living, but like Lazarus when I die."

The fact is that men cannot live in the promised land *and* in Egypt at the same time. Men are not saved by grace *and* by works. We cannot go to hell *and* to heaven!

So it was here. A choice had to be made. Choose Barabbas—a robber, insurrectionist, seditionist, and murderer—or choose Christ, in whom was no fault, no guile. He went about doing good, healing the sick, cleansing lepers, giving sight to the blind, casting out demons, and raising the dead.

There was no cloudy gray area here; the issue was clearcut, but the world loves its own. The member of the partisan resistance movement was preferred to the Prince of Peace. The man of glamor, the fighter of the Romans, the criminal—he was chosen over the lowly Galilean peasant.

Surely a selfish world chooses that which it calculates best serves its interests. Lazy, it seeks the easy way out. Thankless, it bites the hand that feeds it. Hateful, it curses the very God who loves it. Evil, it hates righteousness, and invariably picks a Barabbas rather than the Christ.

To choose Christ is to choose life eternal and abundant, to have your sins washed away, to have the authority to call God your Father, to be a citizen of heaven, and to fulfill your purpose in life.

July 4

Priority. Eventually all graves will be opened (John 5:28–29), for the resurrection of Jesus Christ guarantees it (1 Corinthians 15:22). However, here we have only the graves of *believers* opened after the resurrection of our Lord.

Thus we see a priority. We learn from other scriptures that Christ is the first to be raised, never again to die. Given a glorified body, He lives forevermore. When the Lord returns for the true church only the graves of believers will be disturbed at that time.

Power. The exertion of force was necessary to open those graves during the death of Christ (although the bodies of those raised did not come out until *after* His resurrection). Supernatural power was needed.

The God who opened up Adam's rib to form Eve, who opened up the heavens to rain forty days and forty nights, who opened up the Red Sea for Israel to cross, who opened the earth to swallow rebellious Korah, who opened the mouth of a great fish to swallow Jonah—that same God opened the graves there at the crucifixion.

Purpose. God's purpose was not just to show us that we have priority or preference as participants in the first resurrection (Revelation 20:6) or to demonstrate His power. The graves were opened that we might better know who Jesus Christ is—Lord over death and the grave.

Through the open grave He speaks peace to our hearts. He exhorts, "Have no fear!" He bids us rejoice. Hold on just a little longer, and we too will see monuments topple, tombstones roll away, mausoleums demolished, and well-kept cemeteries ruined. Keep looking up!

July 5

Sir, we remember, while He was still alive, how that deceiver said, "After three days I will rise." (Matthew 27:63)

It came to the minds of the enemies of Christ that Jesus had said, "After three days I will rise." In bringing that prediction to the attention of Pilate, they called Christ "that deceiver," whereas they addressed the governor as "Sir." What arrogant blindness to call Jesus Christ a deceiver (John 7:12, 47).

What had Christ done while alive to warrant being called a deceiver? The miracles He wrought were genuine. His healings were real and without price. No phony cripples were in the audience or on the payroll, working in cooperation with Christ. No blessed healing cloths were mailed out for a donation; no holy water from the River Jordan was sold.

Those who had been deaf still could hear; those who had been dumb were still praising God at the top of their lungs. The woman bent over for eighteen years still stood straight. And the man born blind was still rejoicing and going through the streets of Jerusalem singing: "Amazing grace! how sweet the sound that saved a wretch like me! I once was lost, but now am found, was blind, but now I see."

Thank God that the Lord Jesus is not a liar or a deceiver, but truth. "Indeed, let God be true but every man a liar" (Romans 3:4). He did just what He said He would do. In spite of the seal, the soldiers, the skepticism, the stone, the Sanhedrin, and Satan, Jesus Christ rose from the grave. An angel rolled away the stone. The sepulcher was empty. Jesus Christ lives.

Because He lives, we also live. We have eternal life right now, having been drawn to Him who said, "And I, if I am lifted up from the earth, will draw all peoples to Myself" (John 12:32).

July 6

He is not here; for He is risen, as He said. Come, see the place where the Lord lay. (Matthew 28:6)

Note the *Proposition*. "He is risen." Skeptics, unbelievers, and atheists have originated many ideas, opinions, and beliefs concerning the resurrection of Christ; but all of their theories and speculations end up on the junk pile of humanism and anti-supernaturalism. According to the Scriptures, Jesus Christ is alive.

Hear now the *Prediction*. "As He said." Indeed, Christ had informed the disciples earlier that He would rise from the dead. The resurrection was no mere sudden afterthought on God's part (Matthew 16:21; 17:22–23; 20:18–19). At the time they were told, it did not register upon their minds. Now the words of the angel struck home. The women had no trouble believing the Lord had kept His word.

"Come," said the angel, "see the place where the Lord lay." The loyal women were in the wrong place—looking for the living among the dead. Of course, it is customary to find dead men in a cemetery. But not *this* man! In spite of the certainty of His death, the binding of the graveclothes, the stone at the entrance of the tomb, the seal of the Roman government, and the soldiers placed on watch—Jesus was not there.

Finally, consider the *Proof*. The rolled-away stone, the broken seal, the terrified guards, the empty tomb, the words of the angel—those are proofs that Jesus rose. Had His enemies been able to produce His body, surely they would have done so.

Later there were many witnesses. Seen first by the women—a reward for their love and loyalty—Christ was then seen by Simon Peter and later by other apostles, more than five hundred brethren, James, and Paul. The changed lives of multitudes of people who claim Christ as their Lord attest that He lives. He lives in our hearts.

July 7

I say to you, arise, take up your bed, and go to your house.
(Mark 2:11)

Those words spoke Christ to the paralytic man lowered down to Him from the roof of the house. It is a command more of us need to hear, for some of us are paralyzed by fear. We are scared saints lying upon beds of fearfulness. Hear the Lord command, "Get up and walk!"

Some saints are shackled by misplaced loyalties. We cannot get up and stand tall because we associate with folks whose minds are mixed up and whose hearts are bad. Some are paralyzed by feelings of guilt. The specter of evil deeds unconfessed haunts us still.

Weighted down thus, our witness is hampered; our usefulness is negligible; our service is limited; our joy almost nonexistent. We look like the prodigal son in the pig pen, walking in the mud of immorality, viewing life from a garbage can level, and smelling like the stench of the sty.

Oh, how we need to hear the message of freedom—get up, pick up your mat, go home, you're free! You are no longer paralyzed by what men think about you, no longer shackled by bad habits. Get out from under peer group pressure and follow the Prince of Peace.

Through Christ you can tuck your affliction under your arm and walk home free; through Christ your enemies will hang on the very gallows they prepare for you. Through Christ you can leap over walls and run through troops. Through Christ burdens are lifted.

The cross is God's answer to solve man's sin problem. When God gives you the victory, opens a door, breaks a shackling fetter, then rise up, pick up your bed, go on home, glorify God, and walk in newness of life until your walking days are over.

July 8

And no one puts new wine into old wineskins. (Mark 2:22)

The dual parable of the old garment and the old wineskins is told in all of the synoptic Gospels. It was our Lord's purpose to teach the Pharisees that He had not come to patch up Judaism. It was not His intention to try to keep the old by adding a little of the new.

Christ made it known that the old and the new were not to be confused—and not just because their outsides were different, but there were irreconcilable differences on the inside. There were essential differences between what Christ taught and what the religious leaders of the day taught. Any attempt to bring them together would result in an explosion. The right thing to do was to put new wine in a new wineskin.

Biblical Christianity is not an attempt to regulate conduct from the outside. Christ works from within. It is because of that internal operation that some wineskins are headed for a bursting out, a spilling over, a perishing.

Being in Christ is to be a new creation. God's folks are people who have been born anew from above, given a new name with a new Spirit living in them—folks who have put off the old man and put on the new. We obey a new commandment to love one another—new because it is based on the love shown at Calvary, that new event in history that was earthshaking in consequences, cataclysmic in effect, universally beneficial, and the epitome of love.

In Christ we have new treasures that moths cannot eat, rust cannot corrupt, nor thieves steal. Let us practice the new life in Christ in the strength of the Holy Spirit.

July 9

Then He took the child by the hand. (Mark 5:41)

In Numbers 5:1–4 God commanded Moses to maintain the purity of the Israelite community by removing certain people from the camp: (1) lepers, (2) those afflicted with certain diseases, and (3) those who had touched dead bodies.

From a health point of view, such cleanliness was necessary. So far as hygiene was concerned, the spread of disease was prevented. From a ceremonial point of view, the ritualistic purity of the congregation had to be maintained.

Israel was to be separate from sin and defilement; she was to realize through her rituals that a holy God would not tolerate uncleanness.

Now follow the earthly ministry of the Lord Jesus Christ. There came a leper to Jesus, begging Him, falling down, kneeling before Him, and saying, "If You are willing, You can make me clean!" (Mark 1:40). Moved with compassion, the Lord put forth His hand, touched him, and said, "I am willing; be cleansed."

In another incident, at the home of Jairus (one of the rulers of the synagogue), that leader's twelve-year-old daughter died. Having entered in where she was lying, Jesus took her by the hand and said, "Little girl, I say to you, arise." Immediately she awakened from death.

Christ did not shrink away in horror or separate Himself or tell those people, "Go away from Me; you're unclean!" No. He touched them, and by the contact they were healed.

> Have Thine own way, Lord! Have Thine own way!
> Wounded and weary, help me, I pray!
> Power—all power—surely is Thine!
> Touch me and heal me, Savior divine!
>
> *Adelaide A. Pollard*

July 10

For from within, out of the heart of men, proceed evil thoughts.
(Mark 7:21)

If our thoughts are on the level of a housefly, we will have a garbage-pail view of life. It is not difficult to see how evil thoughts come out of an evil heart. Here is one difference between the carnal Christian and the spiritual Christian. The carnal saint is more apt to give way to his thoughts; he is more likely to give away a piece of his mind; he is more prone to carry out the evil he thinks.

On the other hand, the spiritual saint finds that the nearer he draws to Christ, the greater becomes his battle with evil thoughts. The spiritual saint partakes of the power given by the Holy Spirit to *not* carry out the evil he thinks. However, the inner struggle with evil thoughts does continue.

R. B. Munger told of a stranger who was chatting one day with an old mountaineer. This mountaineer had two dogs that happened to be about the same size. The dogs were fighting each other continually. The visitor asked the old man which dog usually won. The man chewed his tobacco for a while in silence, and then he said, "The one I feeds the most!"

God has seen fit to suggest themes for our thoughts (Philippians 4:8). We need to focus our minds on the Word of God and thank Him for His Word, which elevates our thoughts and makes us more like the Lord Jesus Christ. Repeatedly God exhorts us to have the mind of Christ (1 Corinthians 2:16); to be renewed in the spirit of our minds (Ephesians 4:23); not to think too highly of ourselves (Romans 12:3); to set our thoughts on things above; and to remember that to be spiritually minded is life and peace (Romans 8:6). Thank the Lord Jesus Christ for cleansing our hearts, enabling us today to think His thoughts.

July 11

He has done all things well. He makes both the deaf to hear and the mute to speak. (Mark 7:37)

See here not just any deaf and dumb man, but see every man. For that man was a picture of all men. Every one of us is born into this world deaf to the things of a holy God (1 Corinthians 2:14). Some men will not accept this painful diagnosis, but that is because they are deaf.

God speaks, and we do not hear. He speaks in the thunder, the winds of the hurricane, the tremors of the earthquake, the eruption of the volcano, the devastation of the flood, the roar of the lion, the chirping of the bird, and the cooing of the baby. Said the psalmist, "The heavens declare the glory of God, and the firmament shows His handiwork. Day unto day utters speech, and night unto night reveals knowledge. There is no speech nor language where their voice is not heard" (Psalm 19:1–3). He speaks, but we do not hear.

He speaks not only in nature but in history. He speaks in experiences—heartbreak, accident, joys, and sorrows. He speaks in the conscience. He speaks through His prophets and angels; He speaks through His Son, the Lord Jesus Christ. He speaks through the Bible, His Word. Yet we do not hear. We are like the men who killed Stephen; they stopped their ears (Acts 7:57).

The wax of sin is hardened in our ears. All the while, in love, God pleads with all of us to accept His Son who loved us so much that He paid the penalty for our sins and shed His own blood at Calvary. Open your ears, and God can work on some other parts of you.

Once you get your hearing straightened out, it affects the rest of your body and being. The Lord will put a spring in your step, send angels to guide your feet, put running in your legs, music in your spirit, a ring on your finger, clapping in your hands, joy in your heart, a crown on your head, wipe tears from your eyes, and put heaven in your view!

July 12

Immediately the father of the child cried out and said with tears, "Lord, I believe; help my unbelief!" (Mark 9:24)

The child's condition. The boy was in bad shape. The accounts given in the synoptics (Matthew 17; Luke 9) show it is not difficult to understand why the father of this child was so distraught. We learn that the boy was possessed with a vehement, foul, unclean spirit that made the child have seizures, cry out, foam at the mouth, gnash his teeth and pine away.

The father's faith. The father's heart was deeply stirred with anguish as he sought help for his only child. Having heard of the power of the man Jesus, the father believed that the boy could be healed by Him. First he brought the child to the disciples, but they could not help him.

Then he brought the son to Jesus and said, "But if You can do anything, have compassion on us and help us" (v. 22). He had shown faith, but it was weak. He must be made to recognize that such doubt hinders prayer. Full faith places the power of God at the disposal of the believer.

The Savior's success. "If You can do anything" is then thrown back to the father by Christ, who said, "If you can believe, all things are possible." With those words still ringing in his ears, the father of the boy replied: "Lord, I believe; help my unbelief!"

Then the Savior said, "Bring him here to Me" (Matthew 17:17). They did, and the Lord Jesus rebuked the demon, which then left the child. The boy was cured from that very hour. You see then what kind of a Savior we have. When He shed His blood at Calvary and then rose from the grave, He proved His ability to be our Savior. Since He has done the greater thing already, what is there now He will not succeed in doing?

July 13

Let the little children come to Me, and do not forbid them.
(Mark 10:14)

Some parents and other relatives brought little children to the Lord Jesus, hoping He would lay His hands upon them, pray, and bless them. Perhaps some who were brought were infants, as well as children old enough to get about on their own. However, the disciples stepped in and rebuked those who had brought the children.

Possibly they thought the Lord's time was too valuable to waste on children, or that it was belittling to deal with little people. Perhaps some felt it was an imposition, abusing the Lord's good nature, taking advantage of Him. Perhaps their concept of the kingdom of God was a poor one.

Whatever the cause for attempting to drive away the children, obviously their sense of a child's worth was inadequate. God is the One who decides who are the inhabitants of His kingdom. Men make up all kinds of rules, restrictions, regulations; but when they get finished with their requirements, God has the final say as to who will and who will not see or enter into the kingdom.

A child does not have to become an adult in order to be accepted by the Lord Jesus Christ. That is the marvel and joy of these words, "Let the little children come to Me, and do not forbid them; for of such is the kingdom of God." In fact, we learn that grown-ups must become as children. Christ said: "Whoever does not receive the kingdom of God as a little child will by no means enter it" (Mark 10:15).

Adult hardness must give way to softness; independence must become dependence; skepticism must give way to faith, and indifference must become eagerness. May this day be filled with that simple childlike faith that we may experience the arms of Christ around us, proving that He is still in the blessing business.

July 14

And Peter, remembering, said to Him, "Rabbi, look! The fig tree which You cursed has withered away." (Mark 11:21)

Having lodged at the house of Lazarus overnight, the Lord returned to Jerusalem the next day. Becoming hungry along the way, He spied a solitary fig tree planted by the roadside. From a distance He saw leaves, but when He got closer He discovered there were no figs on the tree.

"Let no one eat fruit from you ever again," said Christ. The next day when the disciples passed by, they discovered the tree dried up from its roots, utterly destroyed.

Because there were leaves on the tree, Christ believed He would find fruit there also. Whether the season had come or not, a fig tree with leaves is expected to have fruit. The Lord's expectation was not unreasonable. The fig tree was a symbol of Israel (Hosea 9:10; Joel 1:7). At that point in history the nation was described as a fig tree with leaves but no fruit.

Gentiles were barren too but not as guilty as Israel. Much is expected of him to whom much is given. If you have leaves, then you should have fruit. If there is no fruit, then judgment is in order.

We Christians have many leaves that point to our profession of faith, but there should be fruit produced also in our lives. If we are not becoming more like Jesus Christ, if the fruit of the Spirit (Galatians 5:22–23) is not being manifested, are we not in danger of being pruned (John 15:2)? Emphasis is upon service, so there is no thought of losing salvation. Yet we are impressed with the seriousness of the failure to bring forth fruit.

July 15

A second time the rooster crowed. Then Peter called to mind the word that Jesus had said to him, "Before the rooster crows twice, you will deny me three times." And when he thought about it, he wept. (Mark 14:72)

Sometimes when a word of warning is remembered it stops us dead in our tracks. We are turned around. A word stored in the heart enables us to please the Lord; it prevents us from sinning against our God. Sometimes a word recalls the love the Lord has for us. We remember what we used to be and where we were when the Lord found us; we remember His grace.

We remember the precious blood shed at Calvary, and our hearts are broken. We remember how often we have stumbled and fallen, and yet the Lord picked us up each time and started us on our way again. We remember that every time we cried out He heard our cry and pitied every groan.

With open hearts the crowing of the cock, the circumstances of life, can be used of the Lord to bring to our minds His will and His Word for our lives. We are thankful for the convicting presence of the Holy Spirit, for the realization that we have sinned, for the genuine sorrow we feel for our sin.

Praise Him, for "The LORD is near to those who have a broken heart, and saves such as have a contrite spirit" (Psalm 34:18). "A broken and a contrite heart—these, O God, You will not despise" (Psalm 51:17).

In Isaiah 57:15 we read, "I dwell in the high and holy place, with him who has a contrite and humble spirit, to revive the spirit of the humble, and to revive the heart of the contrite ones." Then said the prophet, "But on this one will I look: on him who is poor and of a contrite spirit, and who trembles at My word" (Isaiah 66:2).

July 16

Then the veil of the temple was torn in two from top to bottom.
(Mark 15:38)

What was the specific meaning of that supernatural event at the crucifixion? It meant that whereas only the priest could enter into God's presence on behalf of the people in the old dispensation, God through His High Priest, Jesus Christ, had now removed all barriers.

Before Calvary nobody could enter freely into the presence of the Most High God to worship. Now there are no restrictions. No more sacrifices and offerings for sin are needed, for the one offering of Christ Himself satisfied or propitiated God. The Holy Spirit witnesses to this.

God Himself opened a new, living, permanent way into His presence. Now the humblest, poorest believer can enter in. Thanks to Christ we have the free right to enter in boldly to the throne of grace. What formerly only the high priest could do once a year the Christian can do anytime.

The throne of grace is open; the presence of God is freely entered into—all because of what Christ did at Calvary. What joy to know your heavenly Father is available at any time—day or night, early in the morning or in the midnight hour. He is available in church at prayer meeting or at home in your secret closet. He is available when you are in trouble, in emergencies, whether healthy or sick. He is there.

Through the blood of Christ the door to heaven is open. You can call on Him anytime. Because of His love for you demonstrated at Calvary He will answer. Rejoice then because of Calvary. All you need do to make contact with heaven is to say, "Father!"

I bring you good tidings of great joy. (Luke 2:10)

Announcing the birth of Jesus Christ to the shepherds keeping watch over their flocks by night, an angel of the Lord said: "Do not be afraid, for behold, I bring you good tidings of great joy which will be to all people."

The Saxon word *godespell* means good story, and from it we have derived the modern word *gospel*, often rendered "good news" or "glad tidings."

Christians everywhere proclaim the fact that God the Son became a man, died on the cross for our sins, was buried, then rose from the grave to live forevermore. That is the gospel.

The text in Luke (2:10) is limited to the incarnation, or birth, of the Savior who is Christ the Lord. Christmas reminds us of that fact, even though we do not know the exact year, month, or day Jesus Christ was born.

That He was born is a certainty. We are sure that He grew into manhood, then died on the cross of Calvary for our sins. What better gift than salvation through faith in Him? What better news could anyone ever hear? Imagine, here is a gospel that expels fear, brings enjoyment, and is meant for everyone!

I am reminded of the story of a five-year-old boy in South Carolina who had one line in a kindergarten Christmas play. He was to appear in angel's garb to say, "I bring you good tidings!"

The lad had a little trouble learning his line until his mother explained that *tidings* meant "news." On the night of the performance the little angel became stage-struck. After a long embarrassing silence, he finally blurted out, "Hey, I got news for you!"

July 18

And behold, there was a man in Jerusalem whose name was Simeon. (Luke 2:25)

Simeon was a very common name, and what little we do know about this particular man we learn from this passage in Luke. His background is not mentioned; no titles, no genealogy, he held no high position or office, possessed no great wealth—he was just "a man in Jerusalem."

Yet something more is said. He was righteous, just; he was right with the Lord, having trusted in the coming Messiah and having shown that faith by offering in faith those sacrifices required by the law.

He was also devout, literally "taking hold well." Carefully, surely, cautiously, reverently, circumspectly, he devoted his life to the Lord.

Note that Simeon waited for the "Consolation of Israel." Consolation of Israel is another title of Jesus Christ denoting His Messiahship. In the Greek it is *paraklēsis* ("Paraclete"), elsewhere translated "comforter, advocate." It is interesting too that Simeon's "waiting" is the same verb rendered "looking for" with respect to that blessed hope, the glorious appearing of Jesus Christ (Titus 2:13).

Simeon was also blessed to have the Holy Spirit resting upon him, as did Bezaleel to work on the Tabernacle, Balaam to prophesy, Othniel, Gideon, and Jephthah to judge; Samson to judge and be strong; Saul to rule; and Ezekiel to receive visions. Upon Simeon there was a holy influence from the Holy Spirit.

One of the blessings from the Spirit was the revelation that Simeon would not die before seeing the Messiah. See Him Simeon did! What a blessing it is to serve the true and living God.

July 19

Now there was one, Anna, a prophetess . . . of a great age.
(Luke 2:36)

As a prophetess, Anna followed in the footsteps of Miriam (Exodus 15:20), Huldah (2 Chronicles 34:22), Noadiah (Nehemiah 6:14), Isaiah's wife (Isaiah 8:3), and others. Married perhaps at fifteen, widowed at twenty-two, she had been a widow nearly eighty-four years. That would make her approximately one hundred six years old.

Now there were in Jerusalem at that time four kinds of people: (1) The Pharisees, who expected a political deliverer, (2) the Sadducees, who expected nothing, (3) the majority of the people who expected whatever was expected of them, namely, whatever their religious leaders looked for, and (4) a small group of pious folks, a blessed few, who looked for, longed for the spiritual deliverance, or consolation, of Jerusalem. God always has a witness. Judaism was bankrupt, but there were those who believed. Anna was one of them, a remarkable woman, dedicated, loyal to the Temple, serving God night and day with fastings and prayer.

God blessed Anna by assuring she was there when the baby Jesus was brought in. The Holy Spirit made Simeon come (Luke 2:25, 27), but God knew Anna would be in the Temple anyway. He fixed the timing. She arrived at the exact moment.

The result was that her testimony was added to that of Simeon's. She celebrated the praises of the Christ child in answer to this act of God that she experienced in her old age. She talked about the child to all who were looking for the liberation of Jerusalem. She publicly proclaimed the Messiah's arrival to all.

Thank God we too met Jesus Christ one day—not as a babe, and not as a dead man hanging on a cross. We met Him not as an angel spirit. We met Him as a living Savior with all power in His hands, resurrected from the dead to die no more.

July 20

But say the word, and my servant will be healed. (Luke 7:7)

The centurion, held in high esteem by the Jews, had a servant boy, possibly his only slave, who was sick with paralysis (Matthew 8:6) and about to die. The Lord Jesus was on His way to the man's house when friends of the centurion stated that this professional soldier felt neither ceremonially clean nor morally worthy to come to Jesus or have Him come to his house.

Through the messengers the soldier said, "Speak the word only, and my servant shall be healed. I am myself a man under authority, but also one *in* authority. Those under me instantly obey me. I say to one, 'Go,' and he goes; to another, 'Come,' and he comes; to my servant, 'Do this,' and he does it."

What he implied was this: If he, a centurion, could issue orders that were immediately obeyed, how much more would Christ, who has all authority, be obeyed.

God's word is *efficient*; it does successfully whatever it is sent out to do. His words are not wasted puffs of hot air (Isaiah 55:11). God's word enlightens; through the Bible the invisible is seen, the unsearchable is revealed, the mysterious is taught.

God's word is *essential*; first, because it is true. Truth is fundamental. Second, because it creates. Without the word of God the world could not continue to exist, for His creative word also sustains.

God's word is *effective*; Jesus Christ spoke the word and the centurion's servant was healed, sight unseen. So it is with us. We believe in Him whom we have not yet seen. By taking Him at His word our sin-sick souls have been healed.

~

July 21

Our Lord had been very busy healing, preaching, and teaching. The opposition of His enemies and the interference of relatives undoubtedly added to His weariness and fatigue. When evening came He said to the disciples, "Let us cross over to the other side of the lake." Utterly tired by the events of the day, He fell asleep in the stern of the boat.

Suddenly there came thundering down the narrow gorges dividing the hills around the Sea of Galilee, a great windstorm, shaking and churning the water. Huge waves covered the boat, beating it back and forth, filling it with water.

Then the Lord arose and rebuked the wind with a single word, "Peace!" The wind ceased. To the raging waters of the sea He said, "Be still!" There was a great calm. A thousand years earlier the psalmist had written: "He calms the storm, so that its waves are still" (Psalm 107:29). Jesus Christ is the Lord of all nature. "And no waters can swallow the ship where lies the Master of ocean, and earth, and skies."

"How timid you are," said Christ. "Where is your faith?" It must be understood that they had some measure of faith. But it was not enough; it was inadequate for the crisis. To successfully face the storms of life you need a *patient* faith, one willing to leave everything in God's hands. It is not a do-nothing faith but one that does not try to hurry God.

Second, a *powerful* faith is needed; a weak faith entertains fears and is cowardly. Third, a faith to face adversity must adequately recognize the significance of the *presence* of Christ. With Him on board the ship of life, you cannot go wrong.

July 22

But as He went, the multitudes thronged Him. (Luke 8:42)

There is really nothing new under the sun. Over nineteen hundred years ago the crowds that followed Jesus Christ did so with a variety of motives. Some people hoped He would be their leader, a revolutionary to kick out the Romans and reestablish the kingdom of Israel in the heyday glory of David and Solomon.

Some followed merely to get a free meal of bread and fish. Even today some of those in city missions are there just for a bowl of soup or a place to sleep; some of these in churches are there just to get a vote at election time, a customer at their store, bank, beauty salon or funeral parlor.

Some followed Christ hoping to see a show, something spectacular performed, a miracle—blind eyes opened, deaf ears unstopped, dumb tongues loosened, crippled limbs straightened, the dead raised.

Some were there to spy on Jesus Christ and report His activities to the religious rulers. It would appear some were anxious to see Christ and the Pharisees "git it on," mix it up, battle it out, and such people—instigators and trouble-makers—mixed in with the crowds.

Such people still are found in our churches. Not content to see things run smoothly, they insinuate, gossip, spread rumors, tell half-truths, and impugn motives. On the lookout for trouble, when they smell it they are as happy as a bedbug in a blood bank. All kinds of people were in the crowds; undoubtedly there were genuine truth-seekers included.

Interrupted on His way to the house of Jairus by the healing of the woman with the issue of blood, the Lord finally reached the synagogue ruler's house. "Do not weep; she is not dead, but sleeping," He said. The crowd there laughed Him to scorn. But the Lord put out the crowd and went on to do what only He could do—raise the dead.

July 23

*Do not be afraid of those who kill the body, and after that have
no more that they can do. But I will show you whom you
should fear: Fear Him who, after He has killed, has power to
cast into hell; yes, I say to you, fear Him! (Luke 12:4–5)*

When one of our very active and prominent church
members was murdered, the question came up, "Why did
God permit such a good Christian to die in such a manner?" That reminded me of the story of a very talkative
lady seated beside a minister on a plane. Suddenly the
plane lurched because of wind turbulence.

Said she to the preacher, "You have an answer to everything. Why don't you do something about this terrible ride?
You're a man of God; this is your department!"

The preacher turned and said calmly, "Lady, this is not
my department. I am in sales, not in management."

Indeed, God is sovereign. He does as He desires when
and where He pleases. As manager He is not obligated to
explain His actions to us. Job was a righteous man, but
God permitted Satan to afflict him; Job's seven sons and
three daughters and many servants were killed. Naboth
was a good man, but Jezebel saw to it that he was slain so
Ahab her husband could have Naboth's vineyard.

Tradition states Isaiah was sawn asunder; Jeremiah was
stoned to death in Egypt. John the Baptist was decapitated;
James was killed by King Herod with a sword. Stephen
was stoned to death. There is nothing new about the murder of believers.

What is important is this: Where do we go from here?
Christ answers: "My friends, don't be afraid of those who
want to kill you. They can only kill the body; they have no
power over your soul. You fear God, who has the power to
kill and then cast into hell." In an age where human life is
not held sacred, let us not fall into a spirit of fear, but let us
trust God that He will take care of His own.

July 24

If anyone comes to Me and does not hate his father and mother, wife and children, brothers and sisters, yes, and his own life also, he cannot be My disciple. And whoever does not bear his cross and come after Me cannot be My disciple. (Luke 14:26–27)

The Lord Jesus made here a deliberate attempt to check the unthinking multitude. He turned and said to them, "If you want to be My disciple, you must hate—that's what I said, hate. Hate your parents, your wife and children, your closest relatives, indeed, hate your own soul!"

The hatred here is not that psychological sense of vindictiveness, that personal "I'll get you if it's the last thing I do" kind of thing. The Jews were admonished in Leviticus 19:17: "You shall not hate your brother in your heart."

The New Testament saint is warned that hatred is a work of the flesh (Galatians 5:20); any man who hates his brother while professing to be a Christian is a liar, walks in darkness, and is a murderer (1 John 2:11; 3:15; 4:20).

Perhaps the negative way of expressing that characteristic of discipleship might be made clearer by a positive expression recorded in Matthew 10:37: "He who loves father or mother more than Me is not worthy of Me. And he who loves son or daughter more than Me is not worthy of Me."

To love here is *phileō*; it signifies affection, fondness. Basically the point is this: God wants first place. Natural affection, blood ties, or race relationships must not be allowed to weaken your relationship with Jesus Christ.

In other words, your love for Jesus Christ is so strong that whatever it is you feel for others is likened unto hatred. By comparison, whoever and whatever is in second place fades into insignificance because Christ is in first place.

July 25

. . . my sheep which was lost . . . the piece which I lost . . . he was lost. . . . (Luke 15:6, 9, 24)

What does it mean to be lost? Read the fifteenth chapter of the Gospel of Luke and you will discover that, basically, lostness is *separation*. Christ told the parables of the sheep, the silver coin, and the son to illustrate the truth that God desires to save the very ones whom the Pharisees rejected and despised.

First, understand that lostness is a state of *stupidity*. The sheep is indeed a stupid animal. Head down, it wanders about, nibbling and paying no attention to where it is going.

"All we like sheep have gone astray; we have turned, every one, to his own way" (Isaiah 53:6). Separated from the shepherd, the sheep is unprotected, defenseless, and at the mercy of wolves.

Second, lostness is *worthlessness*. In this parable the woman lost her silver coin. What good is money that is lost? As a boy I used to walk up and down Broad Street in Philadelphia and fish money out of the subway grates, using a fishing sinker attached to chewing gum made sticky with fire from a match. The coins I lifted up were useless until they got into my hands.

Money that is lost gains no interest; it is useless. The man who is without Christ likewise is without a purpose in life.

Third, lostness is *misery*. By choice the young man widely known as the "prodigal son" left home. He got in with a bad crowd, lost all he had, and was reduced to the role of a beggar with a garbage-can view of life.

That is what lostness means: stupidity, uselessness, and misery. Above all, it is separation from God. Such was our condition when Jesus Christ shed His blood for us. I am glad He found me. Did He find you too? Then rejoice.

July 26

So Jesus answered and said, "Were there not ten cleansed?
But where are the nine?" (Luke 17:17)

That question has haunted me. Why did the other nine
not return? What makes one man grateful and another
thoughtless? Why does one man give thanks and another
show ingratitude? In this case all were healed, all were
cleansed of their leprosy. All had faith and stepped out at
our Lord's command to go to the priests. Why then did
not the other nine return and give thanks?

Once healed, did the nine then remember their Jewish-
ness and separate themselves from the Samaritan? Were
they simply forgetful? Were they overly concerned about
obeying the law and fulfilling their ceremonial duty? Or
was it maybe pride?

Did their remembrance of hard times fail to be erased
by the new blessing? Did an attitude that emphasized how
long they had had leprosy, and how rough it was to live as
a leper, overwhelm them and smother the joy of the present
cure and cleansing?

Faith they had—otherwise they would not have taken
one step to go to the priests. They believed in the power of
Christ but seemingly did not surrender to Him. They had
faith—but lacked the spirit of thankfulness for the outcome
of that faith.

How sad! Ingratitude makes men ineligible to receive
further blessings. The other nine men would never hear
the Lord Jesus say to them, "Your faith has made you
whole." In other words, if this man would maintain his
faith, he would see still further blessings from the Lord.

May you be a grateful Christian today, experiencing
anew what it means to be made well or whole by faith.
Discover today that gratitude for *one* blessing obtains *another* blessing.

July 27

For the Son of Man has come to seek and to save that which was lost. (Luke 19:10)

Zacchaeus was a rich man, having used well his office of chief among the tax collectors, or publicans. However, his wealth did not bring him happiness; something was missing in his life. By the grace of God, the Holy Spirit moved him to seek Jesus of Nazareth. So this little man, unable to see Jesus over the crowd, climbed up into a sycamore tree to see the Lord as He passed that way.

Christ met the need in the life of Zacchaeus, for the very object of Christ's appearing was the salvation of Zacchaeus and all like him.

When I was a boy I loved to play such games as "Hide and Go Seek," "Hot Beans and Butter," and "Kick the Can." In those more-or-less carefree days, all of life was one big game. The Depression, welfare, the Second World War—those did not hinder us or detract from the fun we had playing in the streets of Philadelphia.

However, God is not playing a game with us. The stakes are too high. His name and character are on the line, so to speak. Our never-perishing souls are up for grabs. It is either heaven or hell. So God seeks out the children of men.

He searches because there are those who hide behind race, skin color, patriotism, tradition, secret societies, education, humanitarian organizations, and the democratic process. Some even hide behind water baptism, church membership, and church service.

Where were you when the Lord Jesus found you, or have you forgotten? Rejoice today as you contemplate the wonderful fact that God became a man and then personally sought you out, found you up a tree, out on a limb—and He saved you.

July 28

Now it was about the sixth hour, and there was darkness over all the earth until the ninth hour. (Luke 23:44)

When you read the Gospels, keep in mind that Calvary was the high point. Do not get bogged down by the healings and other signs along the way. Sure, they are magnificent—blind eyes were opened, tied tongues loosed, deaf ears unstopped, withered limbs restored, shaking hands and trembling legs steadied, demons cast out, and the dead raised.

But the compassion shown was also calculated to speed up the trip to Calvary, to hasten becoming an offering for sin. See then the Lamb of God hanging there on the cross between two robbers. He was crucified about 9:00 a.m. Those first three hours were filled with physical pain.

Despite the terrible torment, Christ never said a complaining word. In perfect communion with the Father, He showed His concern for others. Then the darkness came over the whole land, from the sixth hour to the ninth hour, noon to 3:00 p.m.

Jesus had not complained about the physical pain earlier; now the judgment falling upon Him was not just physical. His soul, His inmost being, His holy, spotless, righteous soul became the great sin offering. The physical suffering, bad as it was—the cruel spikes in His hands and feet, the beating suffered earlier, the crown of thorns mashed down upon the forehead—was not the main issue. The great agony was when He who knew no sin became sin. At that point the demands of the Father's justice were met. Satisfied with the offering, God is satisfied with you—and with all who accept Jesus Christ.

July 29

Jesus said to them, "My food is to do the will of Him who sent Me, and to finish His work." (John 4:34)

After the Lord spoke to the Samaritan woman and she left to broadcast her discovery, the disciples begged Him to nourish Himself with the food they had just purchased. But Christ replied, "I have food to eat of which you do not know." The disciples misinterpreted His response—being so caught up with the physical, they could not see the spiritual meaning of His words.

As they wondered if someone else had given him to eat, Christ said, "My food, my nourishment is to do the will of Him who sent Me, and to finish the work He gave Me to do." With those words He sought to teach them God's priority. The most important thing in the world is the will of God.

Christ knew that He had to be about His Father's business. To do the will of the Father was more than food to His soul. Refreshment and sustenance were His through obedience to the will of God the Father. In talking to the woman at the well Christ was carrying out His divine commission, obeying divine orders.

What a lesson for us to learn today when everyone seeks to do his own thing. Selfishness is the only food some people eat, and they choke on it. When their wills clash, they fight. The saint must earnestly devote himself to doing the will of God and to being strengthened by God to do that will.

Through prayer and through study of the Bible, genuine Christians feast spiritually, and they are blessed. You will discover today that if it is indeed your heart's desire to do the will of God, the Lord Jesus will feed you till you want no more.

Guide me, O Thou great Jehovah, Pilgrim through this barren land;
  I am weak, but Thou art mighty; Hold me with Thy pow'rful hand;
Bread of heaven, Bread of heaven, Feed me till I want no more,
  Feed me till I want no more.

William Williams

July 30

Therefore if the Son makes you free, you shall be free indeed.
(John 8:36)

"You're charged with assault and battery," declared the judge severely.

"But, Your Honor, I was only swinging my arms in fun, and my hand hit his nose," protested the prisoner. "I've got a right to swing my arms, ain't I?"

"That's true," agreed the judge. "But your right to swing your arms stops where the other man's nose begins."

What some people call liberty is really license. Murderers want to be free of the death penalty. Some children wish they were free from their parents' discipline. Some parents want to be free of their responsibility to their children.

Homosexuals desire to be free of their guilty consciences—a guilt not imposed by man-made restrictions on their "freedom" but created by violation of God-given commandments.

Then there are church folks who want to be free of the God-ordained authority of the pastor (Hebrews 13:17). Some women strive to free themselves of the yoke of male dominance (Genesis 3:16).

What an age we live in! Everybody wants to do his own thing. Yet with all of the cries for liberation, men remain slaves—to sin, self, and Satan.

Why? Because only Jesus Christ can set men free. Only He can break the power of the sin that enslaves us. Patrick Henry was right when he cried, "Give me liberty or give me death!"

Without Jesus Christ the liberator, death is exactly what you get; but if the Son of God shall make you free, you shall be free indeed. If you are free indeed, enjoy your freedom!

July 31

. . . before Abraham was, I AM. (John 8:58)

The verb used for Abraham is "to become" (*ginomai*), so that we might render the verse, "Before Abraham became"; "before he came into existence." That suggests, as is true of all humans, that there was a time when Abraham was not.

In the minds of His inquisitive hearers the words Jesus spoke pointed to the title *Jehovah,* revealed to Moses in Exodus 3:14. Understanding therefore that the Lord claimed deity, but unwilling to accept that claim, the Jews believed Him guilty of blasphemy and picked up stones to kill Him.

We rejoice, however, that the Lord Jesus is the I AM of the Bible. Christ is a here-and-now Savior. He who says to you right now, "I am with you," will say tomorrow at twelve noon when you cry to Him, "Hey, I'm *still* with you!" He is not dead, but is "He who lives, and was dead, and, behold, I am alive forevermore" (Revelation 1:18).

When your way appears blocked and opportunities are slammed shut in your face, hear Him say, "I am the Door." When liars tell falsehoods about you and spread rumors that would ruin you, Jesus Christ says, "I am the Truth." When the darkness of sin encroaches and you begin to stumble, hear Him cry: "I am the Light of the world."

When preachers disappoint you, Christ states, "I am the Good Shepherd." When trouble arises and you are overwhelmed and do not know which way to turn, hear Him say, "I am the Way!" When depressed by the death of loved ones, He says, "I am the Resurrection and the Life."

He stands by your side right now. When your tomorrow becomes your today, Jesus Christ will be there. He who has brought you safe thus far will carry you home.

August 1

But they did not understand the things which He spoke to them. (John 10:6)

So often the Lord Jesus was not understood. The very ones He sought to save seemed not to understand. On one occasion He said, "Destroy this temple, and in three days I will raise it up." Not understanding that He spoke of His body, the Jews murmured, "It has taken forty-six years to build this temple, and will You raise it up in three days?" (John 2:19–21).

Again Christ said, "You must be born again." Not understanding He spoke of a spiritual rebirth, Nicodemus questioned the physical possibility of reentering his mother's womb (John 3:3–4). Again Christ said, "Whoever drinks of the water that I shall give him will never thirst. But the water that I shall give him will become in him a fountain of water springing up into everlasting life" (John 4:14). Not understanding He spoke of the indwelling Holy Spirit, the Samaritan woman at the well said, "Sir, give me this water, that I may not thirst, nor come here to draw" (John 4:15).

Later Christ said to His disciples, "I have food to eat of which you do not know." Not understanding that He spoke of His desire "to do the will of Him who sent Me, and to finish His work," the disciples said one to another, "Has anyone brought Him anything to eat?" (John 4:32–34).

When the Lord said, "And you shall know the truth, and the truth shall make you free," the Pharisees, not understanding He spoke of their spiritual bondage, replied, "We are Abraham's descendants, and have never been in bondage to anyone" (John 8:32–34).

Our Lord was often misunderstood. We who love Him must continue to ask the Father for help to better understand the Word of God and thereby better serve the Lord Jesus Christ, the Good Shepherd.

~

August 2

Jesus knew that His hour had come that He should depart from this world to the Father. (John 13:1)

The Lord Jesus knew His *hour.* In the Bible, *hour* must be interpreted according to how it is used in the context. At the wedding at Cana of Galilee it was not yet His hour (John 2:4)—the time to show Messianic power by working miracles was not for Mary to decide. When the angry mob sought to lay hands on Him, He slipped from their presence, for it was not His hour to be taken (John 7:30; 8:20).

There in the upper room the Lord referred to His physical death. Yet His *hour* embraces more than His death; it includes all the following events including the resurrection and the ascension.

The Lord referred also to His *home.* To depart from this evil world system was to go to the Father in heaven. Christ yearned to be back home with the Father. This is no prodigal son in a pig sty who one day said, "I will arise and go to my father." No. Here is the only begotten Son: holy, righteous, without deceit or guile found in His mouth; one without sin about to become sin for you and for me; one who says, "Father, the hour has come . . . I have finished the work which You have given Me to do. And now, O Father, glorify Me together with Yourself, with the glory which I had with You before the world was" (John 17:1, 4–5).

The Lord Jesus had a *hope.* He knew what awaited Him here on earth. There was treachery afoot, imminent denial, physical pain, mockery, death. Worse, He who knew no sin would be made sin. Yet Christ loved His own who were in the world and loved them unto the end. Rest assured that He loves you still, now that He is glorified and in heaven. Rejoice because you too have the hope of a home in heaven when your hour comes.

August 3

Peace I leave with you, My peace I give to you; not as the world gives do I give to you. (John 14:27)

What men cannot give, God gives. For God's method is first of all to deal with the inner person and inner peace, not that outside thing that so much depends upon circumstances. Note that the Lord calls this peace His own. In a peculiar way this peace is His legacy, something handed down, bequeathed; it is a bequest. So His distinctive brand, the only true peace, He leaves as a legacy. That which is His He leaves to His own.

It is also a gift; "I give to you." As the Prince of Peace whose Father is the God of Peace, He is ultimately qualified to give peace. The peace Christ leaves as a legacy and gives as a gift is one that will calm troubled hearts, regulate disordered minds, set your spirit at ease, banish your fears, take away agitation, dissolve frustration, and remove cowardice, making you bold as a lion.

There will be peace even when afflicted by the wiles of Delilah, the wickedness of Jezebel, the evil of Alexander, the taunts of Goliath, the magic of Jannes and Jambres, the dementia of King Saul, the haughtiness of Rabshakeh, the selfishness of Diotrophes, the pride of Nebuchadnezzar, the vengeance of Herodias, the blasphemy of Belshazzar, the plots of the Pharisees, the schemes of the Sadducees, the treachery of Judas, the carnality of Esau, or the jealous hatred of Cain!

The peace Christ gives abolishes heart-troubling fear and produces hope and joy. But first of all, there must be objective peace with God. Second, the subjective peace of God is available. The entire package is yours!

August 4

I will no longer talk much with you, for the ruler of this world is coming, and he has nothing in Me. (John 14:30)

The announcement that the Lord had but a little time left to converse with the disciples is tied in with the statement "The ruler of this world is coming." By it we learn that Christ knew what the devil was up to; He was aware of Satan's schemes. Reference is made to Judas and the men who would be sent out by the Sanhedrin to take Jesus.

Although wicked men are the tools, Satan behind the scenes is the manipulator. Christ had come to die, and no one could thwart His plan. What Christ did was voluntary; He wanted the disciples to understand that He knew what was happening.

Satan's inability to tempt Jesus to do evil is emphatically put: "and he has nothing in Me." The devil could not even get to first base; there was no old nature in Christ to be stirred up.

The devil is coming! That cruel creature comes with centuries of cunning craftiness; demons bow down before him; the prince of this world system, the deceiver of the nations, the grand liar, the power behind all tyranny, slavery, dope traffic, racism, and crime syndicates—he comes!

Let him come. For we stand hidden and protected in Christ, the Lamb of God, in whom the prince of the world could find no spot to set up a base of operations.

Our hope is built on nothing less than Jesus' blood and righteousness. Our hope is a person in whom the devil has nothing. Over the announcement that the devil is coming may we hear the words of that blessed hope—Jesus Christ returns! May we rejoice, for greater is He who is coming for us than he who is in the world. Even so, come, Lord Jesus!

August 5

But I have called you friends, for all things that I heard from My Father I have made known to you. (John 15:15)

They were called His friends because He disclosed certain facts to them. From the day He called them He taught them. That was the mark of genuine friendship. They did not always understand what He taught or preached, but that did not alter their relationship. He loved them and wanted them to know.

He made known to them that He was the Lord of nature when He changed water into wine (John 2:11); that it was His Father's house He cleansed (John 2:16); that He would rise from the dead (John 2:19); and that men must be born again (John 3:3).

He made known unto them that He could heal the impotent, give sight to the blind, walk on water; that He was the sent one from heaven, the Bread of life, the Light of the world, the liberator who sets men free indeed. He made known to them that He was the Good Shepherd, the Way, the Truth, the Resurrection and the Life, who raised the dead.

Today, making known the things of the Father is done by the Holy Spirit in the name of Jesus Christ. Though we are blood-bought slaves of Christ, we are also His friends. We do not always act like His friends, but our failure does not cancel the bond between us.

For the Lord Jesus is a friend who sticks closer than a brother (Proverbs 18:24); a friend whose wounds are faithful (Proverbs 27:6); a friend who loves at all times (Proverbs 17:17); a friend who gladly laid down His life for you and for me (John 15:13).

> Jesus is all the world to me,
>   My Friend in trials sore;
> I go to Him for blessings, and
>   He gives them o'er and o'er.
> Jesus is all the world to me,
>   And true to Him I'll be;
> O, how could I this Friend deny,
>   When He's so true to me?
>   Will L. Thompson

August 6

You did not choose Me, but I chose you and appointed [or-dained, KJV] you that you should go and bear fruit. (John 15:16)

We did not choose Christ; He chose us. It had to be that way because we were too dumb, too depraved, and too dead to have chosen God. He moved when we were dead, found us when we were lost, opened our eyes when we were blind, spoke when we were deaf, and loved us when we hated Him.

Not only were we *picked*, but we were *placed*. The word rendered *ordained* in the King James Version means "to put, place, appoint." The picker is also the placer. When I was a boy I picked blackberries for my aunt living in Elmwood. I did not leave the berries just any old place; I put them in a jar. When my aunt got through making blackberry dumpling, I put them in my stomach!

The God we serve appointed day and night, He ordained the seasons of the year, He placed the sun and moon in the sky, He named the stars and put them in their galactic sockets, and placed the planets in their orbits. Surely having bought us with Christ's own precious blood, He has the right to do with His property as He pleases.

Third, we see His desire that we be *productive*. Despite the cold snow of lethargy and lack of cooperation, the poison ivy of ingratitude, the weed of greed, the caterpillars of envy, the beetles of anxiety, the squirrels of covetousness, the gypsy moths of deceit, the groundhogs of gossip, and the high winds of adversity, the people the Lord picks and places are to be productive.

Our fruit is to become more like the Lord Jesus Christ. There is to be more and more evidence in our lives of the fruit of the Holy Spirit: love, joy, peace, longsuffering, gentleness, goodness, faith, meekness, self-control. Let us praise God, and let the fruit of our lips give thanks to Him for picking, placing, and producing.

August 7

Nevertheless I tell you the truth. It is to your advantage that I go away; for if I do not go away, the Helper will not come to you; but if I depart, I will send Him to you. (John 16:7)

Christ would remind us today that sometimes stumbling blocks, oppositions, and traps are put in our way, and we are often displeased, annoyed, discouraged, and made angry. Consequently some of us give up and quit instead of standing and withstanding.

Still others, trusting in their own ability, their own strength and strategies, try to fight their own battles. The result is all too often misery, despair, defeat, and ruin.

So hear the Lord saying, "I'm telling you these things now, because I won't be here with you later. I'm going away, and I want you to remember these things."

The talk about leaving them was unwelcome news to the disciples. Their reaction was one of sorrow. Preoccupied with their own sense of loss and despair, they simply could not grasp the full import of Christ's departure.

His predictions concerning His death were unheeded; likewise any talk about a resurrection was untenable. The joy of the Son returning to the Father was of course incomprehensible to them (John 14:28). The followers of Christ remained down in the dumps, disheartened, in deep sorrow.

Because He is the Truth, Christ said: "Nevertheless, I tell you the truth. I must go away. Indeed, it is to your advantage, to your profit that I go away."

Christ could not lie to them in order to try to cheer them up. For He knew that however much adverse circumstances might seem to shackle them, only the truth could set them free. Thank God for the Holy Spirit, the Spirit of truth, now living in us!

August 8

Jesus therefore, knowing all things that would come upon Him, went forward and said to them, "Whom are you seeking?" (John 18:4)

Betrayal. Christ knew whom Satan had inspired; He knew that the religious leaders conspired, and He knew what transpired between Judas and the priests. Yet Christ went forth to further bring about that which He had come to do.

Boldness. Judas was allowed to carry out his prearranged plan. Hypocritically, he repeatedly, fervently embraced the Lord and kissed the Master. But Christ undermined the impact of Judas' deceitful act. When Judas stepped back into the company of the armed crowd, the Lord with a bold stroke of courage asked the question that destroyed what Judas had hoped to accomplish.

Bewilderment. "Whom are you seeking?" The question took them by surprise, momentarily stopping them. Christ knew why they had come. They answered, "Jesus of Nazareth." With poise, majesty, and confidence Christ replied, "I am He."

Immediately they went back; they fell down, unnerved, befuddled, recoiling in confusion and fear. They picked up their deflated egos, dusted themselves off, and with trembling fear and loss of dignity again stood before the Lord. Again He asked, "Whom are you seeking?"

And they said a second time, "Jesus of Nazareth."

The Lord replied, "I have told you that I am He. I am the man; take Me!"

So it was—*betrayal* by Judas, the *boldness* of Jesus, the *bewilderment* of the Jews and the Romans. Jesus Christ had come to die, and that scene in Gethsemane was but another step toward Calvary.

August 9

Jesus said to him, "Thomas, because you have seen Me, you have believed. Blessed are those who have not seen and yet have believed." (John 20:29)

Thomas refused to believe that his fellow disciples had seen the risen Lord. But Christ understood Thomas; He knew the very nature of the man was so upset over the turn of events that he found it nearly impossible to believe the tragedy had been reversed.

It was absolutely necessary for the resurrected Savior to be seen. Such eyewitnesses would then become fantastic evangels. Sight has its place, but that scene took place over nineteen hundred years ago. Today God's plan calls for us who hear or read the Bible to believe it.

Faith comes by hearing and hearing by the Word of God. Faith takes God at His Word, without necessarily feeling, seeing, or experiencing anything. Those who demand such proof do not realize that their requirement of a sign indicates spiritual immaturity.

In addition, we learn that the life of faith is a blessing. Believe first; step out on God's promise. Then assurance will follow. Whoever at any time believes without seeing is blessed. If we can experience joy inexpressible now (1 Peter 1:8), not having seen Christ, what shall we experience when we do see Him? Rest assured, we *shall* see Him. For our citizenship is in heaven. We are right now the children of God, and it has not yet been revealed what we shall be, but we know that when He is revealed, we shall be like Him, for we shall see Him as He is (1 John 3:2).

> What rejoicing in His presence
>   When are banished grief and pain;
> When the crooked ways are straightened
>   And the dark things shall be plain.
> Face to face! O blissful moment!
>   Face to face—to see and know;
> Face to face with my Redeemer,
>   Jesus Christ who loves me so.
>
>   *Carrie E. Breck*

August 10

To whom He also presented Himself alive after His suffering by many infallible proofs. (Acts 1:3)

Passion. Our Lord's passion included ridicule, scorn, unbelief (even His own brothers did not believe), traps, spies, lack of faith, perjurers, hypocrites, ingratitude by those healed, would-be disciples, testing by Satan, false accusations, misunderstanding, hatred, envy, injustice, expediency, betrayal, denial, scourging, and mocking.

He was spat upon, slapped, cruel spikes were hammered into His hands and feet, a crown of thorns mashed upon His head, and a spear thrust into His side. More than all of those physical and mental torments, He who knew no sin became sin.

Presentation. The resurrected Christ appeared only to believers during the entire forty-day period. The very suddenness of His appearances, their total unexpectedness, their variety so far as time, place, and audience was concerned, and the fact that He gave different speeches for different purposes—all those things indicate that He did not stay with anyone for any length of time. Indeed, it was not His intention to be with them as in the days of His earthly ministry.

Proofs. The particular word used only in the New Testament and translated "proofs" was employed technically in medical language. It means indubitable evidence, that from which something is surely and plainly known. That is why the King James Version adds the word *infallible*. And several other translations use the word *convincing*, which is almost as strong a term.

You recall that Luke was a doctor. Perhaps better than all of the other New Testament writers he knew from his medical experience that it was absolutely impossible for a dead body to come to life again by itself, by its own power. Yet Jesus Christ *showed* Himself alive.

August 11

Be saved from this perverse generation. (Acts 2:40)

The King James translation says "Save yourself"! How strange that command sounds. For the Bible teaches that men cannot save themselves. If by "save" you mean escape from the penalty of sin or avoidance of hell, it cannot be done. If by "save" you mean weaken the power of sin in your life, it cannot be done. If by "save" you mean the eradication of the presence of sin, it cannot be done. We simply cannot save ourselves.

The point Simon Peter made is this: the deliverance, or salvation, you need is available. But it is appropriated only by those who hear and accept the gospel of the shed blood of Jesus Christ. Merely to hear is not enough. Some folks hear but do not heed. Some have eyes but do not really see.

Be saved at once! is the force of the tense used. It means to take advantage of what the Lord has done for you. Let God save you by us. We are His messengers. Pay attention to the gospel we preach! Be saved from this perverse generation!

Simon's message was aimed at his own people. The purse-picker Judas had betrayed the Lord. Christ was arrested. He was tried by men whose minds were made up ahead of time. He was beaten, bruised, slapped, His beard plucked. He was spat upon, mocked, insulted, ridiculed, and blasphemed. A crown of thorns was pressed down upon His brow; cruel spikes were driven into His feet and into His holy hands.

So it was that a crooked, perverse generation put Jesus Christ to death. Yet beyond all the physical pain, the heart of what happened at Calvary lies in the fact that He who knew no sin became sin for us. To this generation then came the exhortation: Repent! Believe that Jesus is the Messiah! Be saved!

August 12

Then Peter said, "Silver and gold I do not have, but what I do have I give you: In the name of Jesus Christ of Nazareth, rise up and walk." (Acts 3:6)

There at the gate of the Temple that was called Beautiful was a certain man who had been born lame. Forty years old or more, he had never walked a single step in his life. His condition was a picture of all men: congenitally deformed, born helpless, at the mercy of wickedness within and without, a nuisance, poor, a miserable beggar.

When he saw Peter and John about to go into the Temple, he stretched out his hand and began asking for money in his usual way. Both of the disciples fixed their gaze on him, and Peter said: "Look at us!" As the man anticipated receiving a coin, Peter said: "Silver and gold I do not have, but what I do have I give you."

Well, what did Simon have? He had Jesus Christ—God become man, the Light of the world, the Ancient of Days, the Word made flesh, the Alpha and Omega.

Leaping up, the man stood upright and began to walk; there was no need to go through physical therapy to learn to use his limbs. The cure was instantaneous. That is the way salvation is. The split second God saves you, you can begin your journey up the King's highway.

The man entered the Temple with Peter and John, walking and leaping and praising God. The blessing he had received was worth far more than silver and gold. What he got from God was greater than that for which he had begged. But this is the way of our Lord; He is able to do exceedingly abundantly above all that we ask or think.

God made this man rich in the name of Jesus. There was no more of the old life, helpless and begging in the streets. This same God speaks to our hearts today. "But what I do have I give you."

August 13

Nor is there salvation in any other, for there is no other name under heaven given among men by which we must be saved. (Acts 4:12)

Soon after the healing of the man born lame, Peter and John were put in prison. Held overnight, the next day the two apostles were interrogated by Annas, the high priest, by Caiaphas, and other members of the Sanhedrin. "By what power or by what name have you healed this man?" Simon let his fellow countrymen know that Jesus Christ was the stone that they had rejected.

The apostle taught the unbelieving council that this new way, later to be called Christianity, was not something hid in a corner; nor was it a narrow, parochial faith; it was *universal*. The lame man's physical impotence symbolized man's spiritual undoneness. As he was lame from birth, so all men are sinners from birth.

The salvation the apostles preached was *unique*. There was not another name under heaven except the name of Jesus associated with that salvation. It is not then a salvation based upon a particular church, denomination, religious system, or good works, but upon a person—Jesus Christ.

That salvation was *uncommon*, wonderful, remarkable. First, because it cannot be earned; it was "given among men." When multitudes seek to work their way to heaven through their good deeds, philanthropic acts, civic and social awareness, human morality, racial advancement, or by abstaining from certain meats, praying so many times a day, worshiping on certain days, and so on, how refreshing to hear we are saved by grace.

Here is an uncommon salvation for the common man, a universal salvation for all men, a unique salvation just for you! Believe on the Lord Jesus Christ, and you will be saved.

August 14

Now when they saw the boldness of Peter and John, and per-
ceived that they were uneducated and untrained men, they
marveled. And they realized that they had been with Jesus.
(Acts 4:13)

Peter and John were going to prayer meeting when a
man lame from birth, sitting at the gate of the Temple,
begged them for money. Calling the man to look at them,
Peter said: "Silver and gold I do not have, but what I do
have I give you: In the name of Jesus Christ of Nazareth,
rise up and walk!"

The man was instantly healed; he leaped, walked, ran,
shouted, and praised God. A crowd gathered. With
newfound courage Peter took advantage of the moment
and preached the gospel to them. *Boldness* is the word used
to describe the change in Simon. Literally, the word means
"freedom of speech, unreservedness in speaking." From
that it came to mean "free and fearless confidence, cheerful courage, boldness, assurance."

Simon called the Jews to repentance. That stirred up the
religious leaders, who arrested Peter and John. On the next
day the two disciples were questioned. "By what power,
or by what name, have you done this?"

Filled with the Holy Spirit, Simon Peter preached to them
Christ crucified, buried, and risen. He concluded: "Nor is
there salvation in any other."

The Jewish authorities were surprised by the candor of
the men because they were men without letters—ignorant.
Their boldness was not that of men whose training had
given them rhetorical ability. That bold and open speech
was given by God; it was the ability to preach openly and
eloquently to a hostile world.

When you spend time with Jesus Christ, it will be said
of you too, "But the righteous are bold as a lion" (Proverbs
28:1).

August 15

I have heard from many about this man. (Acts 9:13)

When the Lord ordered Ananias to receive Paul, who had been blinded on the road to Damascus, Ananias replied to Christ: "Lord, I have heard from many about this man, how much harm he has done to Your saints in Jerusalem."

Paul's bad reputation preceded him. What a terror he had been—a blasphemer and a persecutor (1 Timothy 1:13)! But upon meeting the resurrected Jesus Christ, Paul became a new creation. The persecutor of Christians became the preacher of Christ.

Later, the apostle wrote that the Christian minister should have "a good testimony among those who are outside"—a good reputation and well-thought of by people who are outside the church (1 Timothy 3:7).

What is your reputation? What is your standing in your community? It is said that what a man stands for makes character, and what he falls for makes reputation. Of course, there are folks who do not care what others think of them. They show it by their deeds.

But Christians must realize that none of us lives to himself, and no man dies to himself (Romans 14:7). No man is an island. We blood-bought children of God must be concerned not only with character but with reputation also.

People will talk. The question is, What are they saying about you? More important, is what they say true? Remember then today: "A good name is to be chosen rather than great riches" (Proverbs 22:1).

August 16

Then the churches throughout all Judea, Galilee, and Samaria had peace and were edified. And walking in the fear of the Lord and in the comfort of the Holy Spirit, they were multiplied. (Acts 9:31)

One ingredient for church progress is peace, or rest. With the loss of its head man, Saul of Tarsus, organized persecution of the church ceased temporarily. Although there were other historical factors involved, the conversion of Saul played a major part in the rest and peace experienced by the church. In such an atmosphere the church made progress.

The second ingredient of church progress is the fear of the Lord. Without this reverence and respect of God there can be little growth. Where you have people with a tender conscience, unwilling to grieve the Holy Spirit, who revere the Word of God and dread to offend Him, there will be progress.

Such folks respect His Word, His church, and know how to behave in church. They love God's people, His servants, His hymns—yea, His very presence and name. The Lord honors their reverence with strength and abundance.

A third ingredient necessary for church progress is the comfort of the Holy Spirit. The word rendered *comfort* means encouragement, consolation, and exhortation.

Here an assurance, an awareness, a consciousness of our relationship with God through Jesus Christ is meant. The Holy Spirit is the one who makes this a reality to us.

It is our Lord's desire that His church be edified and multiplied. Let the process begin with each individual believer who finds a genuine rest in Christ, has a genuine fear of the Lord, and maintains a genuine comfort and strength.

August 17

To Him all the prophets witness that, through His name, who-ever believes in Him will receive remission of sins. (Acts 10:43)

In this portion of the sermon Peter preached to the Gentiles there in the home of Cornelius, three basic things may be seen. First, there is the requirement for salvation. Cornelius was a good man, devout, fearing God, and had a good reputation among the Jews. He was religious but lost.

His sins were still on him. No amount of prayer or giving alms to the poor would remove his sin. He needed to believe in Jesus Christ. Some ridicule what they call "easy believism." Yet the text states, "Whoever believes in Him." That is the only condition for salvation.

Second, see the resurrection of the Savior. Peter preached about Him whom the Jews slew and hanged on a tree, whom God raised up the third day and showed openly to certain believers (Acts 10:39–40). The early church did not wait until Easter Sunday morning once a year to celebrate the resurrection.

Every Sunday was resurrection Sunday. Every sermon proclaimed the risen Savior. Modern-day preachers would be well advised that they have no message from God that does not include the shedding of blood at Calvary and the rising from the grave of an everlasting, ever-living Lord.

Third, there is the remission of sins. Through faith in the resurrected Savior our sins are remitted. The noun *aphesis* speaks of a release as from punishment, a prisoner freed from jail, a slave from bondage.

The best synonym for remission is forgiveness. We learn that the basic idea in forgiveness is the removal, the sending away of sins, separating the sin from the sinner. God has done that for everyone who believes in the shed blood of Jesus Christ.

August 18

These were more fair-minded than those in Thessalonica, in that they received the word with all readiness, and searched the Scriptures daily to find out whether these things were so. (Acts 17:11)

The verb translated *searched* means "to distinguish, investigate, examine, inquire into, scrutinize, sift, question, interrogate, estimate, judge." The people at Berea examined, discerned, judged, asked questions, and searched the Old Testament to see whether Jesus Christ fulfilled in His person, works, sufferings, and ministry the promises and types given in prophecy.

What they had heard was not a take-it-or-leave-it thing with them. It was too important. Today we spend much time, money, and energy searching and researching in the various fields of science. Tremendous amounts of money are spent on education.

But when it comes to the study of the Bible by the average church member today, that is another matter altogether. Yet note the priesthood of all believers here in today's devotion text. Those people at Berea were not overwhelmed by the apostle Paul. They exercised the right of private judgment.

Whereas prejudice had closed the minds of the people in Thessalonica, here at Berea no preconceived notions were allowed to stop them from thoroughly investigating the claims of the gospel. Their investigation was not a superficial thing, either in time or quality. They diligently searched; research was done daily. They were real in their desire to know the truth.

Just as the people at Berea were open-minded to truth and gave God's Word an opportunity to work, let us show by our conduct and disposition that we are genuine Christians.

August 19

Therefore take heed to yourselves and to all the flock, among which the Holy Spirit has made you overseers, to shepherd [feed, KJV] the church of God which He purchased with His own blood. (Acts 20:28)

The *people* of the church are designated by the apostle Paul in his farewell speech to the elders at Ephesus as "all the flock." As, in the Old Testament, Israel was the flock of Jehovah the Shepherd, so in the New Testament Christ is the Chief Shepherd of the church. We are His sheep.

The *pastor* of the church is exhorted here to be on guard, to constantly take heed to himself. As a bishop, one who oversees, he must be careful to maintain a life of prayer, Bible study, morality, and diligence in the work to which God has called him.

One *purpose* of the church is to be a restaurant for the righteous. We come to church to be fed the Word of God, which is described elsewhere as milk, meat, honey, and bread. In a balanced diet, given with regularity and fully digested, a man can really live (Jeremiah 15:16).

The *purchaser* of the church is God. Here *to purchase* means "to save or preserve for one's self." The church is God's property. We take what Jehovah said to Israel and apply its truth to the church: "This people I have formed for Myself; they shall declare My praise" (Isaiah 43:21).

The *preciousness* of the church is established when we consider what it cost the purchaser. It cost blood, the precious blood of God's Son, Jesus Christ. Thank God for the church, the Body of Christ, the temple of the Holy Spirit, the light of the world, the house of the living God, the ark of safety, the spotless, virgin bride of Christ, the pillar and ground of truth. Rejoice today that you are a part of the true church, a sheep safe within the fold.

August 20

. . . except for these chains. (Acts 26:29)

Many notable saints suffered imprisonment: Joseph (Genesis 39:20); Micaiah (1 Kings 22:27); Hanani (2 Chronicles 16:10); Jeremiah (37:15–16); John the Baptist (Mark 6:17, 19); the apostles (Acts 5:18; 12:3–4).

The text finds Paul the apostle making a personal appeal to Agrippa, as Festus sat nearby. How often mention is made of his bonds and prison experience (2 Corinthians 11:23; Ephesians 4:1; 6:20; Philippians 1:7,13,16; Colossians 4:3, 18; 2 Timothy 1:8, 16; 2:9; Philemon 1, 9, 23)!

Some critics of Christianity believe such imprisonments are uncalled for, unnecessary, inane, and, indeed, the result of fanaticism. They claim that, in addition to this physical aspect, Christianity is restrictive and so is intellectually shackling.

From their point of view, to be a Christian is to be a prisoner of man-made legalisms, of medieval morality, of mystical mythology, of stupid superstition, and tragic traditionalism. Some see the preacher as the jailer, the church the prison, and the church members as prisoners who are willing to pay dues in order to be kept in prison. Those critics are not aware of the fact that their own unbelief and their own perverted concepts and ideas are the very things that keep them in spiritual straitjackets.

The greatest prison of mankind is sin, and Satan is the warden. He uses the sin in men's hearts and tempts men to do what they want to do anyway. Jesus Christ came to break that power by paying the penalty Himself in His own body, that whosoever believes in Him should be set free from the prison of self, sin, and Satan and made a servant of the Savior in whom alone there is true freedom.

August 21

. . . for I believe God. (Acts 27:25)

Because Paul appealed to Caesar (Acts 25:11), it was necessary that his case be tried in Rome. Earlier he had been arrested, described as a general disturber of peace all over the world, and accused of sedition. Now he was on a ship headed for a winter port. Paul had warned the captain and the centurion: "Men, I perceive that this voyage will end with disaster and much loss, not only of the cargo and ship, but also our lives."

Paul admonished them to stay at Fair Havens near the city of Lasea, but the captain and his crew sailed on. Soon a terrific storm came upon them; a tempestuous, violent wind drove the ship at will. The crew in frantic haste undergirded it, lowered sails, threw cargo, provisions, and equipment overboard—all to no avail.

After many days amidst dashing waves, when neither sun nor stars could be seen, when hunger gnawed, shipwreck was certain—and all hope of being saved was gone.

How often calamity must come into our lives to get us to heed the voice of God. How often trouble seems to be the only thing that will open our ears to God's Word. That time Paul found a willing audience.

"And now I urge you to take heart, for there will be no loss of life among you, but only of the ship. For there stood by me this night an angel of the God to whom I belong and whom I serve, saying, 'Do not be afraid, Paul; you must be brought before Caesar; and indeed God has granted you all those who sail with you.' Therefore take heart, men, for I believe God that it will be just as it was told me" (Acts 27:22–25).

Thus two hundred seventy-six souls were saved from a watery grave, blessed by Paul's God because of Paul. The Lord meant for Paul to stand before Caesar.

August 22

For since the creation of the world His invisible attributes are clearly seen, being understood by the things that are made, even His eternal power and Godhead. (Romans 1:20)

The blizzard of 1978 was an unforgettable experience. Our plans were disrupted, meetings canceled, money lost, patience tried, heating bills escalated, and fenders crumpled. We were forced to agree with the psalmist who said, "He [God] sends His command to the earth. . . . He gives snow like wool; He scatters the frost like ashes. He casts out His ice like morsels; who can stand before His cold?" (Psalm 147:15–17).

Surely no one in his right mind would argue with Job, who said that at God's command amazing things happen, wonderful things that we can't understand. He commands snow to fall on the earth, and sends torrents of drenching rain. He brings the work of men to a stop; He shows them that He is at work (Job 37:5–7).

Sometimes natural phenomena are frightening, awesome. I remember that in 1954, when my wife and I were on our honeymoon, a hurricane came up, and I thought the winds would lift our '46 Plymouth coupe and fly us to Niagara Falls. Earthquakes, volcanic eruptions, and floods can create great fears in the hearts of men.

I wondered as I looked out the window at the myriad white flakes swirling madly past the trees and lampposts, how many folks will see the hand of God in all this? When things return to normal, the snow melts, cars are dug out, their motors are started, and workers' schedules are resumed, we are prone to forget what it was like when traffic was paralyzed, schools were closed, and work was brought to a standstill.

Did men see God's hand in the blizzard? What about His face? Thank God that we have indeed seen His face in Jesus Christ, and it has helped us to be impressed with His handiwork.

August 23

Professing to be wise, they became fools. (Romans 1:22)

Their claim. The apostle Paul denounced those who claimed they were wise. He made it known that men hid behind a façade of wisdom. Their subjective professions of cleverness are objectively false.

Their confusion. Sin makes men foolish. To compound its evil effects, sin makes a fool think he is smart. While egotistically proclaiming how wise he is, man commits folly. While he is in the very process of bragging about his cleverness, God pins a donkey's tail upon him. Man does not even feel the pin pricking him. Sin is so deceptive that men become fools without even knowing it.

Their change. Here is the proof that men claiming to be wise are crazy. They change, or exchange, the glory of God for that which is not glorious. If the real thing is rejected, a substitute must be made. Get rid of a holy God, and you will put in His place a homemade god.

Whatever man chooses outside of Jesus Christ is corruption and decay; it is rottenness. Man makes a bad bargain when he changes the glory of the incorruptible and only wise God for the images of corruptible human beings, birds, beasts, and bugs.

The truly wise man accepts the shed blood of Jesus Christ who is the wisdom of God (1 Corinthians 1:24). Jesus Christ alone is exempt from wasting and wearing out. All else shall perish and become old as a garment; although all else shall change, Christ remains the same. His years shall not fail.

Today let your prayer be:

> Change and decay in all around I see;
>
> O Thou who changest not, abide with me.

H. F. Lyte

August 24

For if by the one man's offense many died, much more the grace of God and the gift by the grace of the one Man, Jesus Christ, abounded to many. (Romans 5:15)

We must look for the meaning of "much more" not in numbers but in the quality of the thing done. Adam deserved what he got. He had been warned but willfully disobeyed God. We die for a reason—sin, the sin of disobedience. God had told Adam what He would do and followed through when Adam sinned.

That remains to this day. The death we die we deserve. God's judgment is according to truth. If you die and drop into hell, it will be justice. You deserve it. You earned it by association with Adam as well as by the fact of committing your own brand of iniquity.

The "much moreness" comes in the fact that whereas we deserve death, we do not merit grace or the gift of grace. It is free. Through the one man, Christ Jesus, has come forgiveness, mercy; God's love has overflowed for the benefit of all men. The verdict of acquittal is much more than the verdict of condemnation.

God is just when He punishes all men for Adam's sin. He gives us what we deserve. When He saves us, He gives us what we do not deserve and cannot ever earn. His grace is all out of proportion to the fall of Adam. That is why the poet could write:

> Marvelous grace of our loving Lord,
>> Grace that exceeds our sin and our guilt,
> Yonder on Calvary's mount outpoured,
>> There where the blood of the Lamb was spilt.
>
> Sin and despair like the sea waves cold,
>> Threaten the soul with infinite loss;
> Grace that is greater, yes, grace untold,
>> Points to the refuge, the mighty cross.
>
> *Julia H. Johnston*

Surely, that is grace greater than all our sin!

August 25

For if by the one man's offense death reigned through the one, much more those who receive abundance of grace and of the gift of righteousness will reign in life through the One, Jesus Christ. (Romans 5:17)

Like a king upon his throne, death reigned. How gruesome that sounds! Imagine death's exercising great power and authority, ruling and influencing the lives of billions of people. Since the murder of Abel the death rate has been one per person. Sheer force of numbers lends credence to the totalitarian, despotic influence of death's reign and rule.

We can thank the Lord, however, that death can be deposed, impeached, forced to resign, and made inoperative. As death began to rule because of the one man, Adam, so through the one Man, Jesus Christ, life abundant and eternal has been made available. God the Son became a man in order that the chilling finger of death might touch Him, who in becoming our sin, paid the penalty of sin.

That sinful connection we had with Adam was broken and replaced with a righteous connection with Jesus Christ for all eternity. Where death used to reign, Christ is King. He is the King of kings, and we are the kings. In the fall of Adam sin worked itself out and produced death. The right to reign in life eternal and abundant is freely bestowed by a merciful Savior. In Him we are enabled to live like kings and queens.

Where there used to be bitterness, now there is sweetness. For darkness, Christ gives light. For sorrow, He gives rejoicing. For cursing, there is blessing; for shackling, there is liberty; for slavery, there is freedom.

Whom the Son of Man sets free is free indeed.

August 26

Likewise you also, reckon yourselves to be dead indeed to sin, but alive to God in Christ Jesus our Lord. (Romans 6:11)

You died to sin, said Paul (Romans 6:2, 7–8, 11); so also said Simon Peter (1 Peter 2:24). Here is a positional truth that needs to become conditional reality, truth that needs to be practiced.

In April 1959, the German and Austrian people generally ignored the seventieth anniversary of the birth of Adolf Hitler. "Hitler? Who is he?" replied a twelve-year-old German schoolgirl when asked what she knew about the former führer.

"Leave me alone; Hitler is dead, so let him be dead," a prosperous German businessman said angrily to an inquiring newsman. Dead, but there is still anti-Semitism in Germany and elsewhere; we even have Nazis in America.

Some things that are supposed to be dead are not. Spurgeon, the great English preacher of yesteryear, told of a cat that once sprang at his lips while he was talking and bit him savagely. His friend in whose house the incident occurred decreed that the poor creature should die. He personally carried out the execution to the best of his ability and threw the carcass away. To his surprise, the cat walked into the house the very next day.

You died to sin. Reckon it to be so. Sin need not rule in your life; sin need not move you because your affections and treasures are located where sin cannot reach—heaven.

You died to sin. Today claim this paradox for yourself. You are dead *but* alive; you are dead *and* alive—alive unto God through the living Lord Jesus.

August 27

. . . conformed to the image of His Son. (Romans 8:29)

Because He is the Prince of Peace, the more I am like Him, the more peace I will have. That makes sense, does it not? Father, make me more like Jesus, the Light of the world, and I will not stumble in this darkness below. Make me more like Jesus, the Head of the church, and the enemies of the church who are in the church will have to step back.

Make me more like the great Shepherd of the sheep, and I shall not want for any good thing. Father, make me more like the Balm of Gilead who makes the wounded whole, who heals the sin-sick soul. Father, make me more like Jesus the Liberator who sets men free, and no shackling habits or enslaving philosophies can bind my soul. Make me more like Jesus, the Bright and Morning Star, and I will walk with my head held high looking up for His blessed return.

Father, make me more like Jesus, the Manna come down from heaven, and I shall be more satisfied day by day. Make me more like Jesus, the Joy of my salvation, and gloomy vicissitudes of life will never overshadow my joy. Make me more like Him who is full of grace, and I shall never stop singing of the amazing grace that saved a wretch like me.

Make me more like Him who loved me and gave Himself for me, and that love will make me love others with a love that melts hearts, covers faults, and moves mountains. Father, make me more like Jesus, a rock in a weary land, a shelter in time of storm; I will not despair when the storms of life begin to rise and the strong winds of adversity blow.

> More like Jesus would I be,
>   Let my Savior dwell in me;
> Fill my soul with peace and love,
>   Make me gentle as a dove;
> More like Jesus, while I go,
>   Pilgrim in this world below;
> Poor in spirit would I be;
>   Let my Savior dwell in me.

Fanny Crosby

August 28

Christ . . . who is even at the right hand of God, who also
makes intercession for us. (Romans 8:34)

The story is told that a well-known entertainer took her
daughter to church, and they sat near the front. Studying
a large crucifix there, the girl ascertained that it was Jesus
hanging there and asked, "Mommy, can't He come down?"
The mother replied in the negative. After a moment the
little girl suddenly cried out, "Jump, Jesus, jump!"

Unfortunately, multitudes of people know only of a dead
Christ hanging on a cross. They do not know that Christ
lives forevermore. Though buried, He was raised on the
third day, seen by the disciples and many others, and ascended into heaven. What is He doing there now?

He is making intercession for us. He is our lawyer in
heaven, our Advocate right now (Matthew 26:64; Mark
16:19; Acts 7:55; Ephesians 1:20; Colossians 3:1; Hebrews
1:3; 1 Peter 3:22; 1 John 2:1).

To be on or at the right hand of anyone is to be in a place
of power, preference, privilege, or honor. Romans 8:34 expresses this truth: the man Christ Jesus has been exalted in
His humanity, after having gone through the stage of humiliation, shame, ignominy, agony, and suffering here below.

His primary mission on earth was finished, and to be
placed at the right hand of the Father is evidence of the
fact that the Father accepted the Son's earthly ministry. We
Christians need help; we are always in trouble. All who
desire to live godly in Christ Jesus will suffer persecution.

Thank the Lord that, in the midst of trials and troubles,
we have Someone who cares, Someone who pleads for us,
and Someone who is able to argue our case successfully.

August 29

Let their table become a snare and a trap, a stumbling block and a recompense to them. (Romans 11:9)

Symbolically the table stands for blessings. The food and drink placed on the table indicate a measure of material prosperity. God's blessing, of whatever sort it is, is your table. Now the question comes, How can a blessing be turned into a curse?

Tables tend to lull people into a false sense of security. We may be pounced upon even while eating at the table, or treacherous enemies could poison the food. Consider Judas in John 13:18, 21–31.

Sometimes our greed can get the best of us. Years ago a man was carried from a Swiss airplane in a coma. Within minutes he died of suffocation. Authorities discovered that he was a thief, a smuggler to be exact. The corset he wore had fifteen hundred small watch mechanisms stuffed in it. But he had pulled the corset too tight and messed up his own timetable!

When General McArthur and the American troops entered Japan and took over the Japanese War Department archives, they made a startling discovery. Before the war an eminent Japanese professor of psychology visited all over America, studying our national character. He was searching for a weak point in our way of life.

He concluded that our most vulnerable spot was early Sunday morning. From that it was decided that a Sunday morning following a Friday that was payday for both the Army and Navy would be our weakest moment. It was after just such a weekend of carousing, drunkenness, and debauchery that the Japanese struck—December 7, 1941. May God deliver us from causing our tables to be turned into traps.

August 30

For of Him and through Him and to Him are all things, to whom be glory forever. Amen. (Romans 11:36).

The study of Romans chapters 9–11 is essential for a correct understanding of Israel's place—past, present, and future—in the plan of God. Paul wanted it known that the Lord had not reneged. Men do not understand the ways and thoughts of God (Isaiah 55:8–9), but all who have faith in the shed blood of Calvary must learn to trust the Lord. The God of history knows what He is doing, and any criticism of Him is at best a demonstration of ignorance. It is *our* knowledge that is at fault, not God's mercy or compassion.

Some people claim there is no God. Some who do not say it act like there is no God. But many poor, illiterate slave grandparents knew better. They believed that the Lord "sees all you do, He hears all you say, my Lord's awritin' all de time." Surely the Bible says that "all things are naked and open to the eyes of Him to whom we must give account" (Hebrews 4:13).

Jesus Christ is the source (*of* Him), the sustainer (*through* Him), and the sum (*to* Him) of *all things*. Hallelujah, what a Savior! God the Father gave Christ to us; we can rest assured He will now with Christ also freely give us *all things* (Romans 8:32), for He works *all things* according to the counsel of His will (Ephesians 1:11).

Since *all things* were created by Him and consist or hold together because of Him (Colossians 1:16–17), He has no difficulty as the heir of *all things* upholding *all things* by the word of His power (Hebrews 1:2–3).

At His second coming our lowly bodies will be changed and made like His body of glory through the power whereby He is able to subdue *all things* unto Himself. Remember: Christ has given you *all things* richly to enjoy. As you go to work, to school, wherever you venture this day, believe He is able to make *all things* work together for your good (Romans 8:28).

August 31

Now it is high time to awake out of sleep. (Romans 13:11)

Sleep is absolutely necessary; without proper rest we become irritable and inefficient. But we also are warned: "Give no sleep to your eyes, nor slumber to your eyelids" (Proverbs 6:4). The writer goes on to say, "Do not love sleep, lest you come to poverty" (Proverbs 20:13; see also Proverbs 6:9–11).

Obviously, sleep can also be dangerous. Ask Samson (Judges 16:19). Sleep can be harmful. Ask Eutychus (Acts 20:9). How well do I remember one midnight, returning from my first church in Philadelphia; I fell asleep while driving. The car crossed three lanes there on Route 1, and when it hit the shoulder of the road the vibrations woke me up. God was merciful to me that night.

But even more detrimental is spiritual sleep. For Satan, like some super sandman, sows sand in the eyes of multitudes of men. Indeed, the whole world is asleep in the devil's lap (1 John 5:19).

Unfortunately, some Christians, too, are sleepyheads. To them Paul exhorts, "Awake to righteousness, and do not sin" (1 Corinthians 15:34); "let us not sleep, as others do, but let us watch and be sober" (1 Thessalonians 5:6).

We Christians should be alert because salvation is nearer now than when we first believed. Furthermore, an alert life is part of the abundant life promised us. A wide-awake Christian has a joy of living that the slothful do not experience, the joy of moving on from one good degree of grace to another.

Be vigilant, then. Stay on your spiritual toes. May the appeal to wake up out of the state of worldly carelessness and spiritual indifference touch a responsive chord in your heart because you realize your salvation today is nearer.

September 1

Joy in the Holy Spirit. (Romans 14:17)

During my pastorate a number of the members of my church were blind. I remember one sister well because of her pleasant disposition. Although she could not see, her face would light up when she smiled, and I found myself just enjoying looking at her. Indeed, the profession of her faith in Christ and the confession of her mouth to His lordship were expressed also in her countenance.

When her husband died I stood at the graveside and wondered what it must be like for a blind widow to stand there as the body of her beloved spouse was lowered into the cold clay. Yet, even in bereavement, there was a peace and contentment about her that impressed me and lingered long in my soul.

Sometime later she had a fall in her home, and her face was badly bruised; but she seemed to bear up well. The last time I saw her it was evident that her health was fast failing. Through it all she appeared cheerful.

If only more Christians would learn to rejoice in the Holy Spirit—to rejoice on the inside no matter what is happening on the outside. People who are materialists, whose emphasis falls upon the external, the visible, the temporal, upon the eating of food and drink—theirs is a lifestyle that does not represent the kingdom of God. Nor is there joy in their lives.

We humans have a happiness that depends upon what happens. However, Christian joy is not based upon circumstances. Rather, that joy is a part of the fruit of the Spirit; it is one manifestation of God's kingdom. It belongs to you and to everyone who is a true citizen of heaven now living on earth.

September 2

For whatever things were written before were written for our learning, that we through the patience and comfort of the Scriptures might have hope. (Romans 15:4)

How would you like to be as worshipful as Abel, obedient as Abraham, brave as Daniel, devoted as David, full of good works as Dorcas, and walk with God as did Enoch? Do you desire to be as powerful as Elijah, as helpful as Epaphroditus, as courageous as Esther, or a warrior like Gideon?

Would you like to be as grateful as Hannah, patient like Job, loyal as Jonathan, steadfast as Joseph, and as militant as Joshua? Is there a desire in your heart to be as industrious as Lydia, as humble as Mary of Bethany, to live as long as did Methuselah, be as influential for God as was Moses, as alert as Nehemiah, as prayerful as Paul?

Do you really want to preach like Simon Peter and teach as did Priscilla or be as dedicated as Ruth, upright as Samuel, strong as Samson, a true daughter of Sarah, bold as Stephen, and wise as Solomon?

It is good to read about the lives of the saints of old. They are inspiring accounts. If you take all of the good points of all of those Bible characters and ball them into one, you will get only a glimpse of the beauty of the character of the Lord Jesus Christ.

Today is one more day to read God's Word, to learn about Him, and to hope in Him. Thanks be to God for one more opportunity to become more like Him who loved you and gave Himself for you.

September 3

And the God of peace will crush Satan under your feet shortly.
(Romans 16:20)

To be the God of something is to be the source, the creator, the bestower of that thing. We thus read of the God of heaven; God of hosts; God of wisdom; God of Abraham, Isaac, and Jacob; God of patience and consolation; God of hope; God of love. Here it is the God of peace.

Peace emanates from Him; He alone is the creator of peace. Without Him there is no real, lasting, genuine peace in this world. The God of peace one day took sin, that great destroyer of peace, and put it upon Christ. Smitten, Christ paid the penalty of sin.

He satisfied the wrath of God and thereby made it possible that all who believe in the shed blood of Christ might have peace with God. And those obtaining peace with God have available to them the peace *of* God.

You see then that there had to be some bruising at Calvary by the God of peace in order to establish peace. Strong language is used here when it speaks of *crushing* the devil's head. Used elsewhere, the verb means literally to rub together and is rendered "to shatter, crush, smash, wear out, annihilate, or beat severely."

Thank the Lord that final victory is on the horizon, and when it comes it comes swiftly. The verse promises God's help in fighting demonic forces, the powers of darkness. We are on the winning side. The gates of hell shall not prevail against the church or against the people of God. Walk in the knowledge of such triumph, and let God use your feet.

September 4

For we are laborers together with God.
(1 Corinthians 3:9, KJV)

Paul wanted to show that any concept of the Christian ministry that exalted the man was improper. We are to honor and respect the man called by God, but not worship him as a god or consider Christian ministers as competitors one with another.

Calling is indicated by the word *laborers*. The apostle did not use this title *fellow-laborer* indiscriminately but applied it only to those saints actively engaged in the Lord's service. Aquila, Aristarchus, Demas, Clement, Epaphroditus, Justus, Lucas, Marcus, Philemon, Priscilla, Timotheus, Titus, Urbane—they were dedicated people, filled with hospitality, fervent in prayer, sacrificial givers, and zealous witnesses to Calvary.

Cooperation is suggested by the word *together*, although "laborers together with" is one Greek word. Spiritually-minded, mature saints recognize and accept differences of personality, physical appearance, race, abilities, gifts, and the very grace of God in the lives of others—and they still work together.

Condescension—"with God." The original is: "For of God we are co-workers." Placed first in the Greek for emphasis, the word *God* reminds us that the Lord is our boss. It is His program; it is in His cultivated field that we are privileged to work.

As you go about your daily tasks, remember you have been called to labor—to work, not shirk. Cooperate with other Christians and praise God for condescending to enlist you as a co-worker with Christ.

September 5

For no other foundation can anyone lay than that which is laid, which is Jesus Christ. (1 Corinthians 3:11)

Many people at Corinth had a false concept of true wisdom. Wrong ideas of wisdom lead to pride. People who think they know and do not know they do *not* know are often puffed up with pride. Their pride moves them to develop parties in the church, each faction thinking it is wiser, smarter, and more spiritual than the other, and each group exalting its leader above other leaders.

One contributing cause of cliques in the church at Corinth then was the wrong concept of the Christian ministry. Preachers are not in competition, said Paul; we are not fighting one another or seeking self-glory. The truth of the matter is that we are all working on the same building.

The one and only foundation of that building, the church, is Jesus Christ. He alone is the basis of all life and reality. The quality of your foundation determines how well you stand the test of life and the coming judgment of a holy God. If you have built upon sand, when the rain descends, the floods come, and the winds blow and beat upon your house, it will fall; great will be the fall of it (Matthew 7:26–27).

Jesus Christ died once for all, rising never again to die; He became the once-for-all-laid foundation upon which true life is lived. Paul looked upon his own work as foundational only in the sense that he was called of God to start, or found, churches.

Wisely he knew that no architect can build without some foundation, and no expert contractor will build without a sure foundation.

September 6

Now if anyone builds on this foundation with gold, silver, precious stones. . . . (1 Corinthians 3:12)

These first three items—gold, silver, jewels—may be put into a special group whose major characteristic is durability and performance. There is no consideration that they would actually be used in constructing a house. If graffiti artists deface and scavengers vandalize houses of stone and brick, imagine what would happen to houses made of literal gold, silver, or rubies.

No. Those materials are *fireproof*; what is stressed is the kind of service given that is composed of such material as will stand the test of God's fire and meet His divine approval.

Three things should be said here. First, *do right.* If you preach, teach, serve, sing, usher, or administrate, then what is done should be correct, true, and right. The deed done, the service performed must be holy, unquestionably right, and moral. What you do is based upon what you believe. That is why good doctrine is so essential.

Second, *do in a right way.* It is possible to do a right thing in the wrong way. Never forget that the Lord is also concerned about your methods. What we do for Christ must be done in His strength, not ours, and in ways pleasing to Him, not our homemade, jackleg, patched-up methods.

Third, *do for a right reason.* There must be a right reason or motive for our service. Gifts and talents that God has given us are to be exercised for His praise and glory, not ours. We are to work because we love the Lord Jesus who loved us first.

Those three principles should be kept in mind: we are to do the right thing in the right way for the right reason. That advice will help us build with gold, silver, and precious stones.

September 7

We have been made as the filth of the world, the offscouring of all things until now. (1 Corinthians 4:13)

In the eyes of the world the early Christians were a sad sight, a spectacle, fools, weak, despised, hungry, thirsty, naked, knocked about, having no certain dwelling place, reviled, persecuted, and defamed.

The words *filth* and *offscouring* come from verbs meaning "to cleanse all around on all sides, to wipe on every side"—that which is rejected, the scrapings, the crumbs, refuse, trash, filth, dirt, dung, scum. That is graphic language, but it expresses the attitude of the world system.

How blind the world is! The very thing men despise is what they most need. That which they treat with contempt is to be most respected. That which they put down is the thing that would lift them up. That which they consider scum and filth is the very thing that would cleanse them and make them whiter than snow.

That which they curse is in reality a blessing. That which is held as worthless is more precious than silver and gold. That which is scandalous and a stumbling block is indeed the chief cornerstone. How blind is the world in its estimation of the people of God.

I am glad that what people say about me does not make it so. God takes nobodies and makes somebodies out of them. Once you are a somebody in Christ, nobody can ever make you a nobody again. When you are placed into the body of Christ, the family of God, it does not matter what the world thinks.

You are a new creature, a citizen of heaven, watched over by angels, sealed with the Holy Spirit. May such knowledge stir up your heart to a more vigorous and dedicated service for Him who loved you and gave His life for you.

September 8

Flee sexual immorality. Every sin that a man does is outside the body, but he who commits sexual immorality sins against his own body. (1 Corinthians 6:18)

There are times when it is wise to flee. When Sarah dealt harshly with Hagar, Hagar fled from her face (Genesis 16:6). After Jacob had cheated Esau and their mother, Rebekah, had heard Esau's promise to kill Jacob, she commanded Jacob to run away to her brother Laban's house (Genesis 27:43).

After killing the Egyptian, Moses fled from the face of Pharaoh (Exodus 2:15). King Saul, possessed by an evil spirit, threw a javelin at David, and David fled; he escaped that night (1 Samuel 19:10). After the warning by the angel that King Herod sought their lives, Joseph and Mary with the young child Jesus fled to Egypt (Matthew 2:14).

But here is something more dangerous than the wrath of a woman, the murderous hatred of a cheated brother, the anger of a pharaoh, the spear of a madman, or the destructive powers of a troubled king. For every sin that a man does is outside the body; but he who commits fornication sins against his own body.

God's advice is: flee fornication. Literally, seek safety in flight, physically run away. We are to escape from the clutches of immorality—do a disappearing act as far as fornication is concerned.

Shun immorality. Flee from impurity. Avoid sexual looseness as if it were the plague. Surely this is good advice. We are to make a habit, or practice, of fleeing fornication. There is to be no letting down of the guard, for the moment you relax may be the very moment you fall. Remember today and every day: Your body is the temple of the Holy Spirit. Keep it clean!

September 9

But beware lest somehow this liberty of yours become a stumbling block to those who are weak. (1 Corinthians 8:9)

Keep in mind that at the time the apostle Paul introduced the gospel of the shed blood of Jesus Christ there were many pagan temples in the city of Corinth. Idol worshipers would bring animals for sacrifice to their gods, and the priests of those temples would burn part, eat part, and sell the remainder to the butcher in the marketplace.

Now the problem was this: Should Christians eat food that had been previously offered up to idols? Some Christians said no (Paul called them weak); others said yes (Paul called them strong).

Some were eager to prove their liberty to eat even food that had been offered up to idols, and they elevated self-advantage over the welfare of others who thought that such food should not be eaten. That resulted in conflict.

The kind of food you eat is an amoral matter. The saint is at liberty to do as he pleases. However, it is not always profitable for the saint to do that which he is at liberty to do. It may not be profitable for himself (1 Corinthians 6:12) or for others (1 Corinthians 10:23).

In other words, the freedom to seek the good of others involves our ability to give in and give up that which rightfully belongs to us. You will have to be led by God's Spirit; we want only to establish the principle of "giving in."

If it takes not pushing what you have every right to push, if it takes that to win men to Jesus Christ or to strengthen believers, so be it! Such an attitude is not shackling; it is liberty—the freedom to seek the good of others.

September 10

You cannot drink the cup of the Lord and the cup of demons; you cannot partake of the Lord's table and of the table of demons. (1 Corinthians 10:21)

In an age of increasing racism the Christian must not connect himself with those who despise other people because of the color of their skin. Racism is demonic, and we ought have no fellowship with demons. Sin is sin no matter what one's race or skin color; sin is thicker than skin.

The devil does not care what color you are. If he can encourage you to get a white liver, a black eye, a red nose, nicotine-stained teeth, a yellow spine, a green brain, a purple outlook, and sing the blues, he will be happy! That is Satan's color scheme.

If we are to have power in an age of moral weakness, if we are to manifest wisdom in an age of moral ignorance, the church must purge itself from entangling alliances with the world system. The church must be more than a social club, though we believe in sociability.

It must be more than a credit union, though we believe in thrift; more than a recreation club, though we believe that bodily exercise is of some profit (1 Timothy 4:8); more than a fashion show, although we believe in wearing modest apparel and putting on the whole armor of God.

Compromise is dangerous. You remember the story of the hunter and the bear. As the hunter raised his rifle to shoot a great big grizzly bear, the bear called out, "Can't we talk this over like two sober, intelligent beings?"

The hunter lowered his gun and said, "What's to talk over?"

"Well, for instance," said the bear, coming closer, "what do you want to shoot me for?"

"Simple," grunted the hunter. "I want a fur coat."

"Well, all I want is a good breakfast," said the bear. "I'm sure we can sit down and sensibly work this out."

So they sat down to work out an agreement. After a while the bear got up, all alone. They had reached a compromise: the bear had his breakfast, and the hunter now had on a fur coat.

September 11

Do not be deceived: Evil company corrupts good habits.
(1 Corinthians 15:33)

Because there is so much deception today, a man must watch the company he keeps. "He who walks with wise men will be wise, but the companion of fools will be destroyed" (Proverbs 13:20). It is a dreadful mistake to hang out with atheists, agnostics, skeptics, cynics, Christ rejecters, and Bible despisers.

Their folly is contagious even if they do feel the same way we do about the death penalty, civil rights, sports, the job, and so on. The fact is that we become like the company we keep. The influence may be almost imperceptible, but it is there nonetheless.

In our text for today's devotion the bad company ridiculed any idea of a physical resurrection. As far as they were concerned, when you are dead, you are done. There is no resurrection. If there is no resurrection, there is no judgment. If there is no judgment, eat, drink, and be merry, for tomorrow we die. Live it up; you have got nothing to lose, for after all, you live only once. When you die, you will be dead a long, long time. A living dog is better than a dead lion.

Paul fully realized the corrupting nature of the teaching he sought to counter. Associate with deceivers full of skeptical ideas, and it affects you adversely. Do not be deceived; do not continue being persuaded to enter on this course of life. You see, it does matter what you believe. Doctrine sinks insidiously into the human mind and mingles insensibly and imperceptibly with our motives. Bad doctrine gives a man nothing to stand on when he is tested.

Believe the wrong thing and you will *do* the wrong thing! Practice cannot be divorced from doctrine. Guard your minds; do not be influenced by those who are ignorant of the truth. Do not pal around with folks who deny the physical bodily resurrection of Jesus Christ.

September 12

And as we have borne the image of the man of dust, we shall also bear the image of the heavenly Man. (1 Corinthians 15:49)

How humbling it is to be reminded of our lowly beginnings, to be told by the Preacher: "All are from the dust, and all return to dust" (Ecclesiastes 3:20). We are nothing but dust, whether president or peasant, pope or preacher, puritan or priest, pauper or prince, physician or patient—all dwell in houses of clay whose foundation is in the dust.

Bearing the image of the man of dust indicates humanity's frailty. Indeed, it is upon this basis that David could praise God: "For He knows our frame; He remembers that we are dust" (Psalm 103:14).

As children of Adam we were given bodies like Adam's body, suited for life here on earth. We have bodies of clay, mortal, frail, subject to disease and illness, decay and dying. We all have the characteristics of Adam, not only physically, but morally and spiritually as well, for we too have been disobedient, knowingly and willfully.

Paul does not stop here; to do so would be morbid, sad, too funereal. The image we have borne is going to give way to the image we shall bear. The basis is the resurrection of Jesus Christ.

The heavenly Man is the Lord from heaven. He who was in heaven to begin with came down to earth to be born of a virgin. He lived among us, then was taken by cruel hands and crucified.

Whereas it is ours now to wear Adam by nature, through faith in Christ we shall put off this image and wear eternally the likeness of our Lord. Changed daily from glory to glory, we are being conformed to the image of Jesus Christ.

September 13

We shall all be changed . . . we shall be changed.
(1 Corinthians 15:51–52)

It is a fact that man needs to be changed. He is born in need of alteration. Such is his inherited nature, his congenital disposition, that he enters the world with a clenched fist, ready to do battle with both God and man. He is born at war and in due time shows his bellicose nature.

To get rid of the enmity with God, man's entire being must be changed. We call that alteration being born again, born anew from above, regeneration, re-creation. It comes only through faith in the shed blood of Jesus Christ. If any man be in Christ he is a new creation, a changed creature.

But now the Christian awaits another change—one that he would know nothing about if he had no Bible. It was revealed to Paul that not all Christians shall see death; there are some saints who will not pass through death, but will go immediately to be with Christ with changed bodies.

The change of which the apostle spoke is the same word used with respect to taking off one suit or dress and putting on another, making a change of garment or raiment. It is an exchange, a making over, a renovation or alteration.

To *change* means to cause one thing to cease and another to take its place. Indeed, the apostle Paul used a verb meaning "to clothe with" when he went on to say, "For this corruptible must *put on* incorruption, and this mortal must *put on* immortality."

The corruptible is the body of the dead saint and it shall be clothed with incorruption; the mortal is the body of the living saint, and it shall be clothed with immortality. Either way, a change must take place. As Job said, "All the days of my hard service I will wait, till my change comes" (Job 14:14).

September 14

O Death, where is your sting? (1 Corinthians 15:55)

The word rendered *sting* here is anything that pierces. It is used also of the claws of an animal, the venomous tip of the tail of a scorpion, the quill of a porcupine, the spur of the cock, the sting of the bee. Also rendered *goad* or *prick* (Acts 9:5), it is the spur, whip, or wooden stick with a metal point used to urge on a horse, ox, or other beast of burden.

If ever you have been stung by a bee you know it is a painful experience. Now it is sin that gives death its power, its sting. First, there is the sting of *frequency.* Death is a common occurrence. Undertakers are kept busy. Fresh graves are dug daily. Second, the sting of death is its *finality.* There is no reincarnation or second chance. There is no such thing as soul sleep. You live and you die. The moment your eyelids close in death, you will wake up either in heaven or in hell.

Fear is a very painful sting of death. Most men are afraid to die. Strong men, rich men, wise men, powerful men—none want to die. Although death is all around us—in the streets, on the highways, and issuing forth from our television sets, we tend to push it out of our minds.

We read about teenage gang killings. We read the obituary columns and think briefly about the lives of famous men and women who pass off the scene, but we soon shake off the effects.

Until the sting strikes home: a loved one's body is flown in from some distant battlefield; an aged father falls victim to a stroke and dies; a husband of thirty years collapses on his job; or a wife dies of cancer—then the fire of fear is rekindled in our hearts. Remember that Jesus Christ suffered the penalty of sin and thereby removed its sting. Yes, the process of death goes on—it is the last enemy to be destroyed—but the penalty has been paid. We Christians have the victory.

September 15

Be strong. (1 Corinthians 16:13)

In the New Testament the command to be strong is found three times; however, two different Greek words are used. One word means to be made powerful, be endued with strength from a source *outside* of oneself (Ephesians 6:10; 2 Timothy 2:1).

Whatever your situation, whatever the circumstances, God has the strength you need. We can get strength in full measure from His undiminished supply. Power is also found in the grace that is in Christ. The ability to accomplish whatever you have taken in hand comes from God. Let the power that belongs to God be your power.

The second word, used in today's devotion text, suggests a gradual growth or *increase* in strength. Luke 1:80 and 2:40 use it to describe John the Baptist and Jesus Christ as children growing up not only physically, but strong in spirit.

Now the saints at Corinth were urged not to be content with their present state but to progressively move on and grow up. They were to be done with the childish carnality of the past that had so weakened them and at the same time was a sign of weakness. What you need now, said Paul, is that inner strength that befits the grown-up, matured Christian.

The strength is not in us but in the Lord Jesus Christ. We need constantly to be reminded of that, because it is so easy to forget it, to serve God in our own strength, to rely upon our own intellect and reason and experience, upon our professional expertise and previous success rather than upon the Holy Spirit.

May it be yours today to truthfully say: I do all things through Christ who strengthens me.

September 16

For our boasting is this: the testimony of our conscience that we conducted ourselves in the world in simplicity and godly sincerity, not with fleshly wisdom but by the grace of God, and more abundantly toward you. (2 Corinthians 1:12)

Our boast. We have here an apologia, a defense of Paul's authority and apostleship. In spite of his enemies he was able to rejoice, to boast. It was not his lifestyle to toot his own horn, but there is nothing wrong with acknowledging what God has done in your life. Conscience enlightened by the Holy Spirit is a safe guide, and Paul's conscience enabled him to boast.

Our behavior. Because his conscience approved his conduct, Paul could endure the insidious attacks and the subtle innuendos by those who sought to undermine his work for Christ. "We conducted ourselves in holiness, simplicity, honesty, godly sincerity, and purity of motive!" Such was the work of the Spirit of God, the ability of God in Christ living in the Christian.

Our basis. The key to good behavior was not for Paul an earthly, fleshly, worldly wisdom or human cleverness. It was the grace of God. Grace is the source for holiness and sincerity in us.

Paul was no self-made man. He was a Christ-made man. Clean living was not *his* achievement but the outworking of the indwelling Holy Spirit. And so Paul's conscience testified—it was a witness, it endorsed, assured, said with utter honesty: I have been accused of all kinds of things, but by the grace of God I have lived the life that pleases the Lord.

Surely it is not too much that Christ asks of us. Having bought us with His own blood from the slave market, He now owns us. He desires that we live right. And He who gives us the power to live well-pleasing to God will reward us when we do. Surely we have something to rejoice about today.

September 17

Now he who establishes us with you in Christ and has anointed us is God. (2 Corinthians 1:21)

Some people believe that it is impossible to know for sure how you stand with God. But if such knowledge were unknowable it would be sad. Such lack of assurance prompts the old nature to works, keeps men in bondage, impugns their motives for whatever deeds they do, and robs Christians of the joy that belongs to them.

You see, the God of the Bible *does* want you to know how it is with your soul. Paul said to the saints at Corinth: "Examine yourselves as to whether you are in the faith. Test yourselves. Do you not know yourselves, that Jesus Christ is in you?—unless indeed you are disqualified." (2 Corinthians 13:5).

It is not a matter of presumptuousness but of obedience to the Bible. You *should* know whether you are saved or not. Never mind those who *think* they are saved but in reality are hell-bound church members or deluded cultists. "I never knew you" will be the awful refrain ringing in their ears for a Christless eternity.

The fact that there are hypocrites in the church does not mean there are no genuine people in the church. For those of you who are genuinely saved, the fact should be settled in your hearts.

It is God who establishes us, confirms us, makes us steadfast, makes us sure in our fellowship with Christ. "Standing firm on the feet" is the meaning of the word rendered *establishes.*

Consider Paul's point. There were those who accused him of being fickle, because he did not come to them when he promised. They said he was a yes-yes, no-no man, unreliable, playing both ends against the middle.

Paul wanted it known that when God directs a man's life, that man is stable, steadfast, and reliable. In other words, he whom God establishes is not fickle.

September 18

. . . lest Satan should take advantage of us: for we are not ignorant of his devices. (2 Corinthians 2:11)

Description. The devil is clearly described in the Bible. To deny that such a person exists is to deny the veracity of the Scriptures and to impugn the integrity of the Author. Failure to see the picture of Satan leaves men without an adequate explanation of the continued evil that is present in this world.

Desire. Satan's desire is to be like God (Isaiah 14:14). Not only does he desire deity, but he seeks to destroy, devour, delude, deceive, discourage, disrupt, and defraud.

Devices. In Ephesians 6:11 we are warned of his wiles, of his methods. Used in an unfavorable sense, the word means "craftiness or deceitful plan." His devices (plural: *noemata*) are literally "his thoughts, his mental perceptions." Used in a bad sense, the Greek word means "a plot, scheme, design, or evil purpose."

We Christians should be able to read the devil's mind to some degree. That cannot be done in our own wisdom or ability but by the Bible and in the Holy Spirit.

Some of the devices are: (1) tempting believers in many ways, (2) getting the church to cover up immorality, (3) making sinners feel their case is hopeless, and (4) keeping backslidden Christians from repenting and causing other saints to be reluctant to receive the penitent back into fellowship.

Defeat. Remember today that the same devil who was defeated in the past at the resurrection of Christ and who shall be defeated in the future when he is cast into the lake of fire need not have any victory in your life today. Knowing Satan's devices, all you need to do is submit yourself to Christ, resist the devil, and watch him flee (James 4:7).

September 19

. . . not on tablets of stone but on tablets of flesh . . . of the heart.
(2 Corinthians 3:3)

Paul's enemies constantly sought to undermine his authority. They considered him an egotist, a braggart always commending himself, breaking his elbow while patting himself on the back. "Well, okay," said the apostle, "but there are those in your midst who require and seek letters of commendation." Possibly he referred to false preachers who had come to town with all kinds of credentials and who had favorably impressed some of the people there.

On the other hand, said Paul, you saints at Corinth are my letters, composed by Christ but published by me. You were brought into existence through my preaching, converted under my gospel ministry, all by the power and grace of God.

You were written not with black, perishable, blottable, erasable, inanimate ink, but with the Holy Spirit. You are not like the law delivered at Mount Sinai and etched upon cold, dead, stone tablets. Such an external code had no vital power to redeem you and make new creatures out of you.

No—as living letters of Christ you have the message written upon living, pulsating, sensitive, vibrant human hearts. Holy Spirit-controlled, your life is a message, and people are reading you.

Remember that *you* are the Lord's living letter. When they look at you, may they see Jesus Christ! May they see the love of Christ and the grace of God in you!

> O for a heart to praise my God,
>
> A heart from sin set free,
>
> A heart that always feels Thy blood
>
> So freely shed for me.
>
> *Charles Wesley*

September 20

Now the Lord is the Spirit; and where the Spirit of the Lord is, there is liberty. (2 Corinthians 3:17)

True liberty is not the ability to control external circumstances and conditions, for what man has chosen his own parents, date or place of birth, IQ, or race? If you had the power, would you like to control the weather and prevent earthquakes, floods, drought, pestilence, volcanoes, and heat waves? What about the devil, the prince of this world system? You cannot see him, let alone control him. Would you usurp his authority and depose him?

Even if you could change conditions to suit yourself, you still would not be free. Someone has said, "A man's worst difficulties begin when he is able to do as he likes." First of all, no matter how much power you wield, the world system you live in would still be deficient—a sin-cursed globe. The fashion, or scheme, of our earthly cosmos is passing away; it is eaten up with sin.

It is sin that shackles; sin enslaves; sin destroys freedom. Unless you solve the sin problem on the inside you can never have true liberty. True liberty is not freedom to live as we please. What pleases us too often shows how we emphasize the external and ignore the eternal.

It is good that sin is no longer a dominant disposition in the saint. Sin's claims are nullified; its chains are broken even though the pieces remain. Remnants or pieces of the old man in us seek to hinder us from holy living, but the sin principle has been slain.

God has set us free, enabling us to fulfill the purpose of our existence. We are free, not from the presence of sin, but from the bondage of sin *to* sin. True freedom is the ability to do God's will. The indwelling Holy Spirit makes that victorious life possible.

September 21

But we all . . . are being transformed into the same image from glory to glory. (2 Corinthians 3:18)

Purpose. Developing Christian character in us is one of the goals of God. As was true in the time of Moses, so it is today. If you spend time in the presence of the Lord, you become like Him. God left us here after our conversion because He wants to mold us into the image of His Son, Jesus Christ.

Your character is the real you, the true self, what you are in the dark all by yourself. It is the Lord's desire to transform you and make you more like Christ.

Process. "From glory to glory" signifies progress—that a process is taking place. The passive present is used— "We are *being* transformed." For some people "glory to glory" has been in baby steps with long intervals of time between.

Carnality, prayerlessness, failure to attend church regularly, bad company—all indicate the failure to surrender to Christ. Still other Christians, having surrendered their wills to the Lord, take giant steps on the road of glory.

Power. Saved by God's power, it still takes His power to develop Christlikeness. Inner changes in character are not wrought by human strength or self-will. No amount of sincerity, turning over a new leaf, hypnosis, or education can make us more like the Lord Jesus Christ.

That is the work of the Holy Spirit. He is in the Christlike-character-molding business. Hold Christ preeminent in your life. Give Him first place. Contemplate His holiness. Enlarge your vision of Him. Recognize Him as the lover of your soul. See His triumph over death, hell, and the grave. By such power you will fulfill His purpose for your life and make good progress in the process of being changed from glory to glory.

September 22

For we walk by faith, not by sight. (2 Corinthians 5:7)

When you become a Christian you submit yourself to Christ. "Lord, I believe You bought me from the slave market with Your precious blood. I am Yours; do with me as You please." That is faith. It is the only kind of life that counts.

Walking by sight or by feelings is not the key to discovering what really counts in life. You cannot believe everything you see. Yet some people say that "seeing is believing." Well, if your eyes are all you have going for you, you are in bad shape.

Satan is able to disguise himself as an angel of light. Wicked men may have charisma. Deluded men may have sincerity. Thieves can quote statistics. Fools can do some good deeds. Demons can sing like angels. Judas can belong to the band of disciples. Counterfeit money may be expertly engraved. In this age of sham, men may be led astray very easily.

If you do not depend upon the Holy Spirit you will be fooled into making mountains out of molehills. Make sure you are in Christ, connected with Him through faith in His shed blood. Apart from Him men have no purpose, no goal in life.

No matter what value we attach to ceremony, ritual, titles, tradition, church work, raising money, maintaining customs, they have no validity, no strength, and no ability to produce beneficial inward changes.

Without Christ, men dream dreams, grasp after straws, kiss shadows, chase the wind, talk trash, hug delusions, entertain speculations, and shrink their souls. What counts most in life is taking God at His Word. The new creation in Christ expresses his faith in love and shows his love by his faith.

September 23

For the love of Christ compels [constrains, KJV] us.
(2 Corinthians 5:14)

Paul had to defend his Christian ministry and his apostleship against the enemies of the gospel. He discovered early in his work for the Lord that when men did not like the message, they found fault with the messenger.

Some went so far as to call him crazy (v. 13), suggesting as did Festus, "Paul, you are beside yourself! Much learning is driving you mad!" (Acts 26:24). Then too, Paul's motives were impugned. He was forced to argue that his attempt to persuade men of his own integrity as a servant of Christ was not motivated by anything ulterior or evil.

The apostle served Christ because of the love that Christ had for him; *Christ's* love is what motivated Paul. Taken objectively, the statement would mean Paul's love for the Lord; but here it is *subjective*—Christ's love for the *apostle*.

Constrain is a word with Latin roots meaning "to draw tight." The original Greek word means literally "to hold together, sustain." It is translated in various ways in other verses in the King James Version: *constrain* can mean "to take, press, straiten, keep in, or hold in custody." In essence Paul said, "I am *controlled* by the love of Christ— His love *compels* me."

What a philosophy of life! Regardless of what your peers may think about you, irrespective of what your enemies may do and despite all adverse circumstances, Jesus Christ still *loves* you. That is all that matters.

Let His love motivate you; let it compel you, keep you going. See today how that love increases your love for Him, helps you love other Christians, and then overflows to reach the unsaved.

> O Love that wilt not let me go,
>
> I rest my weary soul in Thee;
>
> I give Thee back the life I owe,
>
> That in Thine ocean depths its flow
>
> May richer, fuller be.

George Matheson

September 24

Therefore, if anyone is in Christ, he is a new creation; old things have passed away; behold, all things have become new. (2 Corinthians 5:17)

The new creation is vastly superior to the old. Perhaps you have forgotten from whence you were dug. I do not mean transplanted from the South to the North, from a small town to a big city, or from a barn to a condominium. I mean from Egypt to the Promised Land.

Have you forgotten how miserable life used to be when you were tired of living but afraid of dying? There was no purpose in life. You were weighted down by guilt, shackled by evil, debilitating habits, influenced by wicked companions.

Think about life in Egypt and you will realize indeed how much superior the new creature is to the old. The old man was dead in sin and trespasses; the new person has eternal life in Christ. The old man's feet were mired in clay; the new creature has on gospel shoes. The old man traveled the broad road toward destruction; the new voyager walks on the King's highway.

The old traveler sang the "blues"; the new creation sings the "Hallelujah Chorus"! The new creature in Christ is what life is all about. The old was shackled, the new creature has been liberated by the Son of God who sets men free indeed. The old was headed for hell; the new is a citizen of heaven.

The old was unable to do right; the new creation is empowered by the Holy Spirit to please God. That is what counts in Christ, what really matters—becoming a new creation with a new name, a new spiritual outlook, the Holy Spirit living within, putting on the new man, obtaining a new body, and able to walk into the New Jerusalem to see the Savior face to face.

September 25

For He made Him who knew no sin to be sin for us, that we might become the righteousness of God in Him. (2 Corinthians 5:21)

Jesus Christ is the "not-having-known-sin-at-any-time" one. The tenses used indicate that He knew no sin up to the very moment of His death at Calvary. He knew about sin, and He knew sinners. He himself was tempted, but there was nothing in Him that the devil could grab hold of (John 14:30).

That should come as no surprise, for Jesus Christ is God. Becoming a man did not stop Him from being God; the very idea is absurd. Whatever else He gave up, those essential moral qualities, or attributes, of God that make God God cannot be divested, thrown off, or emptied out. God is always holy, eternally righteous.

God the Father made the sinless one to be sin. Note that He did not make Him a *sinner*. That is unthinkable. Here we have more than being made a sin offering. Christ was made a curse for us (Galatians 3:13). He was charged with all that sin is in us. The Father laid upon Christ the iniquity of us all (Isaiah 53:6). There on Calvary's cruel cross He slew His only begotten Son.

That was done in order that sinners such as we are might become reconciled to the Lord. You see, by that act of God His intense hatred of sin was demonstrated, His wrath vented. The death of Jesus Christ satisfied the anger of God against sin, and all that had made peace impossible was removed.

That is the good news; sin has been dealt with at a terrible price. Jesus Christ took our place, bore our sins, and died the death we all deserved by shedding His blood for us. Rejoice this day! In Christ you are without condemnation.

September 26

For what fellowship has righteousness with lawlessness? And what communion has light with darkness? And what accord has Christ with Belial? Or what part has a believer with an unbeliever? (2 Corinthians 6:14–15)

All of us agree that there is power in unity. It is good to be in harmony in the church, in the home, in marriage, and in society. Cooperation is commendable. However, there is danger in man's seeking to harmonize that which is out of harmony with God. If we are not united in that which is proper, our unity becomes abomination unto the Lord.

Remember that there is no symphony of soul between our Savior and Satan. Satan hates us; Christ loves us. Satan desires to kill us; Christ died for us. Satan is the prince or darkness; Christ is the Light of the world.

Satan, a roaring lion, seeks to devour; Christ, the Lamb of God, seeks to save. Satan deceives; Christ enlightens. Satan accuses; Christ forgives. Satan condemns; Christ pardons. Satan entices us to do evil; Christ encourages us to do right. Satan weakens us; Christ empowers us to do good.

Satan pushes the old nature; Christ strengthens the new nature in us. Satan is the father of lies; Christ is truth. Satan shackles; Christ sets free. To Satan, Jehovah directed these words: "Yet you shall be brought down to Sheol, to the lowest depths of the Pit" (Isaiah 14:15); but to Christ came the words of God the Father, "You are My beloved Son; in You I am well pleased" (Luke 3:22).

Such then are the differences between our Savior and Satan. There are no points of agreement between them— no, not in word, thought, deed, or purpose. Christians ought to have no agreement, accord, harmony, concord, or intimate association with the children of the devil, with those who practice sin (1 John 3:8–10). Be careful of the company you keep.

September 27

Bringing every thought into captivity to the obedience of Christ. (2 Corinthians 10:5)

No man can succeed in the battle of thought who refuses to submit his mind to the Holy Spirit. I know that God gave each of us a brain and expects us to use it to think and to reason. Yet somehow true freedom is in being chained to the Master, Jesus Christ. Only when the Holy Spirit controls our thought life can we thoroughly please God.

Note that it is to be *every* thought. That means all the time—not some thoughts sometime. There is a tendency for some of us to feel that evil thoughts are not so bad as long as we do not carry them out.

I am not suggesting we become zombies, automatons, mechanical men, robots, or spiritual dummies. When Christ controls our minds, they are stayed on Him; we trust in Him, and we are kept in perfect peace. In Christ, the "thoughts of the righteous are right" (Proverbs 12:5). Again: "Commit your works to the LORD, and your thoughts will be established" (Proverbs 16:3).

When Christ controls our thoughts we have sober thoughts and are not high-minded, conceited, puffed up, or do not think too highly of ourselves (Romans 12:3). When Christ controls our thoughts we think on things that are true, noble, just, pure, lovely, of good report and virtuous (Philippians 4:8). When Christ controls our thoughts, we do not think ourselves to be something when we are nothing (Galatians 6:3).

To obey Christ is to do what He tells us—when, where, no matter what! It seems to me that when a person comes to see what Jesus Christ accomplished on Calvary, he comes to want no less than to be totally owned by the Lord—to have even his thought life controlled.

September 28

Examine yourselves as to whether you are in the faith. Test [prove, KJV] yourselves. (2 Corinthians 13:5)

I guess unfair criticism bothers all of us. It certainly made the apostle Paul angry. It seems there were always those constantly observing Paul and trying to undermine his authority, nullify his ministry, and put an end to his preaching.

He was under constant surveillance; his detractors poked fun at his size (*Paul* means "little"), despised his appearance, belittled his speech, doubted his sincerity, questioned his apostleship, and threw in his face the facts of his past life when he persecuted the church. Our text comes as part of an angry response—a caustic reply to those at Corinth who spent their time peering at Paul through a microscope. The command to the Corinthian saints is: Examine yourselves!

Keep testing yourselves to make sure you are in the faith. Are you a Christian or just a church member? Are you just singing in the choir, or do you really have a song in your heart? Is your name merely on the church roll, or is it written down in the Lamb's book of life?

The word rendered "examine" is also translated "tempt." That is because under such testing man often breaks down. The word *tempt* connotes putting to the test with the hope and intention of breaking a man down.

Examine yourself and discover your weak points and your strong points. Inasmuch as the command is given, the obedience is possible. What God orders us to do, He enables us to do. It is possible for a man to test or examine himself and *know* whether he is in the faith. Thank God if you are in Christ and you know it by virtue of the examination. The second step is to prove yourself and show that Christ is in you. *Prove* here means to test for approval. How? By your love of the brethren, time spent in prayer, study of the Bible, and clean living. What a challenge for today!

September 29

It is no longer I who live, but Christ lives in me.
(Galatians 2:20)

Prior to my becoming a Christian my old nature ruled as mayor in the city hall of my heart. All the world revolved around me, myself, and I. Had I been rich, I would have said the same thing the man in Luke 12:16–20 said. But I was poor, and though I could not say what the rich man said, I lived like it anyway. My attitude was the same as his was.

Self-centeredness is natural to the sinner. Unfortunately, millions of other sinners think the world revolves around them. That causes conflict, crime, and war. As the wills of men collide, Satan attempts to force his will upon an unsuspecting world. The entire universe is full of big I's and little you's.

When I became a believer the Holy Spirit was seated in the city hall of my heart to superintend my human spirit. Only in that way can I now truthfully say, "I, yet no longer I." Acceptance of our position in Christ should make us aware that *I alone* is no good. Someone other than *I* is available to help, to guide, strengthen, and preserve; that someone is Jesus Christ.

Christ in me becomes the motive and power for the good *I* do. Note that it is the good *I* do. The tremendous paradox is that it is not *I alone*. Jesus Christ living in me motivates and empowers so that all the credit goes to Him. To the word *I* must be added the words: "Yet *no longer* I." The life lived in my body has hidden roots. They are in Christ.

The saint is to live so intimately with Christ that the Lord controls his life, imparts power and impulse, and transforms him morally and spiritually. Christ works His will through him. God grant that you will have today that spiritual awareness that is needed in order for the doctrine to be put into practice.

September 30

For you are all sons of God through faith in Christ Jesus.
(Galatians 3:26)

You can imagine the consternation of the apostle Paul when he heard that some Judaizers, or legalizers, had come and upset some of the saints there in Galatia. They argued that in order to be a genuine Christian it was necessary to obey the law of Moses—circumcision, Sabbath keeping, kosher foods, and so on. Otherwise, one could not be right with God.

That was false doctrine. If you are going to operate under a law system and be legalistic, you are ignoring the emancipation proclamation of Christ. Paul was led to argue that faith alone put people right with God—not what you eat, what you drink, what you wear, what day you worship, cutting of the flesh, and so on. Paul desired to lift the Christian's point of view above legalism.

Whatever your faults, mistakes, bad ways, whatever your stumblings and falterings, once born again you cannot be unborn; God does not disinherit Christians. The proof that you are a son is the presence of the Holy Spirit in your body.

He lives in you as a result of the redemptive work of Christ at Calvary. God's Spirit in you is the guarantee of sonship, the down-payment of future blessings. We are adult sons and daughters of God, not minors who are under certain controls and restrictions.

The entire Godhead is involved in making each believer a son and an heir. The power to live as sons of God comes only from the Holy Spirit sent by the Father in the name of the Son.

October 1

Therefore you are no longer a slave but a son, and if a son, then an heir of God through Christ. (Galatians 4:7)

If God the Father already has given us the Lord Jesus, the inexpressible, indescribable, unspeakable gift, what is there He will not now give us? It is tragic then for members of the royal family of God to still live and serve in the attitude of a slave. Christians ought not cringe in fear and doubt, afraid to venture out for the Lord, "For God has not given us a spirit of fear, but of power and of love and of a sound mind" (2 Timothy 1:7).

We are heirs of God through Christ, or as Paul states in Romans 8:17—heirs of God and joint heirs with Christ. We are recipients of a marvelous new spiritual heritage through God. I repeat: this sonship and subsequent inheritance is through God.

It is not something we earn or merit. We are not naturally-born sons of God (inward) or children of God (outward). We have to be born again.

If you have been born again, the earth is yours, everlasting life is yours, the kingdom of God is yours, the righteousness of God is yours. You are an heir of salvation with angels to minister to you.

You have inherited the promises, blessings, and incorruption. You are an heir of glory, a joint heir with Jesus Christ and will share in all that belongs to Him.

We are right now heirs of God. It is not a matter of waiting until we die in order to receive anything from the Lord. We are right now justified; we are right now sanctified; we are right now the temples of the Holy Spirit; we are right now citizens of heaven; we are right now accepted by the Father; we are right now possessors of the inheritance.

October 2

Let us not become conceited, provoking one another.
(Galatians 5:26)
Let us provoke one another. (Hebrews 10:24, KJV)

A conceited person is one who is full of bluster, a boaster, a braggart, envious of others, striving after empty honors. A conceited man puts false values on people and things. For him, nonessentials are made matters of life and death. He talks big and establishes opinions without foundation.

Now unfortunately, conceit calls forth a response; it challenges competition. It is this challenging that is called "provoking" in Galatians. It means to incite, goad, dare one another to do things against which there may be conscientious scruples.

It is a "calling each other down." That is how the stronger-natured person responds in kind to his own conceit—he accepts the challenges to combat.

On the other hand, in Hebrews 10:24, *provoke* is not a calling forth as in Galatians 5:26 but a *paroxysm*: (1) a sudden outburst of emotion or action, or (2) a spasm, fit, or convulsion. The Greek is literally "to sharpen or goad, spur to anger, irritate, incense."

How strange it is then to use such a word here, not in the sense of moving to strife, contention, bitterness, and anger, but as an incitement to love and encouragement to good works. That is surely the kind of stirring up that is needed in our churches today!

Keep in mind the needs of your fellow saints—their trials, tribulations, testings, temptations, infirmities, frustrations, and bad circumstances. Why? In order to stir up, provoke, and stimulate one another to love and good deeds.

October 3

Do not be deceived, God is not mocked; for whatever a man sows, that he will also reap. For he who sows to his flesh will of the flesh reap corruption, but he who sows to the Spirit will of the Spirit reap everlasting life. (Galatians 6:7–8)

We read repeatedly in Exodus that Pharaoh hardened his own heart and refused to let the children of Israel go. He thus fitted himself into God's plan of punishment. The Lord in turn speeded up Pharaoh's destruction by sending the plagues. God caused the events calculated to hasten Pharaoh's doom.

God's will came first. Pharaoh's evil conduct ran smack against that righteous will, and he suffered the consequences.

The God of the Bible is prepared for every contingency. Neither man nor the devil and his demons can create any situations that catch God by surprise and compel Him to do something other than He originally intended.

The awesome fact is that God is going to be glorified one way or the other. He prefers that men and women, boys and girls, willingly, free-heartedly honor, magnify, and glorify Him. They should do so in tongue, for God delights to hear men praise, bless, and eulogize Him. They should also do so in deed, for God delights when men practice those things that are pleasing in His sight.

What is more, He has made it possible for us to fulfill our purpose in life. How? Through faith in Jesus Christ. Without faith, it is impossible to please God. That faith must be in the shed blood of Christ; that faith is trust, reliance, and confidence in what God the Son did at Calvary.

There He who knew no sin was made sin for us that we might be made the righteousness of God in Him. Believe that in your heart and you have a purpose in living, a goal in life that guarantees a foretaste of divine glory now and eternal joy later.

October 4

For in Christ Jesus neither circumcision nor uncircumcision avails anything, but a new creation. (Galatians 6:15)

No physical conditions, racial characteristics, educational achievements, intellectual ability, political affiliation, degree of civilization, or attainment of culture—none of those are essential to New Testament Christianity.

That was the lesson to be learned at Galatia, where there were those who emphasized the outward cutting of the flesh. It is a fact that other nations practiced circumcision, but God introduced it to Abraham (Genesis 17:9–14). For Abraham and his descendants God gave that cutting of the flesh a spiritual significance. Circumcision became a foundation sign and seal of God's covenant with Israel.

You can see why the Judaizers wanted to maintain the practice. They argued that Christians must also keep the law of Moses. Paul said no. Outside show and ceremony do not count in Christ. Cuttings of the physical flesh, observance of feast days, holy days, new moons, keeping of the Sabbaths, special diets—those mean nothing in Christ. His work at Calvary was complete. "It is finished!" He cried. Nothing needs to be added.

What really matters in life then is not some outward cutting of the flesh, but an inward Spirit-wrought activity. What counts is a new creation. What is a new creation? It is a genuine Christian. If you are a true saint—if you really believe in Christ—then neither high IQ nor low IQ, neither much culture nor little culture, neither black skin nor white skin will avail you anything with God.

What counts is to be born again—to accept the shed blood of Jesus Christ. Then you will become a different person; old standards and values will be discarded, and life will have a new meaning.

October 5

You were sealed with the Holy Spirit of promise, who is the guarantee of our inheritance until the redemption of the purchased possession, to the praise of His glory. (Ephesians 1:13–14)

The moment one accepts the shed blood of Jesus Christ, the Holy Spirit comes to live in his or her body. The Holy Spirit is given as the first installment of things to come. In other words, the Holy Spirit is given as a down-payment.

He is a pledge of what is in store. He is a security deposit—a guarantee. Having just sold our home and in the process of buying another house, we are familiar with the contract terms. A down-payment of $500 was required to get the process moving.

The contract may stipulate that within ten days more money is to be given in order to bring the total up to at least ten percent. If a mortgage loan is gotten, then the remainder of the money is paid at settlement. The guarantee, or down-payment, indicates good faith in the purchase and that you intend to go through with the deal.

God intends to go through with His contract. God established us; He makes us steadfast in the Lord Jesus Christ by giving us the Holy Spirit to live in our bodies. "By this we know that He abides in us, by the Spirit whom He has given us" (1 John 3:24). Consequently my confidence, said Paul, is in knowing that what God started He is going to finish.

God bound the contract by giving the Holy Spirit in advance. The confidence of salvation is not man-made. Such assurance comes from the Lord alone. It is not worked up by man. It is not based upon emotional experiences or produced by speaking in tongues.

God moves to make us sure in our heart. God gives the confidence. We know that what the Lord started in our lives He is obligated to complete. He will redeem His purchased possession.

October 6

But God, who is rich in mercy. . . . (Ephesians 2:4)

God often reminds us of what we used to be. His purposes for so doing are: (1) that the reminder might help us to keep humble, (2) to deepen our gratitude, (3) to heighten the concept of His grace, and (4) to glorify God who alone is able to take nothing (what we *were*) and make something (what we are *now*) out of it.

We need to hear anew the exhortation Jehovah gave to Israel through Moses: "You shall remember that you were a slave in the land of Egypt, and the LORD your God redeemed you" (Deuteronomy 15:15).

A reading of Ephesians convinces us that in our former state we were in very bad shape—dead in trespasses and sins, walking in iniquity, following foolish fads and fashions, influenced by the devil who is the prince of the power of the air.

We were disobedient, living in lusts, rebellious, governed by the desires of the flesh and the mind, condemned children of wrath, formerly darkness, partakers with the children of disobedience, bound for hell. What a picture of our background!

But God, who is rich in mercy, loved us when we were unlovable and sent His only begotten Son, Jesus Christ, to die for us. He who knew no sin became sin and was smitten by God there on Calvary. There on Golgotha the Prince of Life was struck dead, the Rose of Sharon was plucked up, the Rock of Ages was shattered.

But God is a phrase replete with grace, mercy, and love. Thank God for the reverse of adversity—God Himself!

October 7

For this reason I, Paul, the prisoner of Jesus Christ for you Gentiles. . . . (Ephesians 3:1)

The cause to which Paul referred was the revelation of the fact that Gentiles and Jews are united in one new group, the church, the Body of Christ. Paul was in jail because he preached that the Gentiles were a part of God's house. You see, preaching that Jesus was the Messiah had stirred up the Jews against Paul. When he started talking about Jew and Gentile joined together, it was more than enough to cause a paroxysm among his brethren after the flesh.

The Jews' uproar at Jerusalem started Paul on his way to prison. He was seized in the Temple, rescued, and bound by Roman soldiers. When he sought to defend his action in a speech before the mob, he was interrupted by them at the mention of the Gentiles.

Brought before the Sanhedrin the next day, Paul's appeal to the Pharisees caused a great dissension, and once again the soldiers had to rescue him. At that point a conspiracy to kill Paul was discovered by Paul's nephew, and he was removed by night to Caesarea. Brought before Felix the governor, he was accused by the Jews (Acts 24:5–6), but Paul defended himself.

For two years, guarded by a centurion, Paul remained at Caesarea until the new governor, Festus, came. Once again the Jews "laid many serious complaints against Paul, which they could not prove" (Acts 25:7). Paul then appealed to Caesar, making it necessary that he be sent to Rome.

After his defense and appeal to King Agrippa, after the storm at sea and landing on the Isle of Malta, Paul finally arrived at Rome. There he remained for a number of years as a prisoner before losing his life, possibly about 68 A.D. What has happened to you as a result of your witnessing for Jesus Christ?

October 8

. . . to the intent that now the manifold wisdom of God might be made known by the church to the principalities and powers in the beavenly places. (Ephesians 3:10)

By God's grace Paul was called to preach among the Gentiles the unsearchable riches of Christ. That God would so work as to bring Jew and Gentile together in one body, the Body of Christ, the church, was a mystery, a thing man could never discover.

That which had been hidden in the plan of God from the beginning of the ages is now manifest. It is here the church has a part to play. Its mission is to make known the full measure of the wisdom of God.

The church itself is the example of God's wisdom. The visible embodiment of divine omniscience, the very existence of the church is proof and demonstration of that wisdom. The church is something for the entire universe to see.

Why? Because what God in wisdom had in mind from the beginning is made plain to the angels. In the church God brought together and united that which was most unlikely to be put together. By a multitude of means, influences, skillful designs, God in grace, love, and mercy put together a body of believers in Christ Jesus.

The local assembly, with all of its faults, is still an example of the wisdom of God. In no place else could so many different people come together in one accord in Jesus Christ, whom they have never seen.

God has ordained that the church make it known—to men and to angels—that the church itself is a mirror of God's wisdom. That, said Paul, was the purpose of his preaching the gospel. The church is to be a channel through which is announced the divine wisdom. Nothing else reveals so clearly God's mind in creation as does the church.

October 9

I, therefore, the prisoner of the Lord. . . . (Ephesians 4:1)

Are you a prisoner of Christ? There are indeed some things that we are constrained *to do* and some things we are restrained *from doing*. There are some places I cannot go; there are some things I do not want to do.

Yes, my speech is limited. Certain places are off limits. My diet is restricted. I probably would never wear certain clothing styles. My lifestyle has some limitations.

But in a sense every man is limited by his own likes, dislikes, culture, customs, traditions, mores, and environment. It is in the Christian's favor that he has a different set of values.

Once the Holy Spirit takes over the city hall of your life, new mandates are set forth. A new source of energy is supplied. Somehow the "jailbird for Jesus" finds for the first time in his life that he is really free.

He is free from practicing self-destructive habits, free from character-demeaning outlooks, free from foolish speculation and puny philosophy, free from twisted values, free from overpowering lusts and uncontrollable desires, free from the rat race that leads directly to hell, free from so-called friends who would tear him down, free from vain ideologies, free from false beliefs like evolution or reincarnation, free from sin's dominion, the cancer of hatred, and the fear of death.

The Christian knows that the predestinated boundaries and limits that God has set around him are calculated to make him what the Lord wants him to be. Whatever the vocation to which He has called you, walk worthy of it, and rejoice in the freedom of your calling.

October 10

Endeavoring to keep the unity of the Spirit in the bond of peace.
(Ephesians 4:3)

We have unity already, but it is a positional oneness. God exhorts that we keep what we have already, that we live up to that which the Lord has declared now exists. We *are* united; we *are* one. Now *live* like it!

It is not a man-made oneness or uniformity; we do not all wear the same type of clothing, same color, same material, same style. There are those in our churches who despair our lack of outward cohesiveness, but their suggestions for bringing a church together are naive, underestimating the power of sin or the strong hold Satan has. True fellowship, however, is based upon something we *do* hold in common.

The basis for unity is the fact that we are members of one body, indwelt by one Holy Spirit, called in one hope of our calling. We have one God, in our hearts is one faith, by the Spirit we have received one baptism; there is one God and Father of all who believe. Cleansed by the one blood, citizens of the one heaven, we enjoy the one salvation. True positional unity exists already.

Positionally we have unity. *Practically* that unity may be threatened. So we have to work at maintaining that which the Lord declares is now true of us. When we do work at it we are blessed. We enjoy it. There is power available, and such harmony advances the cause of Christ by striking fear in the hearts of evildoers.

Our greatest example in this unity is Christ. One with the Father, He knew what was ahead for Him. Yet He flinched not. His composure made a shambles out of the prearranged plans of Judas. Indeed, His enemies became all the more angry and determined to do Him in. They succeeded temporarily. Only temporarily! After three days and three nights Jesus Christ rose from the grave with all power in His hands.

October 11

And He Himself gave [many essential gifts] for the edifying of the body of Christ. (Ephesians 4:11–12)

Ephesians 4:11–16 is a very lengthy and complicated sentence. In essence it is saying that God has given the church exactly what it needs to grow and become what God wants it to be. The church is not left an orphan, to make out the best it can by underhanded tactics, manipulations, politics, unholy alliances, inflated titles, ego trips, or mercenary gimmicks.

No. God's desire for the church is: Grow up! If earthly parents want to see their children grow up, mature, become adults, how much more our heavenly Father desires that for us. Our Father, who regenerated us through faith in the shed blood of Jesus Christ, wants us to be adults in our thinking.

Immature Christians are easy prey to spiritual slickers, church charlatans, and devilish cultists. Tossed to and fro, they are easily carried about by all kinds of doctrines. They are immature, weak, unsettled, unsteady, flighty, temperamental, selfish Christians. God does not want us to be that way.

His desire is that we be edified. Note that twice the word *edify* is used. In verse 16 Paul speaks of the building up of the Christian in *love*. Here is the challenge to the church: Grow up! Be edified!

Such a topic as edification is a challenge to us because we live in an age of destructiveness. There is so much seeking to tear us down and nullify our witness for Jesus Christ.

Two things the Christian can do are: (1) speak only that which is good for necessary edification (Ephesians 4:29), and (2) remember that love edifies (1 Corinthians 8:1). Clean language and Christian love practiced by the believer will help build up the Body of Christ.

October 12

"Be angry, and do not sin": do not let the sun go down on your wrath. (Ephesians 4:26)

Anger is not forbidden in the Bible. Indeed, the new man in Christ may very well get angry at times. I am sure the Lord Jesus would like to see more Christians become angry with sin, filth, hypocrisy, racism, and corruption.

Remember too that the Lord Himself became angry (Mark 3:5) when men accused Him of violating the Sabbath and again at the first and second cleansings of the Temple (John 2:15; Mark 11:15). It cannot be said that all anger is sin.

The apostle Paul is here quoting a sentence from Psalm 4:4 and prompting us to obey what at first may seem to be a contradiction. "Be angry, and do not sin" contains two imperatives: (1) be angry, and (2) do not sin. We are urged to be angry and in the same breath urged not to sin in that anger.

That is God's advice to those who believe in the shed blood of Jesus Christ. What He commands us to do, He also enables us to do. Even justifiable anger must not be kept too long. Get it out of your system before the day is over. Otherwise it may fester and grow and control *you* instead of you controlling *it*.

Now how can we obey this scripture? Prayer is the best way. Take it to the Lord, and leave it there. Failure to dismiss such anger gives the devil a toehold. I know that at times Satan influences my thoughts. He whispers, "Are you going to take that? I thought you were a man! You're a chump and a fool to boot. Why don't you tell him off or, better yet, punch him!"

At such times of testing the Bible really helps. I am glad that the Holy Spirit in me prevents me from venting my anger in violence. Consequently I have lived to see many more suns come up—and go down.

October 13

And do not grieve the Holy Spirit of God, by whom you were sealed for the day of redemption. (Ephesians 4:30)

This command is full of good theology for the person washed in the precious blood of the Lord Jesus Christ. For one thing, it indicates that the Holy Spirit is a Person, not just a wind, breath, or impersonal force as is taught by some. The Spirit of God is a person, not an "it."

You cannot grieve a thing, an inanimate object; only personality is grieved, made sorrowful, affected with sadness, or offended. The Spirit is more than an influence.

Second, the command itself indicates a very close relationship between the Spirit and the believer. That is because the Holy Spirit lives in the bodies of all true Christians (1 Corinthians 6:19). Such intimate fellowship exists to make Jesus Christ real to us.

Third, Christians grow in the realization that known, unconfessed sins are the basic cause of God's grief. When we fail to confess—to say the same thing God says about our sin—then fellowship is broken, our witness is sullied, cause for criticism of Christ is given, our strength is sapped, and our prayers become heavy.

Years ago my heart was struck by the words God asked Israel through the prophet Jeremiah: "What injustice have your fathers found in Me, that they have gone far from Me, have followed idols, and have become idolaters?" (Jeremiah 2:5).

Can you imagine a grief-stricken God asking pieces of clay, "What wrong have you found in Me, to break My heart the way you have?" Surely Christians must answer that the failure is not in God but in us. May the blessed Holy Spirit find cause for rejoicing in your life today.

October 14

. . . forgiving one another, even as God in Christ forgave you.
(Ephesians 4:32)

To *forgive* means "to pardon, to extend favor, show grace"; it is to excuse for a fault or offense, to renounce anger or resentment against, and to free the offender from the consequences of his offense. To forgive is to grant pardon without harboring resentment.

Why should Christians forgive one another? Because God commands it. What the Lord commands us to do, He also supplies the strength to do. When you wrong me and *I* hold it against you, I sin against you and against God. When I wrong you and *you* hold it against me, you sin against me and against God.

Why should Christians forgive one another? What is behind such forgiveness? What is its motivation? The forgiveness of God which was heard, seen, and experienced at Calvary is the answer. Christ's shedding His blood at Golgotha is what pushes Christians to forgive other Christians.

We are not asked by the Scriptures to forgive other Christians in our own strength, out of the goodness of our forgiving hearts, but for Christ's sake—because of Jesus Christ, on account of Christ, in Christ.

If we will practice with one another Christlikeness in the church, the Body of our Lord, we become fit vessels to be used of the Lord Jesus in society, on the job, in the neighborhood, at home, and in school. Wherever we are, wherever we go, we take Christ with us. Those outside of Christ will be influenced by the love and forgiving spirit they see among Christians.

October 15

And walk in love . . . as children of light . . . circumspectly.
(Ephesians 5:2, 8, 15)

Your walk is your conduct. Paul used *walk* in a moral sense and taught that it is impossible to become a Christian and yet continue to walk as a pagan. The apostle John taught that the walk refers not only to practical conduct but to the whole stance of the believer. Our walk is our behavior, the way we live, our lifestyle, our conduct.

Walk in love. Our love for the Lord should undergird our behavior. How? We show we love Him by keeping His commandments (John 14:15). We show we love God by reading and studying the Bible. Loving God is a process of growth, and basic to that growth is our knowledge, understanding, and appreciation of the Bible. Then, too, we show that we love God by our love for other Christians.

Walk in the light. Light is holiness, so to walk in it is to live pleasing to the Lord. Light is knowledge. To walk in the light is to do what you know is right, to avoid doing what you know is wrong, and to continue learning which is which.

Light represents the known will of God. When a Christian practices what he knows is right, he walks in the light. As the will and desire of God are made known and we obey, we are walking in the light.

Walk, looking—which is what *circumspectly* means. The saint is to be prudent, heedful of circumstances, mindful of consequences. In short, the saint should watch his step. Many pitfalls and hidden snares exist these days. But if we let the Holy Spirit lead us, we will be more than successful in walking in love and in light. We shall give better witness to all concerned that we are the children of God.

October 16

For you were once darkness, but now you are light in the Lord.
Walk as children of light. (Ephesians 5:8)

Darkness describes the way of the wicked (Proverbs 4:19), the fool (Ecclesiastes 2:14), burglars (Job 24:16), and the ignorant (John 12:35). We are reminded that once upon a time we were in darkness, ignorant of God's will. We walked in darkness because we were blind; we loved darkness because our deeds were evil; and we had fellowship with the unfruitful works of darkness because we had no discernment.

Once we *were* darkness. Being darkness involves the inner person, a darkened understanding, and a foolish heart. Now such a time is behind us; a tremendous change has been wrought, a miraculous transformation has taken place.

Having been born again through faith in the shed blood of Jesus Christ, we are now the children of light. To be a child of someone is to inherit characteristics of that person. God is light, and Jesus Christ is the Light of the world. The child of God reflects that light.

Now Paul says, "Because you are light, walk like it." Intellectually, light is truth; morally, it is holiness; mentally, it is knowledge; spiritually, light is righteousness.

What ecstasy we experience when we contrast what we were with what we are now! Not that we are conditionally perfect. No, our standing is perfect, but our state is imperfect. There are still faults and failures, slippings and slidings, but we rejoice in having another day to let our light so shine before men that our blessed Father in heaven may be glorified.

> I looked to Jesus, and I found
> In Him my Star, my Sun;
> And in that light of life I'll walk,
> Till trav'ling days are done.
> *Horatius Bonar*

October 17

Finding out what is acceptable to the Lord.
(Ephesians 5:10)

One of the great needs of today is spiritual discernment, Christian discrimination, and Holy Spirit insight. These are days when so many professed Christians, let alone the unsaved world, cannot tell right from wrong, truth from falsehood, or the road to heaven from the road to hell.

Forced daily to make decisions, we are dazed by the fast pace of modern society, deceived by self, and deluded by Satan. Consequently our concepts are blurred, our senses numbed, our ideas fuzzy, our spirits dulled, our eyes blinded, and some unbelievers have consciences that are seared.

How easily people are duped by spiritual quacks, self-appointed messiahs, gurus, prophets, bishops, advisors, healers, tongue-speakers, and merchants of materialism. Such lack of discernment is one aspect of darkness. God, who is light, and Jesus Christ, who is the Light of the world, have no desire that we dwell in such darkness (Ephesians 5:8–14). Having been washed in the blood of Christ, we are now the children of light. So walk in the light.

The Lord is not looking for sullen faces of disgruntled, foot-shuffling people given to mediocrity and eye service. He desires folks who are eager, willing, ever-ready, zealous, driven with a burning desire to please the Lord. To please God—that is the motivation. We must ask, "Father, what would You have me to do?"

That is the approach to the life of light, possible when you know and love Jesus Christ in a real, vital, intimate, and personal way. Only in that way can the darkness of the dearth of discernment be dispelled. Strive today to do only that which is acceptable and pleasing to the Lord and thrill to hear the Holy Spirit within you give witness to your spiritual success.

October 18

And you, fathers, do not provoke your children to wrath, but bring them up in the training and admonition of the Lord. (Ephesians 6:4)

This exhortation is found in the practical section of the book of Ephesians and deals with the Christian's walk, one of the major themes in this section. Actually the Spirit-filled walk affects all aspects of life. The three relationships Paul felt led to deal with are: (1) husband-wife (2) child-parent (3) slave-master.

Fathers are warned not to continuously irritate their children or make it a habit of provoking them to anger by vexatious commands, uncertain temper, or unreasonable blame. They are not to exasperate them to resentment.

How is that obeyed? By bringing them up in the training, discipline, wisdom, counsel, and admonition of the Lord Jesus Christ.

Note that this is a command (Deuteronomy 6:7; 11:19; Proverbs 22:6). If for no other reason, the father, as the head of the house, ought to do what the Lord commands him. He is held responsible by God.

One man told me he did not believe religion should be forced on his child. He would let his boy grow up and pick what he pleased. I asked him: "Does the boy choose what he wants to eat, or when he wants to go to bed or get up, or if he wants to go to school? Do you make him wear clothing? Why do you stop at the most important thing?"

The Christian father must live the life before his children and seek to win them to Jesus Christ. If he teaches them and prays for them, he will be a good representative of his Father who is in heaven. To lead a child to Christ is the most important thing any parent can do for that child.

October 19

Grace be with all those who love our Lord Jesus Christ in sincerity. Amen. (Ephesians 6:24)

The Lord said on one occasion, "He who loves father or mother more than Me is not worthy of Me. And he who loves son or daughter more than Me is not worthy of Me" (Matthew 10:37). That is basic. God demands, God commands our love—a love that is genuine, unfeigned, real. As Paul said, a "sincere" love.

A Roman artist named Titus was commissioned to carve a statue of the emperor. He did a good job, and at the unveiling everyone was amazed at the striking resemblance of the statue to the living emperor. Every feature was carved to perfection.

All went well as the statue was displayed in public until the summer sun began to bear down. Then suddenly the nose fell off. When the statue was inspected it was discovered that although the rest of it was carved out of marble, the nose was made of wax.

So Titus was banished from Rome in disgrace, and a law was passed decreeing that from then on all statues of the emperor were to be made without wax.

The Latin words for "without wax" are *sine cera*. From those words we have derived the English word *sincere*.

Love for Christ helps eliminate phoniness. Love for self, office, or other things disappears. Love for Christ inspires us to do our very best.

Love for Christ produces love for others and makes us more considerate of them. Love for Christ is the very heart of life, for if you love the Lord Jesus you love Him who sent Him. When all is said and done, we realize that "In this is love, not that we loved God, but that He loved us and sent His Son to be the propitiation [the atoning sacrifice] for our sins. We love him because He first loved us" (1 John 4:10, 19).

October 20

*. . . that you stand fast in one spirit, with one mind striving
together for the faith of the gospel.* (Philippians 1:27)

There are many values and many benefits for the local
church whose members are united and work in harmony
with one another.

First, the blessings of the Lord are bestowed because of
obedience to the Word and will of the Lord. He commands
us to let our lives demonstrate the actual change of citizenship. We are citizens of heaven. We have been translated into the heavenlies; we should live like it. The gospel
of Christ includes unity, integration.

Second, it is good and pleasant (sweet) for brethren to
dwell together in unity (Psalm 133:1). In a world of strife,
chaos, and turmoil, there is in Christian fellowship a joy
divine. It is like an oasis in the desert.

Third, there is power in unity. When folks are together
in spirit, mind, and purpose, their resources are commonly
available, their efforts directed, energy channeled, and the
concentration makes them effective in whatever they un-
dertake to do.

Fourth, such unity strikes terror into the hearts of the
enemy. After all, the devil is the creator of chaos and confusion. He wants to scatter, divide, form cliques, weaken,
and conquer. The lack of unity in a church emboldens the
devil.

True unity is encouraging. Courage in the face of hostility and fearlessness in the face of persecution stir up fear
in the heart of the persecutor. Unity is used to help quiet
disruptive forces.

Even if the enemy is not fazed by your show of unity,
your unity points to the enemy's destruction. Whether he
sees you are united or not, perdition awaits him. Proof?
Your united stand. It is proof that your enemies are basically powerless to thwart God's work and that they are by
their resistance running to ruin.

October 21

Christ Jesus, who, being in the form of God. . . .
(Philippians 2:5–6)

These words constitute one of the strongest assertions in the New Testament that Jesus Christ is God. Enemies of the Bible who deny that Christ is God Almighty are hard put to properly interpret this passage. At best they must deny the Bible is the Word of God.

Now the expression "form of God" (*morphe theou*) does not speak of mere outward appearance. It is true that in the Old Testament there are many references to God's having, like man, a face, eyes, ears, nose, mouth, lips, tongue, arms, fingers, back, clothes, shoes, and staff. However, these are figurative.

We call them anthropomorphisms—man-forms; we describe God in terms we use to describe ourselves. Obviously these are figures of speech, since there is no image in the worship of Jehovah.

In order for a thing to exist, it must have form. Every being has form. An angel is in the form of an angel, a man in the form of a man, a dog in the form of a dog, and God is in the form of God.

Form is the permanent expression of existence—it is that which manifests or demonstrates essential nature or specific character. To be in the form of something, says Lewis Sperry Chafer, means to possess the essential nature or attributes of that being and to reveal them. Thus Jesus Christ was all and everything that makes God God.

To deny the deity of Christ is to undermine the foundation of biblical Christianity. Man is a sinner and deserves to die. Man as man could not save himself. God as God—God in the form of God—cannot die. Since man cannot atone for his sin and God cannot die, the only solution for man's dilemma is the one we find recorded in the Bible: God became a man in the person of Jesus Christ. "And being found in appearance as a man, He humbled Himself and became obedient to the point of death, even the death of the cross" (Philippians 2:8).

October 22

For our citizenship is in heaven, from which we also eagerly wait for the Savior, the Lord Jesus Christ. (Philippians 3:20)

Man is a creature full of curiosity. He has plumbed the depths of the ocean, trekked to the North Pole, scaled Mount Everest, and landed upon the moon. When asked, "Why climb a mountain? Why travel to the moon?" men have answered, "Because they're there."

I have nothing against those who are so venturesome; however, I have no particular interest in such explorations. But there is a place I heard about a long time ago that I want to visit—indeed, I want to take up permanent residence. Where? Heaven.

> Sometimes I'm tossed and driven, Lord,
>
> Sometimes I don't know where to roam,
>
> But I've heard of a place called heaven,
>
> And I've started to make it my home.

Why? Because it is there. Why search, why yearn for heaven? Because it is from there that we also look for the Savior, the Lord Jesus Christ. From heaven—where it is rent-free, no mortgages to pay; where there are no hospitals, funeral parlors, or cemeteries.

From heaven—a city that has no need of the sun or the moon to shine in it; the glory of the Lord lights it, and Christ is the lamp. It is from heaven, where our citizenship is, that we look to see our Savior come.

When He comes He will wipe away all tears from our eyes. When He comes, He will take us up to heaven where the wicked indeed no longer can trouble us, and our wearied souls will be at rest. There we will see those loved ones who outran us and who presently enjoy their citizenship in a way we have yet to experience.

October 23

Be anxious for nothing. (Philippians 4:6)

According to the Word of God it is wrong for the believer to be a worrywart. Indeed, this text is a command. Christians are not asked, they are told: Be full of concern for nothing. They are not begged or pleaded with, they are commanded: Do not worry about anything!

A worried saint is in disobedience to the Word of God. An overanxious Christian is an anomaly, a contradiction. Because we are washed in the blood of Jesus Christ and sealed by the Holy Spirit, no one can pluck us out of the Father's hand. Indeed, our God makes all things work together for our good, as He determines that good. Why then should we worry? Is it that we fail as Christians to take God at His word concerning daily living?

What good is worry? Dr. Charles Mayo said: "Worry affects the circulation—the heart, the glands, the whole nervous system. I have never known a man who died from overwork but many who died from doubt."

What is accomplished by worry? As one anonymous writer put it: "Don't tell me that worry doesn't do any good. I know better. The things I worry about don't happen!"

Another writer stated: "Worry is interest paid on trouble before it comes due."

The antidote for the poison of anxiety and worry is prayer. Rather than chew your fingernails, try this: "In everything by prayer and supplication, with thanksgiving, let your requests be made known to God."

In short, why worry when you can pray?

October 24

Finally, brethren, whatever things are true, whatever things are noble, whatever things are just, whatever things are pure, whatever things are lovely, whatever things are of good report, if there is any virtue and if there is anything praiseworthy—meditate on these things. The things which you learned and received and heard and saw in me, these do, and the God of peace will be with you. (Philippians 4:8–9)

Paul lists virtues that are generally accepted by pagans. Not only what is true, or real, but whatever is noble, or dignified and reverent; whatever is just, or in accord with what is right; whatever is pure, or not mixed with low, debasing elements; whatever is lovely, or calls forth and inspires love; whatever is of good report, or fair-sounding, or has a good ring to it. If there be any moral excellence or if it is worthy of praise, we are told to think on these things.

The word translated *meditate* here means to take into account, reckon, calculate. We are to estimate carefully, weigh out the pros and cons of those moral values. The exhortation is in the form of a present imperative, or present tense command, signifying practice and continuance.

Start now to think on these things, and keep on thinking about them. That is necessary because the battle for the minds of men is a constant warfare. Simply to reflect, merely to contemplate lightly, is not enough.

Consider these thoughts as if you are calculating the cost of committing yourself to them in action, as if you intend to really be a doer of the Word, not a hearer only.

Do them! Again a present tense command is used indicating practice. We see then that these thoughts are to be translated into holy action. Obedience will result in that peace of God that passes all human understanding.

October 25

All things were created through Him and for Him. And He is before all things, and in Him all things consist. (Colossians 1:16–17)

The ground of all creation. Paul answered the heretics at Colosse by pointing out first of all that Jesus Christ is the Creator. All things (in heaven and in earth, visible and invisible, whether thrones, dominions, principalities, or powers) were made by Him; and without Him was not anything made that was made (John 1:3). All created things owe their existence to Jesus Christ.

The goal of all creation. Now we learn also that "all things were . . . for Him." For His own use and glory were they made. In other words, Christ is the end of creation, the very reason for the existence of the universe.

All things are for Him (Hebrews 2:10), for His praise and glory. Said the writer in Proverbs 16:4: "The LORD has made all things for Himself."

The glue of all creation. Note the words "in Him all things consist." That may sound strange, but the word rendered "consist" means to hold together, cohere, to band or stand together. Because of Jesus Christ the universe is a cosmos instead of a chaos.

I am glad that Christ is the sustainer because so few men seem interested in ecology these days. Because man has a polluted mind and heart, it is only natural that in time he would pollute his environment.

The ground, goal and glue of all creation died in our place on the cross for our sins. The very thought humbles us, gives us confidence to go on, and makes our hearts rejoice. Hallelujah, what a Savior!

October 26

. . . which is Christ in you, the hope of glory.
(Colossians 1:27)

Only the Lord of glory can be the hope of glory. And Christ our Lord is our hope, the expectation of good. Our basis for expecting to one day share in the bliss, happiness, honor, beauty, and majestic splendor of Christ is internal, not external; it is spiritual and not fleshly.

Good deeds, high morals, social concern, and other altruistic contributions are all excellent, but they are not the foundation for the assurance of salvation and life eternal. Only your relationship with Jesus Christ can give you this inner assurance. If you are looking for glory hereafter the Lord of glory must be in you right now.

If the surgeon cuts me open he will not find Christ; if the psychiatrist deeply anlayzes me, he will not find Christ in me. But Christ is there just the same. That is a fact revealed in the Bible and made known to us by the Holy Spirit.

"At that day you will know that I am in My Father, and you in Me, and I in you" (John 14:20). "I in them, and You in Me . . ." (John 17:23). Said Paul in Galatians 2:20: "It is no longer I who live, but Christ lives in me." According to Ephesians 3:17, Christ dwells in your heart by faith.

Christ in you points to your actual physical condition right here on earth at this moment. I repeat: If you are looking for glory hereafter you must have the Lord of glory in you right now.

To be in Christ is to be vitally connected to Him. Rejoice in that. But to have Christ in you is likewise cause for rejoicing, for it is the guarantee of future glory.

October 27

. . . every man . . . every man . . . every man.
(Colossians 1:28)

Pride moves some men to want to belong to something exclusive. A mature Christian always wants others to have what he has. Our Lord makes no appeals to any select group. He is no respecter of persons; He has no favorite races or faces.

The invitation is "Whoever will, let him come." Whenever you hear an appeal made to one special group to the exclusion of another group, you know it is not of God, for the gospel is universal. It is to the rich and the poor, the educated and the illiterate, the black man and the white man.

The true gospel of the one true God and Savior is for everybody. There is no privileged inner circle, no spiritual elite. Every man, every individual has within his grasp that which all others also may reach. There are no exceptions.

Paul, like every true preacher of the gospel, was jealous of the soul welfare of all whom God put in his charge (2 Corinthians 11:2). What he offered was for every Christian. He wanted the best for them.

To that end he preached Christ—not economics, for the silver and gold and the cattle upon a thousand hills belong to Christ. Not science, for Christ is the wisdom of God. Not history, for Christ is the Lord of history, the B.C. and the A.D. Not civil rights, for Christ is the righteousness of God. Not politics, for the kingdom of Christ is not of this world system. Not psychology, for Christ is the mind of God.

No true minister is called to preach man-made legalisms. Jesus Christ is the fulfillment of the law. He is Christ in you, the hope of glory. He is the one the preacher has been appointed to proclaim to every man.

October 28

For you died, and your life is hidden with Christ in God.
(Colossians 3:3)

The primary attack of the enemies of the cross at Colosse was against the belief that Jesus Christ was all-sufficient to redeem. Some heretics taught that God cannot come into contact with matter because matter is evil. Jesus Christ could not be God who became a man.

They taught that there were many go-betweens emanating from God—a series of intermediaries, angels on the ladder from heaven to earth. Christ was but one rung on that ladder.

In addition to that false doctrine taught by *gnostics*—people who claimed to be in the know—there were the errors of the legalizers, or Judaizers. Those people stressed outward ceremony and ritual. They observed feast days, the new moon, circumcision, Sabbaths, and practiced many things calculated to save or keep men saved.

Paul was led to answer: No, all we need is Jesus Christ. We are complete in Him. We are united to Him in such a way that when He died, we died. When He rose from the grave, we rose also. If we are risen with Christ, we should seek those things that are above, where the risen Savior is seated on the right hand of God the Father. Furthermore, we are to set our affection on things above, not on things on the earth.

The reason we should seek heavenly, spiritual things, the reason we should set our affection on things above, is that we died to that which would keep us earthbound. We rose to a new life—spiritual, heavenly, resurrected life.

Our position is right now one of being seated in the heavenlies, citizens of heaven right now. We have eternal life right now. The true you is more than what is seen by others here on earth.

October 29

Therefore put to death your members which are on the earth:
fornication. . . . (Colossians 3:5)

There is nothing wrong with sex in itself. Sex is not sin.
It is beautiful—a gift from God. But we are to control it,
not let it control us. Like all other gifts, sex may be abused
and perverted. Such misuse presents a very real problem
in modern society.

Fornication, a very general term for all sexual immorality, specifically refers to sex relations involving an unmar-
ried person. The same act involving a married person is
called *adultery.* The Bible condemns fornication (Romans
1:29; Galatians 5:19; Ephesians 5:3; 1 Thessalonians 4:3). It
is sin. Sexual indulgence outside of marriage is *sin.*

Why is fornication condemned? Because it is dangerous. Premarital sex increases uncertainty, distrust, disappointment; it may produce disease and death. The terrible
trio remains: detection, infection, and conception. Fornication grieves the Holy Spirit, breaks fellowship with God,
causes heartaches, and handicaps the child born.

Why condemned? It is a robber. It shortchanges. In marriage the two become one; fornication robs sex of the rich
potential for unity. What the fornicator calls love is lust.
True love wants the best for its object. If a man is not willing to accept full responsibility for his action, he is not
manifesting love. The man who wants to have his cake and
eat it too loves only himself.

Something is wrong with a "love" that prefers the secrecy and shame of fornication to the bold public declara-
tion of marriage and the sense of responsibility of the married life. May God in Christ help you this day to live a
clean life in a dirty age.

October 30

Walk in wisdom toward those who are outside, redeeming the time. (Colossians 4:5)

In this practical section we are instructed how to deal with unbelievers, those "without" or "outside." The phrase is used of non-Christians, unbelievers, all who are outside of Christ, outside of heaven, outside of the church, outside of the ark of safety, outside of the Christian brotherhood.

Dealing with unsaved people is an important matter. In 1 Timothy 3:7 it is stated that a bishop "must have a good testimony among those who are outside." In 1 Thessalonians 4:11–12 we read: "Aspire to lead a quiet life, and to mind your own business, and to work with your own hands, as we commanded you, that you may walk properly toward those who are outside, and that you may lack nothing."

So you see we cannot brush aside that matter of the Christian's dealing with unbelievers. How we act in the world, our relationship with non-Christians, is important.

The first thing we are told is to "walk in wisdom." The command speaks of a perpetual, habitual walk, and your walk is your conduct, your behavior. Such a command is needed because some saints do not know how to act in the company of unbelievers.

In Matthew 10:16 we see that the Lord wants us to be wise as serpents and harmless as doves. If so, our lives become living epistles. The world is keenly watching our walk; we are open for all to read. Only as we behave wisely and walk in wisdom will Christ be seen in us.

Today make the best use of your time, for your time is God's time. Use every opportunity to show forth Jesus Christ.

October 31

Let your speech always be with grace, seasoned with salt, that you may know how you ought to answer each one. (Colossians 4:6)

After the walk of verse 5 comes the talk, for speech is extremely important. Nothing really takes the place of the personal warmth of the human voice. There is no substitute for the speaker in person—no, not even the bumper sticker. Perhaps you have read of the preacher who was driving down a road behind a car with a "Honk If You Love Jesus" bumper sticker. While stopped behind the car at a traffic light, he honked and waved. The lady in the car ahead stuck her head out of the window and yelled: "Can't you see the light is red, stupid?"

Two things are said here about the Christian's speech. First, it is to be with grace, in a kindly spirit. The saint's talk is to be gracious. That means pleasing, sweet, courteous, winning favor, pleasant, for that is what impresses the unbeliever. No corrupt (rotten, spoiled, smelling like decayed fish) communication is to come out of the Christian's mouth (Ephesians 4:29).

Second, his speech is to be seasoned with salt (having been seasoned before serving so that it is palatable when served). That means his speech is not to be stale, insipid, pointless, trite; but to the point, fresh, vital, interesting, wholesome, fruitful, appetizing, sensible—appropriate to the time and place and person involved.

In that way good may come. Our walk (wise and not wasted) and talk (sweet and sensible) must reflect Jesus Christ. Our words and actions should be those guided by the Holy Spirit. Then, as Simon Peter said, we always will be ready to give an answer to every man that asks us a reason of the hope that is in us (1 Peter 3:15).

November 1

. . . in power, and in the Holy Spirit and in much assurance.
(1 Thessalonians 1:5)

The gospel Paul preached to the saints at Thessalonica was more than mere words, gossip, or meaningless chatter. First, it was preached with power. Indeed, it is the power of God unto salvation. Since man does not live in a moral vacuum, he must react in some way to the Word preached to him.

It takes a powerful Word, a gospel full of power, to remove a sinner from a broad, downward road of destruction to a narrow, heaven-bound highway; to translate a man from darkness to light; to make alive in Christ one who was dead in sin; to turn people from serving dumb idols to worship the true and living God. It takes *power*.

Second, the gospel came literally "in Holy Spirit." There is no definite article—so it means "Holy Spirit-wise," or in connection with the Holy Spirit. Said Paul: "We preached the gospel in the power of the Spirit." When that is done, the gospel that has power in it also has power *on* it.

Third, the gospel came in assurance. Again, we see that the text refers not to the Thessalonians' reception of the gospel (v. 6) but to the *manner* in which the gospel came to them. We are taught that it was proclaimed with absolute confidence.

Assurance here means literally "a supreme fullness, abundance." The verb from which the noun is derived means "to fill one with any thought, conviction, or inclination," thus, to make one certain, to persuade, convince.

Every preacher ought to be convinced in his own heart that he stands as an ambassador for Christ, a representative of the high court of heaven, called of God. Nothing takes the place of the preaching of the *Bible*.

November 2

For this reason we also thank God without ceasing, because when you received the word of God which you heard from us, you welcomed it not as the word of men, but as it is in truth, the word of God, which also effectually works in you who believe. (1 Thessalonians 2:13)

The first word rendered *received* means "to take hold of"; it is the objective fact of taking what is handed over. Like a loaf of bread from the supermarket, a baton from a relay runner, or a letter from the mailman—you receive God's Word.

Paul and those with him were faithful in delivering the Word of God unadulterated, pure, simple, untampered with. When my wife and I lived in Chicago, I sent several hundred gospel tracts I had written to a minister in Los Angeles. Something happened to the package at the post office and he never received the tracts.

After inquiry, and weeks later, a package was returned to my house with my name on it, but inside were two sets of hot pants. We never found out what happened to the tracts, and because the package had not been insured, I lost eighteen dollars. Imagine, from gospel tracts to hot pants! My wife and I laughed for days about it, suggesting, that since they were bright red hot pants, "you know who" fooled with the package.

Paul said: We handed on God's message, and you accepted it. Here then is the meaning of the word rendered "welcomed." It is to accept. You welcomed it. That denotes an inner, willing appreciation, belief, and subjective acceptance. By taking the Word of God you accepted and got the Word of God.

Note it is God's Word (twice stated), not man's word. When it comes to matters of life and death, heaven and hell, time and eternity, righteousness and wickedness, salvation and lostness—men would be wise to hear God and not listen to men.

November 3

Then we who are alive and remain shall be caught up together with them in the clouds to meet the Lord in the air. (1 Thessalonians 4:17)

After Paul left the city of Thessalonica some of the Christians there died, some possibly because of persecution. The problem then arose: What will be their status when the Lord Jesus returns?

Paul answered that there is no disadvantage for the deceased saints. Indeed, they will rise first and will share in the glory of the coming of Christ. Supernatural power will be required at the rapture. It takes tremendous energy to carry a body through air that is the domain of the devil.

The verb *harpazo* that is used means "to take something forcefully, firmly, quickly, or rapaciously." At the rapture Jesus Christ shall snatch us away, pluck us out, carry us away, take us by force, pull us through the devil's territory. In other words, the earth will be robbed, raped (raptured), spoiled by Christ as we zip through the skies impervious to the resistance offered by spiritual wickedness in high places, for God's power is irresistible.

That space between earth and the expanse of the first heaven is the realm where Satan operates. The air is the abode of all kinds of evil spirits.

Yes, we are surrounded by an invisible host, unseen forces of wickedness. That is why Paul talked about unbelievers walking according to the prince of the power of the air (Ephesians 2:2).

Satan is the ruler of the "government"—those in power —of an organized kingdom of evil spirits. To go through his kingdom requires supernatural power. But when Christ is for you, it does not matter who is against you. And when He comes for you, it does not matter who tries to hold you back.

November 4

And may your whole spirit, soul, and body be preserved blameless at the coming of our Lord Jesus Christ. (1 Thessalonians 5:23)

When Adam sinned, his entire tripartite being—body, soul, and spirit—was messed up. When a man is born again, the first thing that happens is the Holy Spirit enters his body and takes charge of the believer's human spirit. That is immediate upon conversion.

The Christian lives a lifetime being renewed daily in his soul. In other words, once you become a Christian, God's work on you is not finished. The fact that you have been taken out of darkness into God's marvelous light and made alive when before you were dead in sin does not mean God has taken His hands off you to let you make it in life the best you can.

Although becoming a Christian totally changes your position from child of wrath to a child of God, the change in your condition is another matter. The change in your *position* was instantaneous; but the change in your *condition* takes more time.

Now that we are Christians, there are some crooked thoughts to be made straight; some rough attitudes to be made plain; some twisted values to be untangled; some spiritual goals to be achieved. Changes in character, viewpoints, opinions, personality, concepts, and habits take a lot of time. God is working on us and in us, seeking to make us what He has declared us to be already in Christ.

All the while we grow in Christ our bodies decline, deteriorate. What God made first in the creation of man will be made last in the re-creation. Let us rejoice that, through it all, our entire beings shall be guarded, held firmly in God's watchful care, and at Christ's second coming we shall be found without fault.

November 5

Now the purpose of the commandment is love from a pure heart, from a good conscience, and from sincere faith. (1 Timothy 1:5)

Believe the wrong thing and you will act in the wrong way. False doctrine generates useless, endless disputes, fables, and speculations. Keep your doctrine *straight*. Teach no other doctrine than that which you have received from the Lord.

Now the purpose of this charge, the object or thing desired, is love; it is that love that comes from (1) a pure heart, (2) a clean mind, and (3) a strong faith. The one preposition combines the three nouns as a unit; the word *from* is italicized—supplied by the translators—twice.

A pure heart. The Bible has much to say about the human heart, the fountain of the thoughts, passions, desires, appetites, affections, purposes, and endeavors—the inner man. Only the blood of Jesus Christ can cleanse the dirty heart.

A good conscience. Conscience means with knowledge—joint knowledge. It speaks of the soul's ability to determine good and bad, right and wrong, and its ability to prompt man to do or avoid, commend or condemn.

Through faith in Jesus Christ a man's conscience may be described as good, or void of offense and sprinkled and pure, free from guilt and known sin.

Sincere faith. Real, sincere, unhypocritical, not pretended, not mere talk—that is the kind of faith spoken of here. If you stick to the doctrine once delivered to the saints, you will see that it produces love that comes from a pure heart, from a good conscience, and from a faith "without wax" —do you remember the reading for October 19? That is the kind of love with which God so loved you and me.

November 6

This charge I commit to you, son Timothy, according to the prophecies previously made concerning you, that by them you may wage the good warfare. (1 Timothy 1:18)

Timothy is exhorted to fight a good fight based on the prophecies made concerning his ministry. He is charged to keep the once-for-all-delivered-to-the-saints faith, those central doctrines based upon apostolic teachings. What Paul is saying then is this: To wage a good warfare, hold to the basic doctrines: God is holy; He is Creator; the Trinity; the eternal Son became a man, lived on earth, died for our sins, was buried, rose from the grave, and is coming back again.

When people start to handle deceitfully the Word of God, when they begin to compromise on sound doctrine, when they begin to play fast and loose with the Scriptures, they are headed for trouble. You cannot mess around with the Bible and at the same time hold to the faith.

Trifle with your faith and you lose it. There is a vicious circle here. It is also true that phony living leads to false doctrine. In other words, do dirt and you will develop dirty doctrine to go along with the dirt.

Holding onto false doctrine will lead a good man to doing wrong. The Christian soldier must practice what he preaches if he wants to fight the good fight. No man can fight an evil that he himself practices. You cannot curse out cursing. Or drink alcohol to death.

Whatever quality or attribute you seek to enforce, you must have it yourself. It takes an honest man to enforce honesty, a good woman to spread goodness. Otherwise your creed is vain, empty words, and your faith will fail you in the battle.

November 7

Wage the good warfare. (1 Timothy 1:18)

Is it possible that some Christians do not know there is a war going on? As ridiculous and incredible as it sounds, there are professed Christians who do not know that a spiritual battle is being fought and that they are involved. Ignorance exempts no one. It may make you a casualty but does not exempt you.

To be in a war and not know it is foolhardy. To tread a battleground without wearing the whole armor is dangerous. To wield a sword of ignorance instead of the sharp, two-edged Word of God is to become a candidate for a purple heart or will get your name listed among the fallen on the battlefield.

Ignorance of the Bible is one reason more saints are not knowingly engaged in the spiritual warfare. Pulpits and pews are full of people who know more about pills, the Phillies, parliamentary procedure, Pontiacs, port, and pinochle than they do about Proverbs, Philippians, or Philemon. They know a lot about luck at the lotteries, but little about the Gospel of Luke or about the Lord of life, Jesus Christ.

The challenge is thrilling. It is invigorating. You will come to realize that it is best to feel a little pain now, so you will feel better later on. Through the eyes of faith the Christian soldier can see that after the surgeon cuts, there is healing. After the midnight weeping, joy comes in the morning. When the wilderness trek is over, we enter the promised land.

By faith we understand that through death we get to life. Through patient submission we arrive at princely sovereignty. If we suffer because of Him, we shall also reign with Him. Let us, as good soldiers of Jesus Christ, fight a good fight.

November 8

Wage the good warfare, having faith and a good conscience.
(1 Timothy 1:18–19)

In this pastoral letter Timothy is exhorted to fight false doctrine and to campaign against those who teach bad doctrine. Yet he is to be careful in his fight to wear the two pieces of armor called sincere faith and a good conscience (1 Timothy 1:5; 3:9).

If true doctrine is denied, that is, disobeyed, it becomes in essence a dead faith. Make sure you believe the right thing about God. Study your Bible, pray, let the Holy Spirit be your Teacher, and you will be sure about your faith, certain of your creed.

The command is to keep your faith and a clear conscience. That is a challenging combination. Faith and conscience are intimately joined. You cannot hold the faith if you are not careful to maintain a good conscience before God.

Paul said, "Some people have disobeyed their consciences and have deliberately done what they knew was wrong" (1 Timothy 1:19, TLB). If you set your own rules and live by them, it is quite possible that your conscience will not bother you. If you follow God's guidelines, however, your underlying motive and direction of life is to obey and please the Lord. Acts of sin are instantly and habitually recognized as such, confessed before God, and forsaken.

In other words, there is no sugar-coating of sin. A good conscience joined with soundness in the faith is a challenging combination. Your doctrine affects your conscience. You will not seek to silence your conscience or try to make it stop crying out against those things that the Bible rebukes.

Once you start ignoring your conscience, it is bound to affect your faith. It is very dangerous to neglect the conscience. Trifle with truth, and you will lose it. Walk in subjection to truth, and you will keep it. You will discover that a good conscience is one that holds to the Bible.

November 9

For bodily exercise profits a little. (1 Timothy 4:8)

Those words are not meant to belittle physical exercise or the quest for physical fitness. Paul had no desire to discourage those who are dedicated joggers and bicyclists.

Nor do we agree with R. M. Hutchins who said, "Whenever I feel like exercise, I lie down until the feeling goes away." C. Depew did not voice our sentiments when he said, "I get my exercise acting as pallbearer to my friends who exercise."

The apostle wanted simply to contrast physical exercise and spiritual exercise. Man's physical makeup is only a part of his total being. No matter how well conditioned you are, disease, accidents, and death still take their toll.

Rest assured also that you will never take your present body with you into God's heaven (1 Corinthians 15:51–52). On the other hand, godliness, or piety, is profitable all the time. It pays eternal dividends. Prayer, clean living, Bible study, Christian fellowship, doing good to your fellow man—those are the spiritual disciplines that please God. It is the heart worship of Jesus Christ who loved us and shed His blood for us that matters most.

May I encourage your heart to continue your devotion to spiritual things. Let others clamor and riot and rave and rage and rant over things that perish. You build your hope on things eternal.

Flex your spiritual muscles as you run the good race, fight the good fight, wrestle against the forces of evil, and press on toward the goal for the prize of the upward call of God in Christ (Philippians 3:14). Spiritual exercise, or godliness, is profitable for all things, since it holds promise for the present life and also for the life to come.

November 10

Lay hold on eternal life. (1 Timothy 6:12)

To *lay hold* of means "to take, possess, seize, overtake, grasp, grab, or catch." *Laying hold* denotes a single complete event; perfect appropriation is the idea. Literally, it is: Lay hold of once and for all for yourself.

What is eternal life? It is the life of God. God is life. Since eternal life is His life, it has neither beginning nor ending. It is the gift of God revealed in Jesus Christ by grace to all who believe in the shed blood of the Lord Jesus. It is not a reward or prize.

Eternal life is Jesus Christ living in the believer. We read in John 17:3: "And this is eternal life, that they may know You, the only true God, and Jesus Christ whom You have sent."

That is not mere head knowledge, awareness of the fact that there was a real, historical Jesus Christ or mere belief there is a God up there somewhere. To *know* here implies and includes intimate fellowship, heart belief, and love.

Take advantage of all that is here and now included in eternal life. To do so is part of fighting the good fight. Keep in mind that eternal life is a present, here-and-now possession.

"You can't live on earth and board in heaven!" Who says so? Lay hold of eternal life right now. There are no acceptable excuses for not living here on earth like citizens of heaven. Lay hold! Laying hold on eternal life is a right-now thing made possible by present knowledge of where you stand with God.

November 11

You therefore must endure hardship as a good soldier of Jesus Christ. (2 Timothy 2:3)

The verb translated *endure hardship* means literally "to suffer evil with someone." Paul exhorted Timothy (and all other real soldiers) to suffer with him: "Share with me in the sufferings for the gospel" (1:8), "endure afflictions" (4:5).

Without doubt Paul was impressed by the soldiers of his day. Perhaps the life of discipline appealed to his mind. The Old Testament, too, could have played a part here. After all, the history of Israel certainly dealt largely with war. God is described as a man of war, a sword, a shield or buckler, a high tower, a battle-ax, and so on.

At the time of Paul's ministry the Jews were under the Roman heel. There were Roman soldiers everywhere to maintain peace and order. Because of his several imprisonments, presumably near army camps, Paul was very familiar with the military (Acts 28:16).

When we read his epistles, we read of weapons of our warfare, pulling down of strongholds, blowing trumpets, fighting a good fight, taking captives, and putting on the whole armor of God. It would appear that he used the term *soldier* to indicate that not all Christians were soldiers.

For the apostle, only dedicated saints, those who were in the fellowship of Christian service, people really devoted to Christ, were called soldiers. The term *soldier* was to him one of honor, reserved for Christians who wholeheartedly resisted the forces of evil.

> Am I a soldier of the cross,
> A foll'wer of the Lamb,
> And shall I fear to own His cause,
> Or blush to speak His name?
> Sure I must fight if I would reign;
> Increase my courage, Lord;
> I'll bear the toil, endure the pain,
> Supported by Thy word!
>
> *Isaac Watts*

November 12

And also if anyone competes in athletics, he is not crowned unless he competes according to the rules. (2 Timothy 2:5)

Salvation is a gift. By the grace of God you are saved through faith in the shed blood of Jesus Christ. Through regeneration you become automatically a potential athlete, and God puts you on the track to run.

However, salvation is no assurance of great rewards. Just being in the race or engaged in an athletic event is no assurance of winning a prize. "If anyone competes" is conditional (aorist subjunctive). Unless you compete fairly and play the game according to the rules, you will receive no crown. Every Christian runs but not all receive prizes (1 Corinthians 9:24–25). Paul's point is to encourage diligence, a busyness about the Lord's work.

Whatever the event, you are required to obey the rules. All games have regulations to follow. So does the game of life. An unholy spirit of competition is harmful; failure to pray, study God's Word, or use Bible methods is detrimental. Failure to compete in the strength of the Holy Spirit is disastrous.

Some years ago eleven members of a high school football team resigned after it was discovered they had broken training rules by smoking marijuana and drinking alcoholic beverages.

Most of the six seniors and five juniors were starters. "You just can't win with sophomores in our league, but I'd rather lose with them than win with bums," the coach said. "We have always set high standards . . . and we're going to keep them."

How much more ought this to be the attitude of the Christian athlete running the race of life for Jesus Christ!

November 13

Remember that Jesus Christ . . . was raised from the dead.
(2 Timothy 2:8)

Promise. First, remember that the Lord kept His *promise.*
After cleansing the Temple for the first time, the Lord was
asked, "What sign do you show to us, seeing you do these
things?"

He answered, "Destroy this temple and in three days I
will raise it up."

And He did. He kept His promise. Early that Sunday
morning when the two Marys came to the grave, the angel
there said, "Do not be afraid, for I know that you seek Jesus
who was crucified. He is not here; for He is risen, as He
said. Come, see the place where the Lord lay" (Matthew
28:5–6).

Power. In remembering the resurrection, keep in mind
that the *power* that raised Christ belongs to you and me
also. In Romans 8:11 Paul states that Christ will give life to
your mortal bodies. If you are a genuine Christian, not just
a church member warming the pew, then the Holy Spirit
lives right now in your mortal frame.

If you believe Jesus Christ rose from the grave, this doctrine has practical results. It is a belief that (1) helps you
take better care of your own body, (2) helps you triumph
over known sin in your life, and (3) helps you cast out the
fear of death, for you have the assurance that as He rose,
you too will rise.

Proof. In the past our Lord kept His promise. For the
present, He supplies power. And, in the future, He will
judge. Remember the resurrection as *proof*—proof that men
will be judged (Acts 17:31). Remember today the resurrection of Jesus Christ and rejoice.

November 14

. . . rightly dividing the word of truth. (2 Timothy 2:15)

The Bible, the mirror that reveals your sin, will help you if you will but let it. It will motivate your service and give you the right reason for the work you do for the Lord. Finally, the Bible will make you more like the Savior.

Now if you rightly divide the Bible, if you straight-cut the Word—do not hook and crook, pick your spots, ignore what you do not like, misinterpret what you despise, mishandle or deceitfully handle the Bible, but do what is right by the Scriptures—it will so work in your life that you will become more like Jesus Christ.

God's Word is a *lamp*. Study it, and your life will light up; you will reflect the radiance of Him who is the Light of the world. God's Word is a sword. Study it, and its cutting, powerful, living, two-edged, discerning power will cleanse your heart and make you like the Righteous One.

God's Word is a *fire*. Study it, and it will cause your heart to burn within while the Author talks with you and opens to you the Scriptures. God's Word is a hammer. Study it, and it will smash sin in your life and please Him who is the sin bearer.

God's Word is sweeter than *honey*. Eat it, and it will sweeten your life and delight your soul with that delight that comes only from Him who is the joy of your salvation. God's Word is truth. Study it and break the shackles of sin. Stand fast with Him who is the Truth that sets men free indeed.

God's Word is *bread*. Eat it—every word that comes out of God's mouth—and like Him who is the Bread of Life, you will be able to resist all the fiery darts and temptations of the devil. God's Word is eternally settled in the heavens. Study it, and the temporalities of life will become as nothing as the Ancient of Days fills your very heart.

November 15

For the time will come when they will not endure sound doctrine, but according to their own desires, because they have itching ears, they will heap up for themselves teachers; and they will turn their ears away from the truth, and be turned aside to fables. (2 Timothy 4:3–4)

Paul predicted that in time church members, not the world, will not endure sound doctrine. They will not tolerate healthy teaching; they will not listen or willingly hear the Word of God rightly divided.

Through Jeremiah Jehovah said: "To whom shall I speak and give warning, that they may hear? Indeed, their ear is uncircumcised, and they cannot give heed . . . they have no delight in it" (Jeremiah 6:10). What happened in Israel over twenty-five hundred years ago is happening today in our churches.

Many seek out preachers and Bible teachers who will make them feel good, comfortable, proud, and contented. Listener and preacher are self-satisfied mutual-admiration societies.

What is wrong with sound doctrine? Possibly we dislike the preacher who preaches it. Bible doctrine punctures the balloon of pride. It destroys the idea of working our way to heaven; it does away with humanism.

Sound doctrine makes folks uneasy and uncomfortable; it convicts, cuts, and condemns. Some preachers are afraid to preach it for fear they become ostracized by their fellow preachers or hit in the pocketbook by the congregation. People will not support that which they do not like.

It is important then that you realize sound doctrine is meat for the soul. It will make you strong. Read your Bible. The Holy Spirit in you will guide you into all truth. Value your soul's welfare; grow, mature, and become more like Him who died for you. In short, endure sound doctrine.

November 16

For Demas has forsaken me, having loved this present world, and has departed for Thessalonica. (2 Timothy 4:10)

Surely there are some things in life we ought to abandon. Forsake foolishness (Proverbs 9:6); confess and forsake sins (Proverbs 28:13). Cease from anger and forsake wrath (Psalm 37:8); let the wicked forsake his way, and the unrighteous man his thoughts (Isaiah 55:7). Here, however, we have the case of a professed Christian forsaking the apostle Paul—Paul, a proved, tried man of God.

Why? What happened? What moved Demas to abandon Paul? Indeed, what prompts men to be disloyal? Personal ambition? Sometimes it is because of envy.

Sometimes friends will leave you because of fear. The disciples are proof of this (Matthew 26:56). So were Paul's friends (2 Timothy 4:16). But Demas left because he loved the attractions of this present age. Love of the here-and-now causes breaks in the fellowship with God and with other Christians. Increased fellowship and friendship with the "now" age means separation and enmity toward God.

Demas returned to his home town, Thessalonica, and probably went back into business there. Hanging around Paul was too dangerous. Physical suffering and even death could result.

Who knows what rewards Demas lost, or how miserable later he must have been! For God has said, "Love not the world or the things that are in the world. If anyone loves the world, the love of the Father is not in him" (1 John 2:15).

In order not to be a disappointment to the Lord or to other saints, set your affection on things above. Remember, if we love the Lord's appearing and look for His return, we will not be in love with whatever this earth affords.

November 17

For the grace of God that brings salvation has appeared to all men, teaching us. . . . (Titus 2:11–12)

The highest example of God's undeserved favor bestowed upon man is the spectacular, miraculous, sudden visible appearance of Jesus Christ. He came at a precise time in history, to a particular place in Palestine, and in a peculiar way—born of a virgin, offering salvation to all men. If men had not needed salvation, Christ would not have come.

That is what we call "saving grace." But grace is not only *saving* for those who accept the gift of God, grace is also *instructive*. Grace trains, teaches, disciplines us. Its school is open for the duration of this present life. There are no summer vacations here, no strikes, no lockouts, no labor troubles, no busing problems. Desegregation is no problem in the school of grace.

You see why the school of grace never lets a person go. One graduates and then goes to another level of schooling. That way one goes from one *degree* of grace to another.

Although the academy of salvation is open for all (it is universal), only those who are saved matriculate at that school. In short, without salvation there is no education. Grace can get nothing else through our thick skulls and hard heads until we accept the number-one offer of grace—Jesus Christ.

Despite the fact that men were so contrary to the holy nature of God, God the Father in infinite love, in mercy incomprehensible, in grace, sent His only Son to pay the penalty for our sin. Guilty men are pardoned, blind men receive their sight, the lost are found, and men deserving to die are given eternal life.

November 18

. . . looking for the blessed hope and glorious appearing of our great God and Savior Jesus Christ. (Titus 2:13)

This sentence begins at verse 11, and the main verb is found in verse 12: "we should live." We are to live good, God-fearing lives day after day in this present evil age. While we so live, we are to continuously expect and look for the blessed hope and appearance of the glory of Jesus Christ. That is the goal we are to have in mind. The very possibility of God's stepping into history excites the senses. The return of Christ is the Christian's hope, his expectation of good.

Then there is the matter of grace and glory. He who was manifested as Savior came the first time in His grace; the second time He will come as God in *glory*. That really is the main thrust of this passage, the heart of the message.

God's grace appeared when Jesus Christ came the first time. Having accepted that grace through faith, we now look for the appearance of His glory when He comes the second time. Finally, we clearly recognize that Christ is God.

B. B. Warfield said that this verse "provides us with one of the most solemn ascriptions of proper deity to Jesus Christ discoverable" in the entire New Testament: "our great God and Savior Jesus Christ."

There is but *one* definite article here in the Greek text, so the natural construction supports seeing the designation "God and Savior" as *one* and applying it to Jesus Christ.

We realize, of course, that His deity does not depend upon this verse alone. Other passages also clearly ascribe deity to Him. It is He "who gave Himself" (v. 14) at His first coming, so that we are "His own special people." And we rejoice in knowing that God our Savior is coming back again for His own.

November 19

Yet for love's sake I rather appeal to you. (Philemon 9)

Philemon actively expressed his faith. He was noted for his hospitality. Indeed, Onesimus had not run away from a cruel taskmaster; he had wronged his master (v. 18). Possibly he had stolen some money or had run away because he just disliked being a slave. We are not sure what Onesimus did, but it seems certain that Philemon was not a cruel man.

He shared his house with the saints, looked after their needs, and ministered to them in their afflictions. Possibly he sent food to the apostle Paul whenever that was feasible. Such hospitality portrayed Jesus Christ, for the word translated *refreshed* (v. 7) means also "to give rest," as Christ used it when He said, "Come to Me . . . and I will give you rest" (Matthew 11:28).

Such active love shown by Philemon assured Paul that his request would be honored. So Paul says, "Now I want to ask a favor of you. I could demand it of you in the name of Christ because it is the right thing for you to do, but I love you and prefer just to ask you" (vv. 8–9, TLB).

Love performs a variety of duties. First of all, *love comforts.* Joseph's brothers thought he would hate them and pay them back for their evil, but Joseph saw God's loving hand in all that had happened. Second, *love controls.* The demoniac at Gadara is proof of this. Lastly, *love changes* things. Paul met love one day, and the persecutor of saints became a proclaimer of salvation. Paul put aside authority, for he knew that the appeal of love and the motivation to love has its own persuasive power.

November 20

For the word of God is. . . . (Hebrews 4:12)

Superior. The Bible is a superior book with a superior message. The theme of Hebrews is the superiority of Jesus Christ over prophets, angels, Moses, Joshua, and so on. He mediates a superior covenant, one ratified in His own blood.

If the Word made flesh is superior, rest assured that the written Word is better than the mere word of mortal men. God's Word is superior because it does that which man's word cannot do. It purifies, sanctifies, illumines; it is truth and settled in heaven. Moreover, it is living, powerful, sharper than any two-edged sword, and it stands forever.

Sword. It parries the thrusts of the devil. It pares, or cuts away, that which is ungodly. It protects, for it is part of the panoply to be worn by the Christian soldier in battle.

Saves. God's Word alone can convict us of sin and point us to Calvary. Faith comes by hearing and the hearing is of the Word of God (Romans 10:17).

A New Hebrides chieftain sat peacefully reading the Bible when he was interrupted by a French trader. "Bah!" the trader snorted, "Why are you reading the Bible? I suppose the missionaries have got hold of you, you poor fool. Throw that book away!"

The chieftain calmly replied, "If it were not for this Bible, you would be in my kettle pot over there by now."

Thank God for the Bible. It is superior to the word of men; it is a sword that pierces the very heart of man. It is a Word that saves men from the penalty, power, and eventually the very presence of sin.

November 21

Let us hold fast our confession. . . . Let us hold fast the confession of our hope. . . . (Hebrews 4:14; 10:23)

Many places in the Bible tell us to hold fast or firm. "Take firm hold of instruction, do not let her go; keep her, for she is your life" (Proverbs 4:13). "Test all things; hold fast what is good" (1 Thessalonians 5:21). "Hold fast the pattern of sound words which you have heard from me, in faith and love which are in Christ Jesus" (2 Timothy 1:13). "Behold, I am coming quickly! Hold fast what you have, that no one may take your crown" (Revelation 3:11).

In Hebrews 10:23 *hold fast* means "to hold down in a firm grasp," thus to have in full and secure possession, to occupy, to maintain. In Hebrews 4:14 *hold fast* means "to master, to control, get possession of by way of your strength, superiority," thus in a sense to subdue, conquer, and vanquish.

Let us hold fast the confession of our hope. I confess with my mouth that Jesus is Lord and believe in my heart that God the Father has raised Him from the dead. If you believe this, hold it fast.

Hold fast? Why? Because we have a great High Priest who has passed through the heavens, Jesus, the Son of God. We are to hold fast not only because Christ is our High Priest, now in heaven working on our behalf, but second, because He is faithful.

Hold fast in confessing your sins, for He is faithful and just to forgive us. Hold fast in sickness, for He is faithful to heal according to His will. Hold fast to His promises, for He keeps His word. Hold fast to His constancy, for Jesus Christ is the same yesterday, today, and forevermore. Hold fast to His hand, for He saves to the uttermost.

November 22

For where there is a testament, there must also of necessity be
the death of the testator. For a testament is in force after men
are dead, since it has no power at all while the testator lives.
(Hebrews 9:16–17)

You know that a will is of no effect during the life of the
one who makes the will, the testator. A will is not valid
until the maker dies. The death of Christ validated the will,
or testament, of Christ. Without His death His will would
have been ineffective, invalid.

Christ died. One has no trouble proving His death. According to the Bible He said, "'It is finished!' And bowing
His head, He gave up His spirit"(John 19:30). Roman soldiers came to break His legs but discovered He was dead
already. Joseph of Arimathea and Nicodemus took His
body and buried it. A guard was set at the tomb. No, you
would have no trouble getting a death certificate from City
Hall proving Christ died.

One more thing was necessary. An executor was
needed—one bound by the terms of the will to carry out
the written desires of the deceased. Christ rose from the
grave in order to execute His will.

How peculiar! Christ made the will; Christ died so that
the will might become valid; Christ rose from the grave in
order to carry out the terms of the will. Wonderful!

If you will take time to read the will you will discover
that our legacy here and now is the promise to supply all
of our needs. Has He kept His word in your life? Our bequest is the presence of the Holy Spirit, living in our bodies, motivating and producing faith in the new man. Our
inheritance is in heaven where a mansion awaits; we have
the assurance that nothing can prevent us from obtaining
the inheritance. The same God who keeps *it* keeps *us*.

November 23

. . . and without shedding of blood there is no remission.
(Hebrews 9:22)

Sin is so deeply rooted in man that the feeling of guilt is naturally a part of our makeup. It is not something occasional, infrequent, or isolated, but is a power that influences our whole being. We may then try to mask our guilt, hide it, transfer it, sublimate it, or rationalize it away, but to no avail.

We may attempt to cry it out, curse it out, circumcise it out, ceremonialize it away, and offer all kinds of sacrifices and libations, but when we get through doing all we can, there is still a tinge of guilt, a suspicion that maybe with all of our self-efforts, something is wrong. We failed to sweep the house clean. Why? Because remission of sins, the forgiveness of sins, is not earned, merited, or achieved by men.

I often hear folks pray, hoping their sins will not meet them at the judgment bar. The thought occurred to me that if your sins *do* confront you at the judgment bar it means the Lord did not send them far enough away.

I do not want my sins hanging around in Philadelphia. I would be in trouble. I am thankful that when the Lord remits sins He sends them off where neither man, demon, nor devil can bring them back to haunt us or condemn us.

According to Isaiah 38:17 God has cast all my sins behind His back; according to Jeremiah 31:34 the Lord has promised to remember them no more. The psalmist said they are removed as far as the east is from the west (Psalm 103:12). Isaiah 44:22 says Jehovah has blotted them out; according to the prophet Micah, my sins were cast into the depths of the sea (Micah 7:19).

My sins have been removed from me; they will never be found again. They will never be brought back and thrown in my face. The blood of Jesus Christ has washed them away. Hallelujah!

November 24

Therefore, brethren, having boldness to enter the Holiest by the blood of Jesus, by a new and living way which He consecrated for us, through the veil, that is, His flesh. (Hebrews 10:19–20)

We first read about the veil in Exodus 26:31–33, which records that Moses was given directions by God concerning the Tabernacle. The fine linen of which the veil was made represented the righteousness of Jesus Christ; the blue, His coming down from heaven; the purple, His royalty as the descendant of King David; the scarlet, His blood shed on the cross.

Now the Most Holy Place, or Holy of Holies, was that part of the Tabernacle into which only the high priest could go and then only on the Day of Atonement that occurred once a year. In the Holiest Place could be found the Ark of the Covenant.

The veil, or inner curtain, therefore separated the Holy Place from the Holy of Holies, the place where God Himself dwelt. Thus hiding the Holiest Place, it signified the way into God's presence was not open (Hebrews 9:1–8).

While Christ hung on the cross, the veil of the Temple split from top to bottom. It was not torn from the bottom up because that would signify the work of human hands. Torn from the top down, the rent signified God's work.

The cup Christ drank came from His Father in heaven (John 18:11). No man took His life; He laid it down freely of Himself. Today we are able to enter boldly into the presence of God. We need no human intermediary. Jesus Christ is the only go-between needed. May we rejoice in that boldness, may we exercise our right as Christians today. Take advantage of the open door. The Lord Jesus will meet you there.

November 25

For yet a little while, and He who is coming will come and will not tarry. (Hebrews 10:37)

Only the intervention of God has saved man in the past. So it is for the future. In this present dispensation of grace, the church age, only the second coming of Jesus Christ will help us, so I look for His coming. Do you? After all, He bought me with His own precious blood, and I belong to Him. Do you?

He is coming back again for His own. You do not make a down-payment on a refrigerator and never bother with it anymore. You either cancel the order and get your money back, or you pay in more money, have the refrigerator delivered to your home, and use it. Well, Christ paid it all. We are fully bought and paid for.

A small boy and his father were in a boat when a storm came up and capsized them. They grasped a plank and tried to paddle, but after a long struggle the father saw that they would not make it to shore. He said: "You stay here and, whatever you do, hold onto the plank. I'll be back to get you." So he struck out for the long swim to shore.

Once in a while he would look back and wave to the boy, bravely holding on. By dark the father reached the shore exhausted. It was too dark by then for the Coast Guard to find the boy, although they tried. Finally, as the first rays of dawn lighted the horizon they saw a speck off in the distance.

As they approached the boy still clinging to the plank, the captain heard him singing. He asked, "Why were you singing? Weren't you afraid?"

The little boy replied, "Why should I be afraid? My daddy said he'd be back."

That is our hope. Christ said He was coming back. Resting on His promise, we too can sing through the night.

November 26

By faith the harlot Rahab did not perish with those who did not believe, when she had received the spies with peace. (Hebrews 11:31)

All of the folks in Jericho were nervous and fidgety, having heard about the marching children of Israel, their conquests, and their God. Only Rahab believed. It was a miracle of grace that a prostitute living in a city full of idolatry, a city that practiced homosexuality, bestiality, and burned babies in sacrifice, should be moved to show her faith in Israel's God (James 2:25).

In the midst of such filth shone her faith. What grace! We do not excuse Rahab's lie, but we must realize the Lord uses us where He finds us. Living in heathendom, a prostitute living the life of a lie, her conscience was just beginning to be awakened.

Though God used her lie to accomplish His purpose, we are not given any principle of lying when we deem it expedient. God will use the devil for His own glory, but that is no excuse for the devil's being a devil. Rahab in her own way provided a shelter for the spies.

She said, "We have heard about your God and what He did for you when you left the land of Egypt, and I know the LORD your God is the true God!" Rahab heard and believed what she heard. *Faith* is the key word here.

After all is said and done, is that not what life is all about—believing every word that comes out of the mouth of God? Rahab acted upon knowledge and sought assurance of deliverance. The God of faith saved her and her family.

> Sinners Jesus will receive;
> Sound this word of grace to all
> Who the heav'nly pathway leave,
> All who linger, all who fall.
> *Erdmann Neumeister*

November 27

Let us lay aside every weight, and the sin which so easily ensnares us. (Hebrews 12:1)

The call to "lay aside every weight and the sin which so easily ensnares us" is indeed a call to the present-day saint. It comes immediately following chapter 11's long list of men and women in the Hall of Faith.

We are told of the faith and the sufferings of the faithful, and then, because we are surrounded as it were by these examples of faithful men and women, we are exhorted to lay aside something.

First, let us lay aside every weight, every burden, every impediment, every stumbling block. Whatever it may be, if it interferes with our service to Christ, or cramps our prayer life, or is harmful to our bodies, it is a weight. It should be dropped.

Second, let us lay aside the sin that so easily ensnares us. Here the writer to the Hebrews is primarily concerned with apostasy. He addresses Jews who professed Christianity, but some of them gave up and returned to their previous Jewish customs and manner of worship and beliefs.

The principle that is applicable is this: We are to lay aside the sin that clings to us. It is as if each of us has a specific monkey on our backs to shake loose. There is some particular sin bothering you with the devil's help. Its weight slows us up in the spiritual race of life.

God is saying, "Lay aside, put off," using the same word used for taking off clothing. Life is a footrace, and we must strip down for it if we are to run successfully. Through faith in the shed blood of Christ we are on God's team. May it be that we will be able to say to our captain, "I have finished the race" (2 Timothy 4:7).

November 28

Jesus . . . for the joy that was set before Him endured the cross.
(Hebrews 12:2)

What if Jesus Christ had not patiently endured such hostility? What if He had run away when chastened for Sabbath healing or had stopped doing miracles because of the sneering skepticism of the religious rulers? What if He had quit the ministry because of the hypocrisy of Judas, or had been scared and run away to another city because men attempted to stone Him? What if He had refused to bear the awful pain of becoming sin when He had known no sin? We all would be on our way to hell.

But He endured. He came unto His own and they received Him not. He was accused of blasphemy, laughed at, scorned, murmured against, and derided. They said He was in league with the devil. His own brothers did not believe in Him. They said He was crazy and had a demon. Others called Him a deceiver. He was challenged to divulge by what authority He healed. When testing Jesus concerning His beliefs on taxes, the resurrection, and the law of Moses on divorce and adultery, His antagonists were all the more stirred up by His answers to their tricky questions.

Eventually that deep-rooted and bitter hatred climaxed at Calvary. He was betrayed, denied, arrested like a common criminal, forsaken, falsely accused, buffeted, and cursed. *But He endured.* Some spat in His face; they chose Him to die rather than a convicted murderer, Barabbas. *But He endured.*

He was whipped, stripped, mocked with a crown of thorns mashed upon His brow, and a reed was put in His hand. They smacked Him while He was blindfolded and demanded that He tell who hit Him. His hands and feet were nailed to a rugged cross where He died between two thieves. *But He endured.* Worse than all physical punishment, He became sin. He endured the cross, despising the shame—thrilled at the prospect of seeing you and me cleansed in His precious blood.

November 29

. . . lest any root of bitterness springing up cause trouble.
(Hebrews 12:15)

Under persecution, the Hebrew Christians had to be warned about their attitudes, especially about bitterness. The writer exhorted, "Pursue peace with all people, and holiness, without which no one will see the Lord; looking carefully lest anyone fall short of the grace of God; lest any root of bitterness springing up cause trouble, and by this many become defiled."

Bitterness can be very dangerous—and damaging—and infectious. Sometimes in a spirit of bitterness we say and do things that are displeasing to God and very harmful to man.

Then later on, after we have changed our attitudes and sweetened our dispositions, we discover it is impossible to undo the great harm done earlier by our bitterness, cynicism, and sarcasm. That is why bitterness is so dangerous.

The writer of Hebrews gives Esau as an example of the danger of bitterness. Having sold his birthright for one morsel of food, Esau later changed his mind. But he could not regain the blessing (Genesis 27:30–37). It was too late. Esau's tears availed him nothing.

Be careful that you do not miss the blessings that belong to you as a blood-bought child of God. Remember: at the cross, Marah becomes Elim (Exodus 15:22–27).

In Christ Jesus bitterness is made sweet. By the power of the blessed Holy Spirit the Christian is enabled to obey the command, "Give bitterness no place in your life. Let it be put away from you" (Ephesians 4:31, author's paraphrase). You will find that the fruit of obedience is joy.

November 30

But do not forget to do good and to share, for with such sacrifices God is well pleased. (Hebrews 13:16)

Doing good and contributing or sharing what you have with others is one way to worship the Lord. In ancient times sacrifices went in part to support the priests, but another part was used to provide meals for the poor. Charitable relief was tied in with the system of sacrifice.

The portion of the animal that was not burned or eaten by the priest was used to help the poor. We do not have any such animal sacrifices today in the church. Yet we are encouraged to continue the aspect of sacrifice that concerns itself with the welfare of others.

Obedience to this scripture is to walk in the footsteps of Jesus Christ. No wonder the Father was pleased. He was well pleased with His Son; when we follow the Son, the Father is pleased with us. To help Christians who are in need is to express the love of Christ.

Surely we cannot forget that the Lord Jesus became poor for our sakes. He gave up His glory and majesty in heaven, became a man, endured the blasphemy, mockery, denial, betrayal, ignominy, disappointment, poverty, hunger, abandonment, and, above all, became sin for us.

What we do for others in the name of Christ we do for Him (Matthew 25:34–40). Rest assured then that the Lord is concerned about our conduct toward saints who are in need. He is well pleased when our sacrifices to Him include benevolence and sharing with others our material possessions and spiritual fellowship.

December 1

But be doers of the word, and not hearers only.
(James 1:22)

Dead. Some hearers are unsaved, *dead* in sin, and naturally you do not expect them to hear. Physically they hear, but spiritually they are deaf.

One minister who complained that he preached a very plain gospel but the people seemed unable to understand, said: "Why, it's as plain as ABC."

A friend piped up, "Yeah, Reverend, but them people is DEF."

Deceived. Some hearers never become doers because they are deluded. They have *deceived* themselves into thinking that church membership and hearing is enough. They are like the man who stands in front of a mirror beholding the face he was born with—dirty, stubbly beard, sand in his red eyes, hair knotty—and then walks away without doing anything to change his appearance.

Doers. That is a matter of the will. The *doer* hears the Word of God and then by the power of the Holy Spirit brings his life and heart into accord with what he heard. It is a process, a becoming, an attitude of heart that manifests itself increasingly as time goes on.

Christian, the Lord Jesus died for you; His blood has washed away your sins. Now He wants you not only to hear His voice, but to become a doer and to live by every word that proceeds out of the mouth of God.

When troubles come, when trials like sea billows roll, and storms, conflicts, adversities, attacks, stress, and strain rage—when the rain descends, the floods come, and the winds blow and beat down upon you—because you heard and obeyed, stability will be your lot and victory your portion.

December 2

Indeed we count them blessed who endure. (James 5:11).

Some people set a time limit on their endurance. Rather than wait for the test to come and then determine to seek God's help to endure, they say: "If things don't get better by next Wednesday at 2:00 p.m., I'm going to call my lawyer." They rant: "If he doesn't apologize by tomorrow morning, I'll call him up and give him a piece of my mind!" They declare: "If things don't change around here by this time next Saturday, I'll pack my bags and move out." And so it goes.

The clock is not the symbol of our faith. Speed is not the test of truth. It must be remembered that with God one day is as a thousand years, and a thousand years as one day. Wait on the Lord. *Wait* on Him. When all seems lost, salvation comes. When things look bad, good shows up.

That is God's way, isn't it? In the darkest hour a light shines. In slavery, a deliverer appears. When it seems that everyone is against you, there comes a friend who sticks closer than a brother. When the storms of life gather round, the sun peeks through the clouds.

When you are stymied and see no way out, God opens a pathway through the sea. When you are shackled and in stocks in the deepest of dungeons, the Lord will shake your prison and loose your fetters. He will let the enemy put you into the fiery furnace, but He will cool the flames.

The blessing comes in sticking it out. By your patience, possess your souls (Luke 21:19). Remember: salvation is a little nearer now than when you first believed.

December 3

To an inheritance incorruptible and undefiled and that does not fade away, reserved in heaven for you. (1 Peter 1:4)

Our inheritance is *incorruptible*. That means it is not prone to decay, ruin, or destruction. It is not perishable.

> Swift to its close ebbs out life's little day;
>
> > Earth's joys grow dim, its glories pass away;
>
> Change and decay in all around I see.
>
> O Thou who changest not, abide with me.
>
> > > *Henry F. Lyte*

We ourselves are perishing among perishables, but our inheritance is incorruptible.

Our inheritance is *undefiled*. That means it is unsullied, without the least stain, unsoiled, free from anything that would deform or debase it. So it is without defect, incapable of pollution.

Our inheritance is one that *does not fade*. The word used here is the same given to a flower, the amaranth, because it never withers or fades, and when plucked off, it revives if moistened with water. So our inheritance is like a flower that never fades.

Finally, we see that our inheritance is *reserved in heaven*. The tense of the Greek verb rendered *reserved* (*tereménen*) means "having ever been and ever continuing to be kept, or safeguarded."

It is a military term suggesting constant watchfulness. Heaven is a good place to have your inheritance. There no moth can eat, no rust can corrode, no burglars can break in, no thieves can steal, no wolves can ravage.

There in heaven no swindlers can defraud, no flimflam artists can trick, no weak guardians can slip up, no unscrupulous lawyers can enter and deprive you of your inheritance in heaven. With such an inheritance, let us rejoice. We are rich in Christ!

December 4

That the genuineness of your faith, being much more precious than gold that perishes, though it is tested by fire, may be found to praise, honor and glory at the revelation of Jesus Christ. (1 Peter 1:7)

Simon Peter said that true faith is more valuable than gold. That is strange, since some people have let the pursuit of gold ruin their faith. He wrote to Christians who were being persecuted; he wanted to strengthen them, encourage them. Adversity and persecution are fires that burn dross from our lives.

A proper attitude is absolutely essential. That is because some of us do not take hard knocks too well. We pout, throw tantrums, scream, kick, seek revenge, even blame God or curse men. Some of us give up.

Simon Peter understood that well. His faith failed when tried. He had boasted publicly that he would never leave Christ, indeed, would die for Him. When the situation got hot, Simon cooled off—then went to warm his hands. Things got too thick, and he thinned out.

As I look back over past experiences and wonder why the Lord let me go through some of the acts of hatred, trickery, ignorance, deceit, lies, sickness, mistakes, blunders, and fiery darts of the devil, I see some things more clearly now. It was to test my faith. It was to refine me as gold.

Admittedly, there were times when I wanted to give up, to resign, take a job with less headache and more money. But note the words in verse 6: "if need be." That means whatever trials you go through, God, who permits them, has a reason.

He is working out some purpose in our lives. He has that right, having bought us with the precious blood of Christ. Whatever we do not understand now, we will understand better by and by. As Job said: "But He knows the way that I take; when He has tested me, I shall come forth as gold" (Job 23:10).

December 5

Receiving the end of your faith — the salvation of your souls.
(1 Peter 1:9)

Keep in mind that the hardships of which Peter spoke are more than ordinary vicissitudes, for even unbelievers experience those. Peter wrote within the context of saints persecuted because they lived like saints. He was not talking about that lot that is common to man nor about the suffering we Christians experience because of our own evil-doing.

If gold needs fire to try it, how much more our faith. We are dealing with eternity. Gold is for temporary use. We learn that faith is proved genuine by the tests of suffering. Anyone can "talk" faith when things go well. But I recognize we all have different sensitivities. Some have had more than their share of natural tragedies.

There have been serious operations, family breakups, divorce, wayward children, houses burned up, and deaths of loved ones in quick succession. Some of you who have suffered because of those things have suffered very little because of your witness for Christ or for convictions of righteousness.

Whereas there is a certain value in maintaining faith through such common testing, how much more when we keep the faith through testings that come because of our stand for Christ. Remember the importance of the end result. Too often we focus on the process and not the end product; we are unduly concerned with the immediate, with no concern for the long term.

God's Word says that while we are going through the trials of this life, think about the future. Once the false and worthless are burned away, the genuine faith, more precious than gold, will be manifested. When Christ returns, the approval of your faith will result in your praise, honor, and glory through Jesus Christ our Lord when He is revealed.

December 6

Therefore, to you who believe, He is precious. (1 Peter 2:7)

That which is precious is *unique*. As the only begotten Son of the Father, there is no one else like Jesus Christ. He is unique—one of a kind. Of no one else did the Father ever say, "You are My beloved Son; in You I am well pleased" (Luke 3:22). Though dishonored by man, He is uniquely honored by the Father.

He has been highly exalted and now sits at the right hand of God the Father, waiting until that time when "at the name of Jesus every knee should bow, of those in heaven, and of those in earth, and of those under the earth, and that every tongue should confess that Jesus Christ is Lord, to the glory of God the Father" (Philippians 2:9–11).

That which is precious is *useful*. Whereas the blood of bulls and goats could not possibly take away sins, Christ washed us from our sins in His own blood. His blood is precious, for we were redeemed not with corruptible things like silver and gold, but with the precious blood of Christ.

That which is precious is *undiminished* by time. Inflation may devalue the dollar, bank accounts may dwindle, real estate values decline. Recessions and depressions come and go. There is unrest, there are wars and crime.

Be thankful that Jesus Christ remains the same yesterday, today, and forever. His preciousness is not altered by time. He may seem to be becoming more precious to me, but that is because I am growing in grace and my fellowship with Him is getting sweeter as the years go by.

December 7

Beloved, I beg you as sojourners and pilgrims. . . .
(1 Peter 2:11)

In the midst of persecution Simon Peter exhorted the saints to live clean lives, leaving the Gentiles without excuse for their persecution of the Jewish Christians. Remember that this old world is not our home. We are but pilgrims passing through.

As we make the journey we discover that water is supplied in time of drought, and manna falls from heaven in time of famine. God supplies our needs and protects us as our shepherd. He fights our battles for us for He is a man of war, the hero of the hour.

As we make the journey to see Him who loved us and shed His own blood for us, we discover that darkness is made light, curses become blessings, crooked paths are made straight, the desert is turned into an oasis, guilt is removed, consciences are cleansed, and sins are forgiven.

We learn that tribulation brings about patience, patience produces experience, and experience produces hope. Hope does not disappoint. We discover too that "the lame take the prey" (Isaiah 33:23), enemies are confounded, traps become tables, stumbling blocks are made stepping stones, mountains are made into molehills, and weaknesses produce His perfect strength.

As we travel along we see light shine forth from broken earthen vessels. Giant problems are slain like Goliath, Jericho walls crumble and fall, prisons become open doors, shackling habits break, and thorns in the flesh prove His grace is sufficient!

God leads His dear children along.

Some thro' the waters, some thro' the flood,

Some thro' the fire, but all through the blood;

Some thro' great sorrow, but God gives a song,

In the night season and all the day long.

G. A. Young

December 8

But when you do good and suffer, if you take it patiently, this is commendable [acceptable, KJV] before God. (1 Peter 2:20)

Sacrifice. "To do righteousness and justice is more acceptable to the LORD than sacrifice" (Proverbs 21:3). Here the word rendered *acceptable* comes from a verb meaning "to choose, select." Literally, to do righteousness and justice is "choicer" to God than sacrifice. Jeremiah 6:20 put it this way: "Your burnt offerings are not acceptable, nor your sacrifices sweet to Me."

Service. "For he who serves Christ in these things is acceptable to God" (Romans 14:18). This text deals with being well-pleasing to God and approved of men. If we serve Christ in righteousness, peace, and joy in the Holy Spirit, we serve acceptably. Is that your desire? It is mine.

Suffering. Simon Peter used the word for grace that is rendered *acceptable* or *commendable* here in 1 Peter 2:20. Peter said that to break a law and then manfully take one's punishment is nothing to brag about. All who do wrong and suffer for their wrongdoing deserve what they get, and their stoicism, patience, endurance, cool-headedness, bravery, and courage signify nothing.

On the other hand, "when you do good"—tell the truth, deal honestly, live a clean life, help people—when one is sincere, keeps the law, preaches the gospel, witnesses for Christ, does an honest day's work on his job—then if he is ostracized and criticized, rebuked, scorned, withheld promotions, lied on, humiliated, beaten, and he endures undeserved punishment without murmuring, complaining, grumbling, or seeking revenge—such suffering is acceptable with God, gracious, or well-pleasing to Him.

Pray today that in sacrifice, service, and suffering you will be acceptable to God in Christ. May acceptability be your goal.

December 9

Let him seek peace and pursue it.
(1 Peter 3:11; see also Psalm 34:14)

Grapple. Grappling is involved in the pursuit of peace. To grapple is to struggle, as in wrestling. Does it sound strange to fight for peace? Paul said: "And the God of peace will crush Satan under your feet shortly" (Romans 16:20). Imagine talking about peace and struggling in the same breath.

God, from whom peace issues—God who is the very source of peace—is going to stomp on the devil's head. The Christian church must learn that discipline is an absolute necessity. One of the ways of securing peace is to knock the devil down every time he rears his ugly head.

Grace. We must develop a deeper awareness of the grace of God in our lives. Grace eliminates the idea of works. The legalistic spirit is wiped away. It is hard for a legalist to be at peace. He never knows when he has done enough work. He may drive himself into a frenzy and frantically wear himself out trying to work out his own salvation.

Grace proclaims that God has done it all; Christ paid it all. Grace gives a high motivation for the work we do, so that those conflicts that would unsettle and disturb us in the service of the Lord are absent.

Gratitude. Thanksgiving is a major ingredient in the pursuit of the peace of God that passes all understanding. Ingrates do not thank God for what He has given them, and they create within themselves attitudes that rob them of peace.

Failure to give God thanks means failure to enjoy what He has given and the inability to receive further blessings. Ingratitude frustrates God's desire for His people to live victoriously.

December 10

Having a good conscience. . . . (1 Peter 3:16)

Christ did not free us to be free to do as we please. His blood was not shed for that. We are to please Him who enlisted us to be soldiers (2 Timothy 2:4). If Christianity were anti-intellectual, you would have no Book to study, no belief to embrace, no doctrine to teach. There would be no need for an enlightened conscience.

If you become callous and careless about your behavior and stifle your conscience when it speaks, you will soon become unfaithful or disloyal to your cause or creed and weak in your beliefs. A good, clear conscience does not mean you are perfect. A good conscience comes from walking in the light—doing what you know is right.

Deliberately doing what you know is wrong and disobeying your conscience, defying God, is presumptuous and deludes a person into thinking that just this one time will not hurt. Do a thing one time, and there is the possibility you will be in trouble.

Fornicate one time, and become pregnant once. Drink one time, and get drunk just once. Steal one time, and get caught one time. That is all it takes. If nothing happens to you the first time, there is still the danger of trouble. If you get away with it the first time, there burns within the desire to try it again. The old nature leads us to become more bold, brazen, and reckless.

Be thankful you possess an enlightened conscience—a conscience superintended by the Holy Spirit. Only with a good conscience is it safe to "let your conscience be your guide."

December 11

*For Christ also suffered once for sins, the just for the unjust,
that He might bring us to God, being put to death in the flesh
but made alive by the Spirit.* (1 Peter 3:18)

You must have the right to come into God's presence.
You must have what is called *access* (*prosagogé*)—"approach,
entrance, a coming to or leading unto." We read in Romans
5:2: "Through whom also we have access by faith into this
grace in which we stand." In Ephesians 2:18: "For through
Him we both have access by one Spirit to the Father." And
in Ephesians 3:12: "In whom we have boldness and access
with confidence through faith in Him."

Second, you need not only the right or privilege of coming into His presence, but you need a way. According to
the Bible there is only one way into the very presence of
God, and that is through Jesus Christ. Edward G. Selwyn
wrote, "Access to God is the be-all and end-all of religion.
. . . Christ's atoning sacrifice brings us to God."

Third, you need not only the right and a way, but you
need someone to take you and introduce you. We did not
open the way or introduce ourselves. We were brought into
the way by Him who is the Way. Christ is the Door.

The one who leads us through salvation's door is Christ.
We have an open door to God through faith in Jesus Christ.
He leads us, or introduces us, into the presence of God the
Father. Christ makes the proper presentation.

What a marvelous thing it is for the Christian to have
free access to God and to confidently approach Him. As
our older folks used to sing in our churches:

> O Lord, I ain't no stranger now,
>
> O Lord, I ain't no stranger now,
>
> I've been introduced to the Father and the Son,
>
> O Lord, I ain't no stranger now!
>
> *Negro spiritual*

December 12

*But let none of you suffer as a murderer, a thief, an evildoer,
or as a busybody in other people's matters.* (1 Peter 4:15)

"The murderer rises with the light; he kills the poor and
needy; and in the night he is like a thief. In the dark they
break into houses which they marked for themselves in
the daytime" (Job 24:14, 16).

"Come with us, let us lie in wait to shed blood, let us
lurk secretly for the innocent without cause. . . . Cast in
your lot among us, let us all have one purse" (Proverbs
1:11, 14).

These passages were taken from the book of Job and
from the book of Proverbs, indicating organized crime syndicates existed more than three thousand years ago. Even
then young men were pressured by hoodlums to join their
gang.

"Let's get together, lay wait for the rich, and snatch pock-
etbooks, burglarize homes, and kill anybody who gets in
our way. We will have one common pot and split up the
loot evenly."

To such an invitation wisdom exhorts: "My son, if sinners entice you, do not consent . . . do not walk in the way
with them" (Proverbs 1:10, 15). No doubt all of us should
heed this advice.

Crime runs rampant in our country with ever-increas-
ing rapidity. The Christian is enabled by the Holy Spirit to
keep himself uninvolved, unentangled with the under-
world. The time will come, said Simon Peter, when the
genuine Christian will suffer enough just for being a good
Christian.

Why add to the misery by doing evil? If we are going to
suffer, then let it be because of Christ's living His life in us.

December 13

Simon Peter, a bondservant and apostle of Jesus Christ, to those who have obtained like precious faith with us by the righteousness of our God and Savior Jesus Christ. (2 Peter 1:1)

It is quite probable that Simon Peter here refers to Gentile Christians rather than Jewish Christians when he speaks of "those who have obtained like precious faith with us." The faith of the Gentile saints is just as valuable and precious in God's sight as the faith of any one or of all the believing Jews.

Note the word *obtained*. It means to attain, usually by lot. It involves no self-effort. What is received is not by your efforts but is like a ripe apple falling into your lap while you are sitting under a tree.

In other words, true faith, faith connected with the righteousness of God, is a gift of God, a gift of His favor, a divine allotment. No one forced God to save anyone. He was not obligated, compelled, or coerced. No one ever threatened to put oil in the clouds and mess up God's waterworks and then demanded, as a ransom, to be taken to heaven.

If salvation were any way other than by grace it would not be based upon true faith.

Here then is a simple message: the faith you exercised to become a Christian was a gift of God, for "as many as had been appointed to eternal life believed" (Acts 13:48).

The same grace, the same faith that Simon Peter and Paul experienced, is likewise yours and is equal in honor, privileges, worth, and value. The humblest believer enjoys a relationship to Jesus Christ equal in saving effectiveness to that of the first disciples of the Lord.

December 14

Grace and peace be multiplied to you in the knowledge of God and of Jesus our Lord. (2 Peter 1:2)

Our future is secure; we are saved, and heaven is our home. We have eternal life right now, but we are still on earth. When we were born again we were not immediately made mature Christians. We were babies. Knowledge about God in Christ helps us mature. Through our study of the Bible the Holy Spirit can work on us, with us, and for us.

Simon Peter wants us to understand what happens when we personally embrace such knowledge. The more we study the Bible, the more we learn of Him who gave us the Bible, the more we know of Him of whom the Bible speaks, grace and peace will multiply in our lives.

Do you want God's grace to be multiplied to you, to be yours in full measure? I do. Let us study God's Word and obtain the full, personal, precise, and correct knowledge about Christ. Know what God's will, God's way, and God's work are, and your heart will be filled with His grace and peace.

"Grace" and "Peace" were common greetings of that day: "*Charis*" among the Greeks and "*Shalom*" among the Hebrews. So note the order here: the Greek *grace* and then the Hebrew *peace*. Grace comes first. If you obtain the grace, then you will have the peace. The grace of God was shown in the shedding of blood by Christ. If you believe in your heart that He died for you, then you will have peace with God. But no grace means no peace. Peace is the result of grace. Only to the Christian is the peace of God available.

Here then is a simple plea: Learn more about the Lord Jesus and give God an opportunity to expand your grace and peace. Since there is no shortage with God, let that which you have received already encourage your heart to ask for more. Grow in grace and peace, and learn by experience that God is good.

December 15

But grow in the grace . . . of our Lord. (2 Peter 3:18)

There are some things in life that you cannot control, things over which you have absolutely no say. All of your education, energy, and experience combined will not help you. At such a time we learn to trust God's grace.

If you fall and do not break a leg or arm, thank God for His grace. If you make a mistake and do not get corrected, thank God for His grace. If you do wrong and do not get caught, thank God for His grace. Do not become presumptuous and think you got away with anything.

You did not. It was grace. If you played with fire and did not get burned, thank God for His grace. Never become arrogant and think you have got away scot-free because of your own cleverness, slickness, and experience. Grace is no license to live in lust and licentiousness.

Understand me. Sometimes we make mistakes in life, but life goes on. If we have the right attitude and recognize the truth about ourselves, then we will not lean on the devil's shoulders, crying the blues about it. We ask the Lord's forgiveness and go on. We grow in grace; we do not dry up in disgrace.

By grace discover in hard knocks a soft touch. Find in the howling winds a shelter in the storm. In sickness, apply the balm of Gilead. In aches and pains, call on the Great Physician. In chaos and confusion, find peace.

If Christ opens a door, go on in. If he digs a tunnel through the mountain of despair, go on through. If He builds a bridge across troubled water, cross on over. If He sends manna down from heaven, pick it up and eat it. Remember that what the Lord *started* in you, by grace He will one day *finish*.

December 16

*Do not love the world or the things in the world. If anyone
loves the world, the love of the Father is not in him.* (1 John
2:15)

Kosmos, "world," means that order or system whose center is man, that by its unbelief, air of independence, lack of
realism, and spiritual blindness demonstrates its evil opposition to God. It is composed of those people, pursuits,
pleasures, purposes, and places where Jesus Christ is not
wanted.

It is that lifestyle that is orientated against God. Such a
system is ruled by the devil, is passing away, and hates
Christians. To conform to such a spirit and such a system
is worldliness.

Now see how John describes the things that are in the
world: (1) Lust of the flesh—that is the desire of the old
nature. It is the attempt to satisfy or pander to the appetite
of the old man who still lives in us.

(2) Lust of the eyes—that is the desire and satisfaction
of looking at something we have no business looking at. It
is the pleasure derived at seeing someone stronger than us
defeated, or seeing someone dressed better than us suddenly impoverished and covered in rags.

(3) Pride of Life—that characterizes the braggart, the
man who swaggers, boasts of race, culture, ancestry, education, intellect, and possessions. That is pretentiousness,
a yearning for the glamor of life, for status symbols, and
the craving of titles and honors.

Worldliness is that set of attitudes and affections that
shows a man's life consists in the possession of things or a
concentration upon things. You can be rich and own many
things, yet not be worldly. Contrariwise, you can be poor,
own very little of this world's goods, and be quite worldly.
It is all in the mind.

John sums it up as "the love of the world." It is not of
God. All of it belongs to a dying, perishing world. The
world is fading away. May we this day determine to set
our affections on things above.

December 17

But you have an anointing from the Holy One, and you know all things. . . . But the anointing which you have received from Him abides in you. (1 John 2:20, 27)

John dealt with heretics and false teachers who called themselves Christians but denied that Jesus Christ is the Son of God. The schism was over doctrine and caused John to call them antichrists (v. 18). Those who remained true to apostolic teaching he encouraged. "Those who left showed they were not really a part of us anyway," says John. "You who remain show you have knowledge of the truth."

"You know all things" (v. 20)—that is, you know who is an antichrist and who is not. You know who is a liar and who is not, once they make known their beliefs. Do not let them make you think you are inferior. The truth is, you are not at any disadvantage. You see, you have been anointed.

The fact that you did not get carried away into error is proof that the anointing remains in you. You do not need them to teach you anything (v. 27). What they claim to have, you have already. The anointing enables you to recognize the truth and refuse falsehood. Nobody outside of the Christian fellowship formed by the Holy Spirit can teach you anything about God or Christ that will either correct or supplement the truth already revealed and believed.

To anoint means "to smear or rub over with oil," to spread oil over. It is an unction. Oil is a symbol of the Holy Spirit, so this anointing symbolizes an imparting of the Spirit. John states that the Holy Spirit in the believer is the most effective safeguard against the antichrists and their heretical doctrines. He is the Spirit of discernment, and He lives in you.

December 18

He who is in you is greater than he who is in the world.
(1 John 4:4)

Literally, a *crisis* is a turning point. It is a crucial point or situation in the course of anything—an unstable condition in which an abrupt or decisive change is impending. One big crisis now facing us in America is the energy shortage, brought on perhaps by a combination of such factors as wastefulness, greed, love of luxury, politics, and shortsightedness.

The result is great concern about wood, coal, natural gas, nuclear power, solar power, and especially petroleum products: oil, kerosene, diesel fuel, and gasoline.

A far greater energy crisis these days, however, concerns the types of energy with which human beings are personally involved. There is, first of all, demonic, or satanic, energy with which deluded men work. The spirit prince of the power of the air seductively energizes the sons of disobedience (Ephesians 2:2).

A second source of energy is human flesh. All of us naturally have this energy. As for the unbeliever, everything he does is in the flesh, in his own strength. However, because the old nature is still in the Christian, there is a great danger that some of our deeds are likewise done in our own strength.

The third source is divine energy. Our Lord energizes or works in us both to will and do for His good pleasure (Philippians 2:13). As we seek to serve the Lord today, to faithfully use the gifts He has bestowed upon us, may we remember that the solution to the spiritual energy crisis is: "'Not by might nor by power, but by My Spirit,' says the LORD of hosts" (Zechariah 4:6).

December 19

We love Him because He first loved us. (1 John 4:19)

Some years ago while making a call at one of the hospitals in our city, I encountered a patient whose filthy language was a source of embarrassment to many other patients, the nurses, and visitors. I spoke softly to him about Christ and sought to show him his need for the Lord Jesus. I knew that the profanity coming from his lips pointed to the evil in his heart.

Sadly, that cancer-stricken man was gospel-hardened. He had heard of heaven and hell; he knew about Jesus Christ—but those things meant nothing to him.

As I left the hospital I pitied the plight of the poor nurses who had to deal with that Christ-rejecter. I also wondered how many performed their duties perfunctorily, like some efficient robot, and how many of them might be motivated by love in their hearts to deal with this sin-sick man.

Often men will perform helpful acts out of motives less than love. A man could be a successful lawyer and not have any love in his heart for his clients. A doctor could be a highly skilled surgeon and yet not have any love for the patients upon whom he operates.

But the love with which Christ loved us is truly incomparable (John 15:13), immutable, and inseparable (Romans 8:38–39). Jesus Christ showed His love for us when we were unlovable, miserable, hateful, mean, and wicked. He went to Calvary bearing our sins upon Himself even though He knew no sin.

It is this love that enables us to love God, to love other Christians, and to love those who do not yet know Jesus Christ in the pardoning of their sins.

December 20

We know that we are of God, and the whole world lies under the sway of the wicked one. And we know. . . . (1 John 5:19–20)

There are those who accuse us of being presumptuous. If there is any one thing we learn from John's first epistle it is this: God wants us to *know*. Fourteen times we find the words "we know." There is no need for the Christian to be timid, uncertain, shaky about his faith. If we have confidence in *Good Housekeeping*'s seal, what about *God's* housekeeping seal? Surely God keeps His own!

We know, according to chapter 2, that we know Him. How? If we keep His commandments. We know we are in Him. How? If we keep His Word. We know that it is the last time. How? Because even now there are many antichrists.

In chapter 3, we know that when Christ appears we shall be like Him, for we shall see Him as He is. We know that we have passed from death to life because we love the brethren. We know that we are of the truth because we love in deed and in truth, not just in word or in tongue. We know God abides in us by the gift of the indwelling Spirit.

We know, according to chapter 4, the spirit of truth and the spirit of error. We recognize them because we listen to the messengers of the Lord. Because He has given us of His Spirit, we know that we are abiding in Him and He in us.

Finally, in chapter 5, we know that we love God's children when we love God and keep His commandments. We know that we have the petitions that we desire of Him because we positively know that He listens to us in whatever we ask. We know that whosoever is born of God does not practice sin. Why? The Christian is kept, watched over, and protected by the eternal Son of God.

These things we *know*.

December 21

The Son of God has come and given us an understanding that we may know Him who is true; and we are in Him who is true, in His Son Jesus Christ. This is the true God and eternal life. (1 John 5:20)

A very popular black athlete, Arthur Ashe, once spoke on the subject of whom he would like to meet in the next world. "Probably Jesus Christ, just to find out if the guy is for real. I would ask him what he thought of his competition—Buddha, Mohammed, Confucius."

There are some things of which you can be very sure—they are guaranteed. One thing that is certain is this: Every human being ever brought into this world is going to meet Jesus Christ. Men do not have to worry as to whether or not they will meet Jesus Christ in the next world. They *will* meet Him, for all in the graves will hear His voice (John 5:28) and shall come forth; and "every eye will see Him" (Revelation 1:7). Yes, every knee shall bow at the name of Jesus Christ (Philippians 2:10).

Jesus Christ has been ordained by God the Father to judge the world in righteousness on that appointed day. The resurrection of the crucified Messiah is the guarantee. You *will* meet Him.

Other world religions provide no personal God; and none solves the problem of sin. All may acknowledge the existence of Jesus Christ, but from their points of view Jesus was just a man, a prophet, a good teacher, but not God Almighty.

We Christians have no doubt in our minds. The Holy Spirit sees to this. We *know* whom we serve. We know He is real, true, genuine. We *know* it! Man's falsehoods do not nullify God's faithfulness. Truth lives on! Those of you with faith in the shed blood of Jesus Christ will discover more and more, from day to day, as you hold on to God's unchanging hand, that God is *real*!

December 22

Beloved, I pray that you may prosper in all things and be in health, just as your soul prospers. (3 John 2)

That was probably a standard greeting in John's day, but it sounds strange today to read that John desired the *physical* health and *spiritual* health of his friend Gaius to be equal. Suppose your physical health depended upon your spiritual health. What would happen?

The Hebrew word rendered *prosper* means "to advance, carry through"; the Greek word translated *prosper* means "to travel a good road or journey." So the one who prospers advances or carries something through to a successful result; he is led along a good road. His fondest hopes are fulfilled.

There are at least three things the Bible has to say about prosperity. First, there is the negative admonition: "He who covers his sins will not prosper" (Proverbs 28:13), "but whoever confesses and forsakes them will have mercy."

Second, "Believe in the LORD your God, and you shall be established; believe His prophets, and you shall prosper" (2 Chronicles 20:20).

Third, it is said of the man who meditates day and night in the Law of God: "Whatever he does shall prosper" (Psalm 1:3). *Law* here means the Word of God, that which reveals the will of God. In other words, if you want to prosper, read and study your Bible.

Prosperity then is based upon (1) confessing one's sins, (2) trusting God's ministers, and (3) studying God's Word. If you will do those three things you will have good spiritual health. Then you will not shake in your boots if someone greets you with: "My heartfelt prayer for you, good buddy, is that you may be as healthy and prosperous in every way as you are in your soul!"

December 23

Mercy, peace, and love be multiplied to you. (Jude 2)

The word *multiply* made me think of the topic "Arithmetic in the Bible and in the Church." Paul spoke of divisions (schisms) in 1 Corinthians 1:10; in the book of Acts many were added to the church (2:41, 47; 5:14; 11:24); Ananias and Sapphira were subtracted from the local assembly (Acts 5:10).

Division. His word came into my heart and split my soul from my spirit (Hebrews 4:12). He broke up the old man in me and separated me from sin and Satan unto Himself.

Subtraction. Jesus Christ pulled out the sting of death; He removed my sins as far as the east is from the west. He cast out my fears, broke shackling habits, and took away all condemnation.

Addition. He put the Holy Spirit in me. He then added me to the family of God; I have been adopted. He raised up new friends, gave me a new name. Through faith in His shed blood I have an eternity to spend with Him in my new home.

Subtraction and Addition. Jesus Christ took away hell and added heaven. He takes away midnight tears and substitutes morning joy. He takes away the ashes of sorrow and substitutes the oil of gladness.

Multiplication. He came that we might have life abundant. Are you growing in knowledge? In grace? In love? Are you thrilled that you serve a Savior who took nothing and made something out of it when He laid His hands upon you?

When men, women, boys, and girls come to Christ they will discover He is the founder of fractions, the creator of calculus, the God of geometry, the author of arithmetic, and the master mathematician!

December 24

But you, beloved, building yourselves up on your most holy faith, praying in the Holy Spirit, keep yourselves in the love of God, looking for the mercy of our Lord Jesus Christ unto eternal life. (Jude 20–21)

Instead of basking in the sunshine of God's love, some of us walk beneath the clouds of confusion and contention, soaked by the rains of self-righteousness, blown about by the blizzards of bickering, backbiting, and bad behavior, swept away by the storms of sensuality, lost in the shaky shadows of selfishness.

We live beneath our heritage, and our favorite song is "Stormy Weather." The above exhortation is needed. Three things must be practiced if we intend to stay within the boundaries where God's love can reach us, bless, and direct us.

First, there must be a continual *building up on your most holy faith*. Strengthen yourself in doctrine, in that once-for-all-delivered body of truth for which you are to earnestly contend.

Second, there is a constant *praying in the Holy Spirit*. That means to fully desire and pray for God's will and way at all costs. Self-righteousness is thus excluded.

The third thing is a continued *looking*. We are to be in the habit of waiting, expecting, looking forward to the day when the Lord Jesus Christ shall return.

That is Jude's message to the Christian. The false brethren, with their false doctrine, were already at work deceiving men and women, leading them astray. He declares they have despised the Word of God and have hardened their hearts to all that He has done.

But *you*—what a contrast Jude makes! You are challenged to thrive in the presence of God, to stay exposed to the sunshine of His favor. Make it possible for the Lord to show you His love right now.

December 25

Now to Him who is able to keep you from stumbling, and to present you faultless before the presence of His glory with exceeding joy. . . . (Jude 24)

Stumbling is a better translation than the word "falling," as the King James reads. One who stumbles may get up again without falling flat on his face. We stumble and then regain our balance. Of course, falling is a possible result of stumbling. But here the "not stumbling" is a "standing firm" or hopefully being "exempt from falling." It is used of a horse that is sure-footed.

The Lord would prevent us from stumbling by providing warnings from the history of unbelief and rebellion. Three examples are given: (1) Israel in the wilderness, (2) angels who were in heaven but who joined with Satan, and (3) the homosexuals of Sodom and Gomorrah.

God exercises His ability to keep us from stumbling *now*; the part of the verse that speaks of being presented faultless points to the *future*. The keeping or guarding from stumbling deals with the nasty here-and-now; the presentation before the presence of His glory is yet to come.

Faultless became a technical word to designate the absence of anything in animals that would make them unworthy to be offered or sacrificed. The Old Testament required that animals without blemish be used. That is a picture of our Redeemer who gave Himself, "who through the eternal Spirit offered Himself without spot to God" (Hebrews 9:14), a lamb without blemish.

The time is coming when we will be perfectly conformed to the image of Jesus Christ. What a time that will be! Victory! Ecstatic delight! Exceeding joy! Rest assured our God is able to do these things—to guard us from stumbling *now* and to present us perfect *later*. That is fact, not fiction. There should be in our souls that conviction that our God is able.

December 26

. . . Amen. And I have the keys of Hades and of Death.
(Revelation 1:18)

The key of David (Isaiah 22:22; Revelation 3:7) speaks of absolute rule over the city of Jerusalem. Jesus Christ—Son of David, but David's Lord—shall reign over the entire earth, with headquarters in Jerusalem during the kingdom age.

The key of knowledge (Luke 11:52) refers to the basic, simple message of the books of Moses, which our Lord declared were being misinterpreted by the religious leaders of His day.

The keys of the kingdom of heaven (Matthew 16:19) refer simply to the fact that God intended to use Peter and other disciples to open the gospel door and make known the grace of God as shown in Christ. To the repentant sinner the door is open. To the hardened and impenitent the door is locked.

The key of the bottomless pit (Revelation 9:1): most likely, here, the "star seen fallen from heaven" is Satan—who is given authority (the key) to call from the abyss a tornado of vicious locust-like demons with scorpion-like stings to torment evildoers. Later, however, in Revelation 20:1, God's angel comes down from heaven with the key of the bottomless pit and imprisons the devil there for a thousand years.

The keys of Hades and of Death (Revelation 1:18): even as hell could not hold Christ's soul, so death could not hold His body. Although the bodies of the saints still lie in their graves, death no longer holds the key. The key is in the hands of Christ.

The hour is coming in which all who are in the graves will hear His voice and come forth. But there are two different resurrections, to be held at different times. First, the righteous will be raised; later, the unrighteous. But both events come about through the resurrected One who has the keys—Jesus Christ.

December 27

Behold, I am coming quickly! Hold fast what you have, that no one may take your crown. (Revelation 3:11)

Some men who start out well do not end up well. King Saul started out well. He had everything going for him. But it was not long before we read of his self-seeking and cowardice, his intrusion into the office of the priest, his rashness, his incomplete obedience, his attempts to murder David, and his consultation with the witch of Endor. In the end Saul fell upon his own sword after being wounded by an arrow from the bow of a Philistine soldier. Saul lost his crown.

Esau is another man who had a wonderful opportunity to be used of the LORD, but he cared little for spiritual things. For one morsel of food he sold his birthright. Later he realized the value of it, but his tears of remorse were in vain. It is quite possible that even then he thought only of the physical, economic aspects, the influence and power that would have been his. He lost his crown.

So did Demas, who forsook God's mighty servant, Paul, because he loved this present world (2 Timothy 4:10). How sad!

Make no mistake about it, Jesus Christ is coming back again. "I am coming quickly" does not mean "I am coming right away" necessarily, but it means, "I will come rapidly; that is, whenever I do come, it will be a sudden coming!"

In the meantime, you hold fast! Carefully and faithfully keep your crown. Hold it in your power. This is an exhortation for the saint tenaciously to hold onto that which he has struggled so long to achieve and obtain. The secret of success depends upon how highly one values spiritual blessings and future rewards.

December 28

You are worthy, O Lord, to receive glory and honor and power; for You created all things, and by Your will they exist and were created. (Revelation 4:11)

> There are a number of us creep
> Into the world to eat and sleep;
> And know no reason why we're born,
> But only to consume the corn,
> Devour the cattle, flesh and fish,
> And leave behind an empty dish.
> And if our tombstone, when we die,
> Be not taught to flatter and to lie,
> There's nothing better can be said
> Than that he's eaten up all his bread,
> Drunk up his drink, and gone to bed.
>
> *Isaac Watts*

Men set up their own goals and work more or less feverishly to reach them. However, in straining out the gnat they miss the camel. It is like pulling one hair out of King Kong and expecting him to topple over. The larger, more important purpose in life is missed altogether. Fulfillment in the lesser areas brings temporary satisfaction at best.

What then is the larger purpose, the most important goal? It is to glorify God. That is why the LORD made us—for Himself (Proverbs 16:4). "All things were created . . . for Him" (Colossians 1:16).

Unfortunately, a man without this particular object in mind makes himself the center of the universe. He becomes his own egocentric god and proceeds to please himself only. But people who want to have their own way and do their own thing often run into other people who want *their* own way and to do *their* own thing. Crash! What a disaster!

Only in Christ can all of life's goals that are set up be properly evaluated and given the correct emphasis. That is when full joy comes. When a man realizes why God put him in the world, why God keeps him alive, what God's purpose is, and when man lives up to that purpose, there is joy unspeakable!

December 29

Fear God and give glory to Him. (Revelation 14:7)

This fear is not that shaking, quaking, trembling kind of thing but reverential awe, trust, and respect. It is a command found often in the Bible, and the man who fears the LORD is blessed. Indeed, the fear of the LORD is the beginning of wisdom and the beginning of knowledge.

Glory is one of those words with many meanings. Originally it was derived from a word that means "what one thinks, an opinion"; then "the opinion that others have." If the opinion is favorable, I have a good reputation; I am in good standing and am therefore to be praised.

Glory came to mean praise, honor, and esteem. That expanded to include grace, wealth, power, worship, transcendence, dignity, excellence, preeminence, importance, majesty, radiance, and brightness. It is the sum of God's divine attributes.

To give God glory is not to give Him something He does not have. It is not adding something to Him not already present. No. To give God glory is to recognize the importance of His deity, to actively praise or extol Him for who and what He is. It is to acknowledge His divine mode of being and what is due to Him.

How? Give glory by taking Him at His word; believing what He says in the Bible. Give Him glory by celebrating His praises. Give Him glory by acknowledging He knows all things; show you believe it by your confession.

Give Him glory by declaring your gratitude for the benefits and blessings you have received from His hand. Give God glory by rendering the honor due to His majesty. May giving God the glory be your goal today and every day.

December 30

There shall be no night there. . . . There shall be no night there. (Revelation 21:25; 22:5)

One of the characteristics of the New Jerusalem and the new paradise is the absence of night. How appropriate this is, for we learn from the Scriptures that nighttime represents a time of evil. It was *at night* that the homosexuals of Sodom pounded on the door of Lot's house brazenly demanding that Lot's visitors be delivered over to them for immorality.

It was *at night* that Lot's two daughters made their father drunk with wine and committed incest. It was *at night* that the enemies of Samson surrounded the city of Gaza, hoping to capture him. Job said that the murderer acts like a thief in the night. The adulterer watches eagerly for twilight, thinking he will not be seen. In the dark, burglars break into houses that they had marked for themselves in the daytime (Job 24:14–16).

It was *at night* that one prostitute who had smothered her baby substituted the dead child for that of her fellow prostitute, and King Solomon had to make a judgment. It was *at night* that King Belshazzar and his cronies drank wine from the vessels that belonged to the Temple of Jehovah. On that night, after the hand had written on the wall, Belshazzar was killed.

Harlots ply their trade *at night*, said the writer in Proverbs 7:8–10. Those who get drunk are drunk *at night*, said the apostle Paul. It is no wonder then that Christ said, "I must work the works of Him who sent Me while it is day; the night is coming when no man can work" (John 9:4).

Judas went to perform his evil mission, "and it was night." We thank the Lord today that we can walk as sons of light and sons of the day, for "we are not of the night nor of darkness" (1 Thessalonians 5:5). We are right now citizens of heaven, where there is no night.

December 31

*He who is unjust, let him be unjust still; he who is filthy, let
him be filthy still; he who is righteous, let him be righteous
still; he who is holy, let him be holy still.* (Revelation 22:11)

Note first that this verse announces the end of *confusion*. It speaks in terms of absolutes. Unfortunately, there
are those "who call evil good, and good evil; who put darkness for light, and light for darkness; who put bitter for
sweet, and sweet for bitter" (Isaiah 5:20). Some argue that
pornography is educational; foul language is therapeutic;
drinking wine is being sociable; telling lies is being tactful;
immorality is "love"; and rotten character traits are merely
"personality differences." However, such confusion and
distorted values shall be brought to an end.

Second, there is *confirmation*. The time is coming when
the book will be closed, the die cast, the mold set, and the
cement hardened. In other words, "In the place where the
tree falls, there it shall lie" (Ecclesiastes 11:3). The words
"Let . . . be" shall become a reality. There will be no further
opportunity for repentance. Men will find themselves confirmed in their beliefs.

Third, there is *conformation*. All of us are being conformed
to some image right now, and the Bible says that whatever
that image is it will be forever. What a joy it is for the Christian to know that daily he is becoming more like the Lord
Jesus Christ. Death will not change the lot of the saint.

If you love the Lord now, you will continue to love Him.
If you delight in the things of the Lord now, if you are growing and becoming more like Him now, what will it be when
you see Him as He is! The righteous and holy shall live on
through *eternity* with Him who loved us and gave Himself
for us.

This book was produced by CLC Publications. We hope it has been life-changing and has given you a fresh experience of God through the work of the Holy Spirit. CLC Publications is an outreach of CLC Ministries International, a global literature mission with work in over 50 countries. If you would like to know more about us or are interested in opportunities to serve with a faith mission, we invite you to contact us at:

CLC Ministries International
P.O. Box 1449
Fort Washington, PA 19034

—

Phone: (215) 542-1242
E-mail: clcmail@clcusa.org
Websites: www.clcusa.org
www.clcpublications.com

DO YOU LOVE GOOD CHRISTIAN BOOKS?
Do you have a heart for worldwide missions?

You can receive a FREE subscription to:

Floodtide
(CLC's magazine on global literature missions)
Order by e-mail at:

floodtide@clcusa.org
or fill in the coupon below and mail to:

**P.O. Box 1449
Fort Washington, PA 19034**

```
┌─────────────────────────────────────────────────┐
│      FREE FLOODTIDE SUBSCRIPTION!                 │
│ Name: _____  │
│ Address: _____  │
│ _____  │
│ Phone: _____  E-mail: _____   │
└─────────────────────────────────────────────────┘
```

READ THE REMARKABLE STORY OF
the founding of
CLC INTERNATIONAL

"Any who doubt that Elijah's God still lives ought to read of the money supplied when needed, the stores and houses provided, and the appearance of personnel in answer to prayer."

—Moody Monthly

Is it possible that the printing press, the editor's desk, the Christian bookstore, and the mail order department, can glow with the fast-moving drama of an "Acts of the Apostles"?

Find out, as you are carried from two people in an upstairs bookroom to a worldwide chain of Christian bookcenters and publishing, multiplied by only a "shoestring" of faith and committed, and though unlikely, lives.

To order your copy of *Leap of Faith*

You may order by:

Phone: 1-800-659-1240

E-mail:
orders@clcpublications.com

Mail: P.O. Box 1449,
        Ft. Washington, Pa 19034

Discount Code: DMB 650

Reg. Price: $11.99

Special Mission Price: $5.40

Shipping in US: 4.00

You pay: $9.40

Name: _____

Address:_____

_____

Phone: _____ E-mail: _____

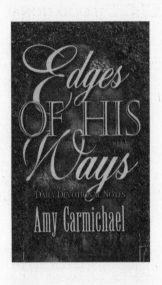

EDGES OF HIS WAYS
Amy Carmichael

These daily devotional notes by Amy Carmichael cover a number of years in which she was unable to have much contact with her fellow laborers in Dohnavur. Despite this hardship, this devotional celebrates the blessings of God, which she recognized as mere whispers of the Greater Power behind them— or, as Job put it, "the edges of His ways" (Job 26:14).

ISBN 0-87508-062-6

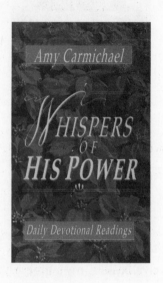

WHISPERS OF HIS POWER
Amy Carmichael

A selection of 366 daily devotional readings culled from Amy Carmichael's previously unpublished letters and writings. Each is based on a verse or short passage from Scripture.

ISBN 0-87508-317-X

DAILY DEVOTIONAL MEDITATIONS
FROM THE MINISTRY OF
WATCHMAN NEE

A TABLE
IN THE
*W*ILDERNESS

A TABLE IN THE WILDERNESS

Rich daily devotional thoughts
from Watchman Nee

When God spreads for us a **table in the wilderness**, when five loaves provide food for five thousand and leave twelve baskets of fragments, **that is blessing**!

Blessing is fruit all out of relation to what we are. It comes when God works completely beyond our understanding, for His name's sake.

Wonder and gratitude have a high place in these meditations, which are drawn from the author's widely varied ministry in China and beyond. They will draw you again to a fresh response to God's superlative grace in the gift to us of His Son.

Trade Paper ISBN 0-87508-699-3

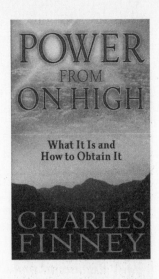

POWER FROM ON HIGH

What It Is and How to Obtain It

Charles Finney

Charles Finney boldly uncovers the awful truth that today's Christians, even Church leaders, are sadly lacking in the critical gift of spiritual power. But he offers hope as he reveals the wonderful fact that this power is available to every Christian who dares ask for it in faith. Finney emphasizes that the Holy Spirit urgently desires to take full control of your life, and he lists certain conditions that must be met before you can be filled with the Spirit and receive *power from on high*.

Trade Paper ISBN 0-87508-189-4

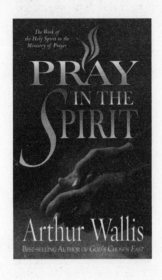

PRAY IN THE SPIRIT

Arthur Wallis

Arthur Wallis sets the pace for a book on prayer that goes beyond general principles to show the role of the Holy Spirit in the life of the praying believer. Through a pointed analysis of our weaknesses in prayer—both our spiritual and practical difficulties—Wallis shows how the Holy Spirit helps us in our weaknesses.

Trade paper ISBN 0-87508-574-1

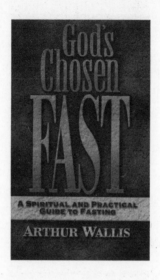

GOD'S CHOSEN FAST

Arthur Wallis

Fasting was practiced in the Old Testament, the early church, and by our Lord Himself. Why then do we not do it today? In a biblical, balanced, and highly practical manner, the author shows the power and blessing released by fasting to God. This book will leave you surprised and challenged.

Mass Market ISBN 0-87508-555-5
Trade Paper ISBN 0-87508-554-7

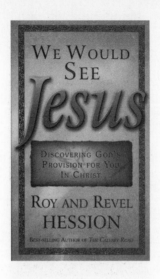

WE WOULD SEE JESUS

*Do you struggle with guilt or
feel like God can't accept you as you are?*

It's easy to forget that nothing we do will make us more acceptable to God. Jesus came to set us free to serve Him in the freshness and spontaneity of the Spirit, and to receive the ABUNDANT blessing God has for us.

Let your life be transformed as you learn to see Jesus, who is both the blessing and the way to that blessing—the means and the end.

Mass Market ISBN 0-87508-586-5
Spanish ISBN 958-9149-25-1

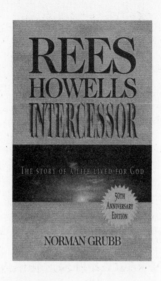

REES HOWELLS, INTERCESSOR

Learn the Key to Prevailing Prayer

Norman Grubb

Rees Howells was a man uniquely taught of God who found the key to prevailing prayer, became the channel of a mighty revival in Africa, was taught the principles of divine healing, and progressed even further in faith until world events were affected by his prayers.

ISBN 0-87508-188-6